THE SOCIAL PHILOSOPHY
OF JANE ADDAMS

The Social Philosophy of Jane Addams

MAURICE HAMINGTON

UNIVERSITY OF ILLINOIS PRESS
URBANA AND CHICAGO

© 2009 by Maurice Hamington

Manufactured in the United States of America

C 5 4 3 2 1

∞ This book is printed on acid-free paper.

Library of Congress Cataloging-in-Publication Data
Hamington, Maurice.
The social philosophy of Jane Addams /
Maurice Hamington.
p.   cm.
Includes bibliographical references and index.
ISBN 978-0-252-03476-3 (cloth : alk. paper)
1. Addams, Jane, 1860–1935—Political and
social views. 2. Sociology—Philosophy.
3. Women social reformers—United States—
Biography.
I. Title.
HV28.A35.H37   2009
61.92—dc22   2008047512

TO ALL REFLECTIVE COMMUNITY ORGANIZERS

WHO MAKE THE CONNECTION BETWEEN

LOCAL AND NATIONAL CHALLENGES AND

BETWEEN THOUGHT AND ACTION.

THIS INCLUDES THOSE OF YOU WORKING

IN THE FIELD AND THOSE OF YOU

IN THE WHITE HOUSE.

CONTENTS

ACKNOWLEDGMENTS   ix

INTRODUCTION:
A REMARKABLE LIFE, A REMARKABLE MIND   I

PART I JANE ADDAMS, PHILOSOPHER

1. Intellectual Influences   15

2. Radical Pragmatism   32

3. Feminist Pioneer   48

4. Sympathetic Knowledge   71

PART II THEORY, ACTION, REFLECTION

5. Ultimate Social Progress: Peace   89

6. Widening the Circle   109

7. The Reluctant Socialist   127

8. Democracy, Education, and Play   149

9. Civic Religion and Utopia   166

AFTERWORD:
COSMOPOLITAN HOPE   181

NOTES   189

BIBLIOGRAPHY   209

INDEX   223

ACKNOWLEDGMENTS

Although my name appears on the cover, many people contributed to the development of *The Social Philosophy of Jane Addams*. In particular, I thank Lisa Heldke, Ann Clark, and Anne McGrail, whose careful reading and thoughtful feedback were invaluable. The reviewers from University of Illinois Press made indispensable suggestions that improved the final product. I also benefited from numerous helpful conversations with Joan Catapano, who stuck with this project through a seven-year gestation. Beth Gianfagna provided meticulous copyediting that made me appear to be a better writer than I am.

On several occasions, I have had the opportunity to present portions of my research at annual meetings of the American Philosophical Association Pacific Division, Association for Feminist Ethics and Social Theory, North American Society for Social and Political Philosophy, Society for the Advancement of American Philosophy, and the National Women's Studies Association. At those meetings, I engaged in beneficial discussions about Addams's work with numerous scholars, but particularly insightful comments came from Marilyn Fischer, Charlene Haddock Seigfried, Hans Seigfried, and Judy Whipps. I am always indebted to Scott Pratt, who first introduced me to the work of Addams while I was in graduate school.

I also thank the Carrie Chapman Catt Center at Iowa State University for funding some of the early research that went into this book through the Catt Prize for Research on Women and Politics in 2002. The resources that it provided allowed me to attend a 2002 conference at the University of Dayton on Addams organized by Marilyn Fischer.

Time is a precious commodity when writing and conducting research, and significant portions of the book were written during a sabbatical I took from Lane Community College from 2003 to 2004. Finally, I thank the University of Southern Indiana for providing me with a research grant that allowed me to participate in a Society for the Advancement of American Philosophy's Summer Institute, where I attended a daylong session on Addams conducted by Charlene Haddock Seigfried and Hans Seigfried.

For the past several years, my supportive partner, Stephanie Hamington, has had to put up with Jane Addams as the "other woman," and my daughter, Rosemary, has come to accept Addams as a ubiquitous figure in our lives.

THE SOCIAL PHILOSOPHY
OF JANE ADDAMS

The standard view, after all, has been that Addams exemplified pragmatism more than she theorized it. And in a discipline cursed by ossified syllabi and glacial stumbling toward new perspectives, violating the "White Guys" portrait of 19th-century American pragmatism requires revolutionary edge.
—CARLIN ROMANO

Introduction

A REMARKABLE LIFE, A REMARKABLE MIND

Interest in Jane Addams has surged since the late 1990s. More than a century after Chicago's social settlement, Hull House, opened, many are finding inspiration from Addams's social ideas, her pacifism, and her feminism. Addams's books are back in print, new collections of her articles are available, and her extant correspondence is being assembled and released. A number of new and insightful biographies have been published. These works recount her extraordinary and inspirational life. In an era when many citizens in the United States are cynical about whether anything can address society's seemingly intractable problems, Addams's life provides a testament to the power of one person to make a difference—locally, nationally, and internationally.

Addams was an inspirational figure who emerged from inspirational times. Understanding Addams necessitates understanding pragmatism and the Progressive Era. *Pragmatism* is the imprecise term given to a main branch of American philosophy that emphasizes experience, instrumental and tenuous truths, fallibility, diverse voices, democracy, and theories in service of social advancement. It is the last characteristic that made pragmatism an appropriate philosophy for the Progressive Era, which ran from the last part of the nineteenth through the early part of the twentieth centuries. During this period, widespread optimism existed that people could improve society. Addams's ideas grew out of this milieu, and ultimately she helped shape the nation's progressive spirit. Following the work of feminist scholars such as Charlene Haddock Seigfried and Marilyn Fischer, I will explore Addams's unique contribution to American pragmatism. *The Social Philosophy of Jane Addams* is not intended as a conclusive work but as an effort to facilitate a wider conversation over this important, yet largely ignored, intellectual figure.

Although I focus on Addams's theoretical contributions, I also draw on her lived experience, because the two are inseparable. As an American pragmatist, Addams viewed experience as an essential component of philosophical reflection. However, I am not recounting her biography.[1] Rather, I am interested in what she has to say to those living in the twenty-first century rather than what she accomplished in the nineteenth and twentieth centuries. Because experience is indivisible from reflection for the pragmatist thinker, I offer the following brief outline of Addams's life.

Biographical Overview

Laura Jane Addams was born in Cedarville, Illinois, on September 6, 1860. She grew up in the shadow of the Civil War and during a time when Darwin's *The Origin of Species* (1859) achieved widespread influence. Her childhood reflected the material advantage she enjoyed as the daughter of John Addams, a politician and successful mill owner. This advantage included the presence of the community library in their home. Her mother, Mary, died giving birth to her ninth child when Jane was two years old. Subsequently, Addams doted on her father and received the beneficial attention of a well-read and politically astute parent. Although John Addams was no advocate of feminism, he did send his daughter to college at what was then Rockford Seminary. Addams became part of a generation of women who were among the first in their families to attend college. At Rockford, she experienced the empowerment of living in a woman-centered environment, and she blossomed as an intellectual and as a campus leader.

Like many women of her time, Addams's prospects following college were limited. After discovering that medical school was not for her, Addams slipped into a decade-long malaise over the direction of her life. The energy and spirit of her college experience did not translate into any clear career path, and she rejected the options of both marriage and religious life. Her unidentified malady was physically and psychologically debilitating and exacerbated by her father's sudden death. As a part of the privileged class, Addams made treks to Europe in search of renewal. On her second trip, she visited Toynbee Hall, a pioneering settlement house in London, which inspired her toward a vocation that would propel her to international prominence.

Toynbee Hall was a community of young men committed to helping the poor of London by living among them. Addams became rejuvenated by a scheme to replicate the Toynbee settlement in the United States. She enlisted a college friend, Ellen Gates Starr, in the plan. However, to identify their vague idea as a plan is a bit of hyperbole. Addams and Starr had little by way of structured concepts for what the settlement would become other than a good neighbor to oppressed peoples. A suitable location was found in Chicago, and on September 18, 1889, Hull House opened its doors. Although it was not the first social settlement, Hull House quickly ascended to a leadership position because of Addams's work and renown. At its height, the settlement movement claimed four hundred such communities across the country.

Hull House was an incubator for social programs. Without any formal ideological or political constraints, the settlement responded to the needs of the neighborhood by starting project after project. The muckraking journalist Ida M. Tarbell captured the spirit of Hull House:

> Hull House is an "open house" for its neighborhood. It is a place where men and women of all ages, conditions, and points of view are welcome. So far as I have been able to discover, genuine freedom of mind and friendliness of spirit are what have made Hull House possible and are what will decide its future after the day of the great woman who has mothered it and about whom it revolves. . . . Hull House serves its neighborhood, and in so doing it serves most fully its own household. Its own members are the ones whose minds get the most illumination from its activities. Moreover, Hull House from its first-hand sympathetic dealing with men and women in its neighborhood learns the needs of the neighborhood. It is and for years has been a constant source of suggestion and of agitation for the betterment of the conditions under which its neighbors—and indirectly the whole city, even nation—live and work. Health, mind, morals, all are in its care. It is practical in the plans it offers. It can back up its demands with knowledge founded on actual contact. It can rally all of the enlightened and decent forces of the city to its help. Hull House, indeed, is a very source of pure life in the great city where it belongs.[2]

The reputation of the settlement quickly grew, bringing women (and some men), mostly college educated, from all over the country to live and work at Hull House. Although Hull House was coeducational, it exuded woman-identified space. A few of the residents married, but many were single, while others were in committed relationships with other women. This environment allowed the women of Hull House to thrive and to succeed at a dizzying array of social and political endeavors in an atmosphere of mutual purpose and support.[3]

From the outset of its operation, Addams wrote about the nature and function of Hull House in a reflective manner and often with philosophical insight. For example, she describes the application and reorganization of knowledge as the fundamental problem of modern life and then claims that settlements are like applied universities: "The ideal and developed settlement would attempt to test the value of human knowledge by action, and realization, quite as the complete and ideal university would concern itself with the discovery of knowledge in all branches."[4] Given the progressive mood of the nation, Addams's work at Hull House sparked widespread interest. She became a prolific author and a sought-after public speaker. Her speeches and articles reflected her valorization of the relationship between theory and action. Starting from local experiences, Addams then extended her cosmopolitan analysis to issues of race, education, and international peace.

Addams was one of the most respected and well-recognized figures in the nation at the turn of the century. She leveraged her celebrity status to play significant roles in numerous progressive campaigns. Addams was a founding figure in the National Association for the Advancement of Colored People, the American Civil Liberties Union, and the Women's International League for Peace and Freedom. When Theodore Roosevelt sought the presidential candidacy of the Progressive Party in 1912, he asked Jane Addams to second the nomination at the convention, a first for women.

There was a gendered dimension to her popularity. Addams transgressed the borders of the public and private spheres to challenge policies and institutions in her work at Hull House but always in ways that were perceived to flow from traditional women's labor (cleaning the streets, opening child-care centers, starting social clubs). After World War I broke out in Europe, her outspoken pacifism and refusal to endorse the war or the U.S. entry into it was greater gender-role transgression than the public could tolerate from a woman. She worked and wrote furiously to prevent the march toward war, and she suffered for her public opinions. Addams's popularity fell, and she became the target of vicious criticism.

Her newfound position as social contrarian gave Addams an opportunity to reflect on the fickle and emotional nature of citizenship and patriotism. Late in her life, Addams's pacifist tenacity was recognized with the Nobel Peace Price (1931), but her popularity mirrored that of the Progressive movement. After World War I, social settlements declined and never recaptured the popular imagination. She continued to work and write in behalf of progressive ideals until her death. Jane Addams died of cancer on May 21, 1935, leaving an under-appreciated intellectual legacy that includes a dozen books and more than five hundred articles.

Was Addams a Philosopher?

In 1961, Merle Curti recognized that Addams had been overlooked by the academy: "It is somewhat curious that in tributes to Jane Addams (1860–1935) occasioned by her centennial year, no serious consideration has been given to her in American intellectual history."[5] In a 2002 essay titled "Mulling (Not Hulling) Jane Addams," Carlin Romano observes that even among those who have contributed to the renewed interest in Addams, there is a tendency to include her without taking her theorizing seriously. He asks, "Was Jane Addams a significant pragmatist, or is she the Queen of Pragmatist Tokens?"[6] Romano notes that, with few exceptions, even the slim number of texts that purport to treat Addams as a serious intellectual fail to acknowledge her as a philosopher. The myth of Addams's lack of original scholarship thrives despite large and growing evidence to the contrary. On one trip to the Jane Addams Hull-House Museum on the campus of the University of Illinois in Chicago to conduct research for this project, I met a young and enthusiastic docent. Despite my efforts at anonymity, she insisted on learning the subject of my research. When I told her that I was writing a book on Addams's philosophy, she emphatically dismissed this as a fruitless endeavor and suggested that I might find a more interesting subject for original philosophy in Ellen Gates Starr or another Hull House resident. The docent, a recently minted Ph.D., merely gave expression to what her instructors and many other scholars continue to explicitly and implicitly perpetuate. The aim of *The Social Philosophy of Jane Addams* is to contribute to the evidence that Addams was an important original thinker and a significant public philosopher.

In 1889, Jane Addams and Ellen Gates Starr opened the doors of Hull House in a mixed immigrant neighborhood on South Halsted Street in Chicago. Addams acted as the resident philosopher. From the beginning, she not only managed the settlement but also wrote and theorized about it and its place in the world. Early in the endeavor, it became clear that Addams viewed the activism of Hull House in terms of social philosophy. She penned articles about the "subjective necessity," "objective value," and "function" of social settlements only a few years after embarking on her grand experiment.[7] In 1899, Addams favorably compared settlement houses to universities. Her concern about academia was quintessential American pragmatism: although both universities and settlements seek knowledge, universities have difficulty applying their discoveries to social life given their insular nature; conversely, the settlement is immersed in communal activity.

Central to her analysis is an epistemological claim regarding settlement work: "it is frequently stated that the most pressing problem of modern life is that of reconstruction and a reorganization of the knowledge that we possess; that we are at last struggling to realize in terms of life all that has been discovered and absorbed, to make it over into healthy and direct expressions of free living."[8] Remarkably, Addams framed the problems of her era not in social terms—poverty, corruption, and apathy—but in epistemological terms: the acquisition, organization, and dissemination of knowledge. She quotes John Dewey: "Knowledge is no longer its own justification, the interest in it has at last transferred itself from accumulation and verification to its application to life. . . . When a theory of knowledge forgets that its value rests in solving the problem out of which it has arisen, that of securing a method of action, knowledge begins to cumber the ground. It is a luxury, and becomes a social nuisance and disturber."[9] Addams contends that the work of settlement houses provides a grounding of philosophical endeavors, not merely as a connection to the life of the community but as a place for significant philosophical theory and reflection.

Not content with quoting Dewey, in the same article Addams references William James on action: "Beliefs, in short, are really rules of action, and the whole function of thinking is but one step in the production of habits of action. . . . The ultimate test for us of what a truth means is indeed the conduct it dictates or inspires."[10] Her use of Dewey's and James's work not only reveals how versed she was in the current discourse of American philosophy but importantly demonstrates how she views settlement efforts as a dynamic mingling of experience and reflection. Her reference to James comes from an address he made before the Philosophical Union of the University of California in 1897 (only two years prior to the work published by Addams), where he first used the term *pragmatism*. In this written conversation among Dewey, Addams, and James, then, we see that like her male counterparts, Addams was on the leading edge of the developments in American philosophy and was helping to construct that edge.

She may have been well read, but was Addams truly a philosopher? Certainly, for the better part of the twentieth century most people would not have given her that label, nor is it a title she claimed for herself. She is not included in mainstream encyclopedias of philosophy or many lists of American philosophers. Yet, her corpus of scholarly and popular writings is a great resource for American philosophy. Biographer Victoria Brown identifies the philosophical content inherent in Addams's writings: "It is perfectly possible, and highly recommended, to read Addams's major works—*Democracy and Social Ethics* (1902), *Newer Ideals of Peace* (1907), *Spirit of Youth and the City Streets* (1909),

Peace and Bread in Time of War (1922)—and encounter there a coherent, co-hesive body of political and social theory that places Addams squarely in the ranks of American leading advocates for democratic, pacifist pragmatism."[11] Furthermore, Addams's contemporaries recognized her intellectual insight. William James told Addams that her book *Democracy and Social Ethics* is "one of the great books of our time."[12] John Dewey assigned Addams's works for his philosophy students to read.[13] Given the esteem in which she was held by her colleagues in academia and her prolific and valued publication record, the question remains: why has Addams not generally been perceived as a philosopher? I suggest four reasons: sexism, the strength of the division between academic disciplines, prejudice against activists, and writing style.

Addams was fortunate enough to have been born into an era when women's education was not thoroughly stigmatized; nevertheless, philosophy at the time was clearly a masculine endeavor. Charlene Haddock Seigfried carefully documents how women are relegated to minor status among the leading texts of American philosophic history of the twentieth century.[14] If Addams is mentioned, she is given a fleeting reference as one who applied Dewey's ideas.[15] For much of the twentieth century, the documents of American philosophy characterize its proponents as exclusively male. Seigfried describes Dewey's attitude toward women as mixed: he argued for women's rights and recognized Addams as a brilliant thinker and writer but maintained traditional views about women as mothers and homemakers. In a 1919 article, "Philosophy and Democracy," written after he had known Addams for more than twenty-five years, Dewey remarkably states, "women have as yet made little contribution to philosophy."[16] The force of gender oppression in society and, in particular, the discipline of philosophy is such that even Addams's good friend, Dewey, who praised her intellect on many occasions and defended women theorists such as Charlotte Perkins Gilman, slips back to the conventional wisdom that women have little to contribute to philosophy. Dewey employs sentiments characteristic of what identity theorists describe as "exceptionalism": women are not as intellectually skilled as men, but Addams is an exception. Seigfried finds Dewey making brief and compartmentalized arguments for women's rights without significantly influencing his overall philosophy.[17] Addams's theoretical work came at a time when society did not accept women as philosophers. Her intellectual legacy suffers from the residue of this prejudice.

Given social opposition, Gerda Lerner suggests that women developed their own support systems to succeed in nontraditional roles: "In order for women to develop feminist consciousness, substantial numbers of women must be able to live in economic independence and see alternatives to marriage as a means of economic security. Only when large groups of single, self-supporting women have been able to conceptualize alternatives to the patriarchal state; only under such conditions have they been able to elevate 'sisterhood' into a unifying ideal."[18] Addams's work at Hull House illustrates Lerner's claim. Addams began to contribute to philosophy only after establishing an intentional community of women living outside the domestic responsibilities normally borne by women. A safe space for women's reflection emerged. Mary Jo Deegan refers to Hull House as a professional women's commune: "These women wrote together, lived and ate together, taught together, exchanged books and ideas, vacationed together, became officers in each other's organizations, developed a pool of expertise on a wide range of topics, and generated numerous changes in the social structure of government."[19] Addams recreated the best of a university environment in terms of intellectual exchange, all the while engaging in a collective project of social inquiry. In this environment, she was highly productive as a writer and speaker; she developed and extended progressive ideas while addressing the needs of the neighborhood. She lacked institutional legitimation as a philosopher in terms of credentials and employment, making the intellectual respect and impact that she achieved impressive. Yet Addams's recognition as a philosopher of note did not occur until the close of the twentieth century, when feminists stripped away socially constructed signifiers of academic legitimation. As philosopher Marilyn Fisher declares, "if philosophy is defined as thinking deeply about questions that matter, Addams is a philosopher of the first rank."[20]

Another barrier to Addams's recognition as a philosopher is her association with the emerging fields of sociology and social work. Mary Jo Deegan effectively argues that Addams was an influential sociologist.[21] However, as thorough as Deegan's argument is about legitimating Addams as a sociologist, it does not preclude Addams's preeminence as a philosopher. Although when John Dewey and George Herbert Mead were at the University of Chicago, disciplinary boundaries were much more fluid, modern scholarship has become increasingly territorial—despite widespread claims of valorizing "interdisciplinary thinking." In particular, many philosophers wish to keep social scientists at arm's length. Philosophers have a tendency to avoid getting their hands dirty with the vicissitudes of social scientific inquiry.

When the Department of Sociology at the University of Chicago first formed in 1892, Hull House played an important role in the nascent field of study. Pioneering works such as *Hull House Maps and Papers* produced some of the first systematic gathering of neighborhood data related to significant social issues. As the Chicago school of sociology grew in stature, it moved away from community concerns to a more abstract, "value free" approach to inquiry. Addams and her Hull House associates were no longer needed or wanted. The feeling was mutual, as Addams had no desire to relinquish the connection between theory and service to society.

The twentieth century witnessed a consolidation and demarcation of academic disciplines. Sociology coalesced into a distinct field of study from philosophy, and the field of social work emerged as a profession. An intellectual hierarchy was mapped onto the sociology/social work distinction, and, not surprisingly, that hierarchy has a gender dimension. Deegan's recent efforts notwithstanding, Addams and most female sociologists are commonly categorized as part of the hands-on field of social work, leaving the academically credentialed men to pursue more highly regarded theoretical interests. Professional sociologists adopt an exclusionary disposition similar to that of their older academic cousins: philosophers.

Despite the turf wars playing out between disciplines on college campuses, the distinction between theoreticians is not always as sharp as some believe. As the editors of *What Philosophers Think* declare, "Philosophy is a subject which crosses borders, and full-time philosophers do not have a monopoly on the subject."[22] The work of Karl Marx, for example, is studied in philosophy, sociology, and political science. Addams's contemporary, William James, is a significant figure in psychology and philosophy, while George Herbert Mead makes contributions to sociology, psychology, and philosophy. As Seigfried states, "Pragmatist philosophy reflects the interdisciplinary approach of its founders, since their careers developed before the hardening of disciplinary boundaries."[23] Scholarly work from various disciplines need not be mutually exclusive. Regardless of philosophic tradition, Addams's role as an important developer of sociology should not preclude her standing as an important American philosopher.

Although philosopher Mary Mahowald declares, "Addams surely fulfills the Socratic definition of the philosopher's role as gadfly of the state," she further claims that social activism is the essential reason why women like Addams were not considered American philosophers.[24] Women pragmatists were usually actively involved in advocating social change, and, given the historical penchant for affixing dualistic labels, activists are not theorists. Activists are generally characterized as people committed to their causes who do not usually have time for the rigors of academia let alone the abstraction of philosophy. Of course, women had few choices. An academic career might be available to an unmarried woman, but it was an uphill battle with few female role models or mentors. Mahowald points out that what interested activist women was usually not the subject of classical philosophical inquiry. Making sure the garbage gets picked up in the neighborhood, delivering babies, and working toward bridging communication between second-generation immigrants and their parents (a few of the issues that Addams addresses) are not the topics philosophers typically confront.

As Curti describes, "Jane Addams did not in any of her writing systematically set forth her social ideas in a way to please the scholars nowadays who set great store on what is called intellectual sophistication."[25] In particular, Addams does not present her philosophy in the linear manner typical of the genre. She writes and thinks from her experience to theory and back again. Her work addresses significant social concerns but couches them in themes and theories that resonate beyond the immediate issue. In Addams's book on prostitution, *A New Conscience and an Ancient Evil,* or teen disaffection, *The Spirit of Youth and the City Streets,* the philosophical content is not as readily apparent as in works such as *The Critique of Pure Reason* or *Meditations on First Philosophy.* Nevertheless, Addams is never simply descriptive. Her writing continually seeks social understanding, clarification, and themes that dovetail with larger ethical or epistemological concerns.

Although defining philosophers is perhaps a worthwhile endeavor, the rationale behind Addams's exclusion from the canon of American philosophers raises another issue. Given pervasive hierarchies of intellect over action, it appears that the title *philosopher* is used as a value judgment as well as a fuzzy term of description. The underlying logic appears to be that women, activists, and social workers are not "good enough" to be philosophers, and therefore someone of Addams's accomplishments is easy to exclude from the philosophical roll call. I hope that this book, as well as other recent works, will make it clear that it is no longer acceptable to ignore Addams's central role in shaping American philosophy.

Furthermore, I believe it is no longer permissible to exclude Addams from the great minds of American philosophy. She should be seen as founding a critical feminist pragmatism that integrates feminist sensibilities, including a robust notion of care ethics with an affective epistemology that makes the boundaries between action and reflection dynamic. The ephemeral Metaphysical Club pales by comparison to the accomplishments at Hull House in generating pragmatist thought.[26] My objective is not to diminish the tremendous work of Dewey, James, or Peirce. American philosophy is a wonderfully rich tradition that is rightfully being rediscovered. The figures associated with the founding of American pragmatism make an undeniable impact on American thought. Nevertheless, the exclusion of Addams constitutes a complex prejudice that must be shed if American philosophy is to fully recognize the extent of its rich history as well as live up to its own ideals.

I want to make it clear that my project of focusing on Addams's philosophy is intended as more *radical* feminism than *liberal* feminism. Liberal feminism, by definition, seeks to acquire equal opportunity and empower women with existing structures. Although this is a worthy goal, radical feminism claims that existing structures must be challenged because of their inherent oppressive systems. My purpose is not to carve another face into the Mount Rushmore of American philosophy in order to reify a feminist pragmatism that traces to the founding of the tradition. Addams is quite critical of founder worship, as is seen in her criticism of the moral presuppositions of the founders of the United States. The inclusion of Addams is symbolic of the dynamism and pluralism that should pervade American philosophy. If American philosophy is to be a departure—a challenge to traditional modes of philosophical thinking—it is appropriate for it to practice its own tenets regarding connection between thought and action in the manner of Addams's philosophy.

The Organization of This Book

The Social Philosophy of Jane Addams is divided into two parts. The first four chapters provide a historical and theoretical foundation for Addams's social philosophy while the last five chapters discuss how Addams applied her social theories to a variety of social issues. Chapter 1 considers Addams's influences, but with a bit of a twist: I simultaneously discuss how she was influential. Historically, many scholars are quick to indicate how Dewey, or Comte, or James, or Tolstoy influenced Addams, but few demonstrate the extent to which her ideas impacted her contemporaries. Others influenced Addams, but she was no one's meek protégé. Ultimately, most of her intellectual heroes failed her in one way or another.

Chapter 2 places Addams within the intellectual narrative of American philosophy known as pragmatism. In particular, her notion of lateral progress, the idea that progress should be defined by widespread gains or improvements, not just the advancement of a few individuals, represents a radicalization of pragmatism not found among her university-based contemporaries. Then, in chapter 3, I discuss Addams's place in feminist philosophy. Her feminism defies traditional categorization. She resists the label "feminist" because she did not want to limit herself to advocating for any one group; however, she viewed the social promotion of women as a necessary part of healthy, robust democracy. Thus, Addams was a pragmatist feminist. These chapters lay the foundation for chapter 4, where I suggest that the centerpiece of Addams's moral philosophy is her concept of "sympathetic knowledge," a unique integration of epistemology and ethics in approaching social issues. Through sympathetic knowledge, Addams viewed citizenship as demanding diverse and rich experiences of others that create better understanding from which to guide moral responses.

The final chapters deal with specific social and political content areas found in Addams's writing. In chapter 5, I discuss her writings and speeches on peace. As someone dedicated to social progress, she found that war represents the ultimate regression. Although Addams never made absolute or universalizing claims, her position in favor of pacifism came the closest. She viewed militarism as divisive and the patriotism fostered in war as a barrier to sympathetic knowledge. She made some of her strongest claims about the need for feminism in the face of war. Like William James, she sought moral substitutes for war in enlisting men *and women* in efforts toward social progress.

Chapter 6 addresses Addams's work on race, culture, and diversity. Living at Hull House, Addams experienced a unique richness and tempo of diversity that led to a cosmopolitan view regarding the value of pluralism. Her writing brings marginalized members of society, including children, adolescents, immigrants, working women, elderly women, prostitutes, and the working class, to the forefront of her philosophy. The chapter concludes with an extended consideration of a revealing public exchange Addams had with anti-lynching activist Ida B. Wells.

Addams found herself in the middle of numerous economic struggles. In chapter 7, her reluctant socialism is discussed. Of course, Addams eschewed such labels, but, despite despising ideology, she often sympathized with socialistic notions. In particular, she supported labor unions, not as an end unto themselves but as a means to widespread social progress. Her much-hailed commentary on the Pullman Strike provides the centerpiece of her economic analysis.

Chapter 8 attends to Addams's comprehensive view of social transactions as fundamentally educational. Hull House sponsored an array of social functions that Addams described as more than civil niceties. Such interactions are occasions to help foster sympathetic knowledge. Accordingly, she viewed settlements as educational endeavors. Her writings on education address diverse topics, such as the importance of physical play in the development of children and the need to make adult education relevant through techniques such as integrating current events. Addams pioneered the concept of adult education.

Addams had a complex relationship with religion. Privately, she harbored doubts about some of the fundamental tenets of Christianity, but publicly she maintained a collegial relationship with Christian organizations so that she could continue important conversations with their constituencies. Ultimately, she created her own version of Christianity, one that was minimalist when it came to dogma and that advocated humanistic social improvement. Chapter 9 reframes Addams's religion as social progress through feminist, pragmatist, utopian thinking.

I conclude with a brief afterword that reinforces Addams's significance for philosophy as well as her position as an icon of social progress. Given widespread contemporary cynicism over politics and social advancement, her work provides a refreshing reminder of the human potential to work collectively and to maintain hope for a better future.

PART I

Jane Addams, Philosopher

Jane Addams writing at desk, ca. 1895–1900.

Although Dewey and Mead were [Addams's] students in that they learned from her experience, criticisms, and insights, they were less inclined to acknowledge her influence than she was to acknowledge theirs. — MARY B. MAHOWALD

CHAPTER I

Intellectual Influences

Addams's philosophical influences cannot be reduced to a simple list of names or schools for at least two reasons. First, Addams was anti-ideological and therefore cannot be understood as rigidly in anyone's intellectual "camp." Although I, like others, suggest that she was a feminist pragmatist, she never claimed either of these titles, and pragmatism is resistant to ideological positioning anyway. At one point or another, Addams broke with her major influences because many of her intellectual heroes (e.g., Thomas Carlyle, Leo Tolstoy, John Dewey) ultimately disappointed her in some significant manner. Second, her thirst for knowledge exemplified the best of the philosopher's spirit of inquiry. She read widely with an open mind. Although she wrote in an era less diligent about attribution than today, her works directly or indirectly refer to a wide spectrum of intellectual influences, some of whom I describe in this chapter. Addams appropriated philosophies as they supported her commitments to social advancement through sympathetic understanding. I offer a brief overview of a half dozen of her more significant influences, but this list is not exhaustive given her fertile mind. Note that because of how well her methodology fits into that tradition, I defer the discussion of her relationship to American pragma-tist philosophy until the next chapter. This chapter continues the work of the introduction in claiming that Addams was a philosopher, but here I establish the rich context for her intellectual work—one that she helped to shape.

Historical Influences

Although the ideas of philosophers are sometimes portrayed as pulled out of time and place to participate in what feminist philosophers have referred to as "a view from nowhere," Addams's theoretical work is so grounded in experi-ence that understanding her social and historical context is crucial. Addams lived through a revolution in American consciousness. During her lifetime, Abraham Lincoln was assassinated, the South endured Reconstruction, the Nineteenth Amendment gave women the constitutional right to vote, the United States entered the Great War, the nation fell into a Great Depression (among many smaller depressions), and sexual mores underwent Freudian scrutiny as the Victorian era faded.

Although Addams was not even six years old at the conclusion of the Civil War, she grew up in the shadow of this nation-defining event. As she recalls, the Civil War "touched children in many ways" including witnessing the mourning of parents and the reading of the names of war dead.[1] It is difficult to overes-timate the influence of the Civil War on the psyche of Americans living in its aftermath. It left more than six hundred thousand Americans dead, more than all other U.S. wars from the Revolution through the Vietnam War combined. Although historians offer various explanations for the motivation and meaning of the Civil War, Addams found inspiration in the human capacity for moral growth and change as the evil of slavery was left behind.

Of the social movements during her time, Addams is most closely associ-ated with the Progressive movement, which roughly covered the period from 1890 to 1920. Like all social phenomena, the Progressive Era was a complex combination of forces that is subject to interpretation by historians and soci-ologists. Progressives believed that society could be changed to improve the general welfare. Although previous populist movements had little faith in grand schemes achieved through governmental efforts, progressives believed govern-ment had the ability to institute programs that could lead to social betterment. An important assumption was that society can and should improve. Addams's philosophy reflects the optimism of the era, but she also shaped the progres-sive ideals of the time by arguing forcefully for the possibility of specific social improvements through collective understanding. She followed through on her social philosophy by repeatedly enacting changes for the betterment of others.

Mirroring the range of social issues that Addams tackled in her lifetime, the Progressive movement was an amalgamation of reform efforts. However, whereas the Progressive movement never coalesced into a single, organized effort,[2] Addams utilized Hull House as the foundation and vehicle for unifying a range of social changes. Hull House exemplified, and often spearheaded, the settlement movement. Settlement workers took progressive ideals and applied them by living in, and working for, oppressed neighborhoods. As Allen F. Davis explains, "they were reformers who served as initiators and organizers and helped to extend the social welfare function of government in the city, the state, and the nation."[3] Poverty, industrial oppression, and unprecedented immigration motivated many people to take personal action by volunteering to participate in communities dedicated to improving conditions.

Although men played major roles, women, emerging from the private sphere and participating in public life, fueled the Progressive and social settlement movements. Historian S. J. Kleinberg describes the gendered nature of settlements: "The settlement house movement was a distinctively female contribution to reform and social welfare in the United States."[4] The late nineteenth century witnessed women's entry into college in substantial numbers. These women, like Addams, were caught in a bind of experiencing their intellectual potential in school but having limited postcollegiate opportunities to apply it. When Addams describes the motives for settlement houses in 1892, she avoids gender distinction but alludes to the dilemma created through education: "We have in America a fast-growing number of cultivated young people who have no recognized outlet for their active faculties."[5] Her claim was more appropriate for women than men, and, by 1902, Addams more explicitly portrays "the college woman" who struggled between the traditional familial role and civic engagement.[6] More than four hundred settlements of various character emerged in the United States.[7] Some were identified with colleges, and some were religiously motivated, but they arose relatively quickly at the turn of the century and diminished just as quickly after World War I. Many women, such as Lillian Wald, Fannie Barrier Williams, Harriet Vittum, Fannie Hagan Emanuel, Ada Sophia Dennison McKinley, and Mary McDowell, started or led settlements, although no one was identified with the movement so much as Addams, who helped to define it through her books, articles, and speeches.[8]

Finally, in considering the various historical forces that impinged on Addams's philosophy, the prevalence of the sexism that she overcame should not be underestimated. Essentialist beliefs about women's inferior intellect, health, and leadership abilities were still common one hundred years ago. Social, political, and institutional limits placed on women were firmly entrenched. Philosopher Nel Noddings speculates about what Addams could have accomplished in a different time period, one that was less oppressive for women: "How many avenues of activity were open to women? Even Jane Addams suffered several years of illness and indecision before she decided to open Hull House with Ellen Gates Starr. Addams became so well known that she was called 'the most dangerous woman in America.' One wonders what she might have done if she had been born some years later."[9] Such speculation is always challenging given the number of variables to consider, but we do know that Addams rose to meet the gender challenges of her era. She was the visible moral and intellectual leader of an unprecedented cohort of accomplished women (and some men) at Hull House that transformed Chicago and then the nation. Robyn Muncy argues that the web of female associations created by Addams evolved into a "female dominion" of social policymaking that spread its influence to the federal government.[10]

Turning from social forces to individuals, there are a number of figures who influenced Addams's philosophy.

Moral Icons: John Addams and Abraham Lincoln

When Addams recounts her childhood, two names dominate her reflection: her father, John Addams, and President Abraham Lincoln, who was assassinated when she was only a few years old. The two men are linked in her mind: "I always tend to associate Lincoln with the tenderest thoughts of my father."[11] Both were public figures, both served in the Illinois legislature, and both were Civil War heroes (although neither participated in combat). They knew and corresponded with one another. For Jane Addams, Lincoln represented a moral icon rather than an important moral theorist. Lincoln was a secular hero for Addams, who repeatedly praises his unwavering honesty and commitment to democratic values. She asks, "Is it not Abraham Lincoln who has cleared the title to our democracy? He made plain, once and for all, that democratic government, associated as it is with all the mistakes and shortcomings of the common people, still remains the most valuable contribution America has made to the moral life of the world."[12] Addams does not often quote Lincoln but invokes him as a beloved secular saint rather than an intellectual.[13] For example, Lincoln receives only a passing mention in *Democracy and Social Ethics*, Addams's most theoretical work. Although he remained an inspirational figure for Addams throughout her life, she sought more reflective depth from the works of philosophers and other intellectuals to develop her social philosophy.

Addams's father was also a moral icon for her, but the reality of the father-daughter relationship makes John Addams a more complex moral influence than Lincoln. Because her mother died when she was two years old, Jane Addams was very much a father-identified child. In her autobiographical account,

Twenty Years at Hull-House, written when she was approaching fifty years of age, Addams devotes the opening to her father in a style that is characteristically humble. She admits, "I centered upon him all that careful imitation which a little girl ordinarily gives to her mother's ways and habits."[14] Intellectually, she emulated his high moral standards, thoughtful consideration of issues, and religious skepticism.

She relates a story about her perplexity concerning Christian predestination in which her father, to her surprise, expressed the view that neither of them had "the kind of mind" to understand predestination. Her impression of the conversation is "that it did not matter much whether one understood foreordination or not, but that it was very important not to pretend to understand what you didn't understand and that you must always be honest with yourself inside, whatever happened. Perhaps on the whole as valuable a lesson as the shorter catechism itself contains."[15] Quite typical of Jane and John Addams, this exchange contains no dismissal of religion or harsh rebuke. Rather, the discussion recognizes the importance of maintaining a disposition of integrity while seeking understanding, even in the face of widely accepted but difficult doctrine. Jane Addams replicated that kind of dispassionate analysis throughout her life.

In an era of separate gender spheres, strong father-identification had the advantage of opening Addams's mind to possibilities that other women dared not pursue.[16] Biographer Victoria Brown notes that John and Jane's relationship blossomed in her teen years. John Addams had retired from politics by that time, and Jane provided him with an intellectual companion not otherwise available.[17] Jane Addams was afforded an unusual opportunity for a young woman of this era: to engage a well-read father. She certainly benefited from the exposure. However, although Addams never publicly expressed anything but admiration for her father, there is some evidence that her intellectual development may have had to overcome some of his ideas. James Weber Linn, Jane Addams's nephew and biographer, notes that she often credited her father with her views on pacifism, yet Linn finds no evidence that he was anything but zealous about fighting in the Civil War.[18] Although John Addams was an important moral model for Jane, their relationship typified her ideas of social progress: the time had come for newer ideals. Nevertheless, John Addams contributed significantly to her intellectual development.[19] One important contribution that her father made was to foster her education not just by sending her to school but also by encouraging reading at home. John Addams was an important citizen in Cedarville and developed the largest library in the town. His own reading brought him to the work of the Italian political philosopher Joseph Mazzini (1805–72), who became an important intellectual legacy to his daughter.

Addams recounts her first tangential encounter with Mazzini when she was twelve years old and walked into a room to find her father in a very solemn demeanor—visibly saddened by the man's death. Her reaction is surprising and has nothing to do with Mazzini's philosophy: "In the end I obtained that which I have ever regarded as a valuable possession, a sense of the genuine relationship which may exist between men who share large hopes and like desires, even though they differ in nationality, language, and creed."[20] However, whether it was because of her father's influence or the power of Mazzini's ideas, Addams referred to Mazzini throughout her career.

During Mazzini's childhood, Italy was in disarray—fractionated and controlled by foreign kings and princes. When he was sixteen, his family was entreated by a revolutionary begging for money, and from then on Mazzini turned his attention to politics. He was an intellectual revolutionary who published articles between terms of imprisonment and exile. While in England, he was befriended by Thomas Carlyle, who introduced him to the political and intellectual circles of England. One of his acquaintances was Joseph Toynbee, father of Arnold Toynbee. Mazzini wrote his most enduring work, *The Duties of Man*, in England but monitored political upheaval in Italy and returned there to aid in the unification of the nation. The success of his efforts is regarded as mixed by historians.[21] John Addams appreciated Mazzini for his political writings and actions; Jane Addams came to value his social as well as his political philosophy. In particular, Mazzini endorsed universal suffrage and freedom for women, national education, and common welfare programs.[22] His new expression of religion grounded in social efforts resonated with Addams's own philosophy: "God has made you social and progressive beings. It is your duty, then, to associate yourselves and to progress as much as is possible in the sphere of activity in which you are placed by circumstances, and it is your right to demand that the society to which you belong shall not impede you in your work of association and of progress, but shall *help* you in it and *supply* you with the means of *association* and of progress if you lack them."[23] In an age without the communication technologies available today, the cross-fertilization of ideas was remarkable. Mazzini, Toynbee, and Carlyle all contributed to Addams's social philosophy, and her father could take credit for introducing her to Mazzini.

Moral Visionaries: From Carlyle and Ruskin to Tolstoy

The 1800s witnessed several thinkers' development of romantic notions of moral leadership. Their ideas about heroism inspired Addams. Her autobiographical narrative, although often humble, implies a sense of personal destiny that fit with the moral visionaries of the era. One such influence was Thomas Carlyle (1795–1881). Addams read his work while at Rockford Seminary: "Carlyle has a way of saying things once in a while that strike, as it were my key-note, just exactly what I have been hunting for."[24] Carlyle's social morality held a particular appeal for Addams. He believed that the universe is ultimately good and moral, and led by a divine will that works through society's heroes and leaders. Mixing in commentary explicating his moral philosophy, Carlyle wrote biographies of social saviors who appeared in the form of poets, kings, prophets, and intellectuals. His *On Heroes and Hero Worship and the Heroic in History* is a series of six lectures delivered in 1840 that describe six archetypes of heroes and gives specific historical examples. Carlyle's heroes evolve over time and reflect a changing society, as different contexts require different leadership. These heroes are able to recognize the social dynamics at work and use them for the benefit of others. However, the duty of self-discovery and social destiny extends to everyone. Because of his emphasis on powerful individuals, Carlyle was not particularly fond of democracy. At first, he wrote about men of ideas but later emphasized men of action, declaring, "the end of life is an action, not a thought."[25] Although Addams shed Carlyle's notion of individualistic heroism, she retained the valorization of moral action throughout her career. Furthermore, Carlyle's morality was grounded in social relations: to be moral was to be in right relation with God and others. One can see a precursor to Addams's notion of sympathetic knowledge in Carlyle's mixing of epistemology and relational ethics: "what we can call knowing, a man must first love the thing, sympathize with it; that is, be virtuously related to it."[26]

Another moral visionary who contributed to Addams's class consciousness and the role of aesthetics in promoting social progress was John Ruskin (1819–1900). The author of more than a dozen books on painting and architecture, Ruskin was recognized as England's leading aesthetic commentator, but in 1860 he turned his attention to social and political issues. His international artistic travels brought him in contact with social inequities, and he wrote sympathetically about the oppressed. Ruskin's fans were outraged by his metamorphosis, and the only encouragement came from Thomas Carlyle. Correspondence between the two led Ruskin to become Carlyle's avid disciple.

Ruskin believed that art and culture reflect the moral health of society: "the higher arts, which involve the action of the whole intellect, tell the story of the entire national character."[27] Although Ruskin maintained a certain elitism in his view that great people produce great art, he also found those works to be a manifestation of society as a whole. The plight of the oppressed is tied to a sense of the aesthetic: "We shall never make our houses for the rich beautiful, till we have begun by making our houses for the poor beautiful. As it is a common and diffused pride, soil is a common and diffused delight on which alone our future arts can be founded."[28] Certainly, Addams's appreciation for art and culture as exhibited in the appearance and activities of Hull House resonated with Ruskin's aesthetics. Her work was also affected by Ruskin's theory of education: "The entire object of true education is to make people not merely do the right things, but enjoy the right things: not merely industrious, but to love industry—not merely pure, but to love purity—not merely just, but to hunger and thirst after justice."[29] Ruskin influenced Arnold Toynbee and other future settlement workers by identifying the problems in large industrial cities and calling for reforms that prefigured the safety net of a welfare state. He also esteemed labor as a noble means of self-actualization. This became a crucial concept for Addams as she sought meaningful labor that matched her high moral standards. Although Addams valued Ruskin's moral imagination, concept of labor, and ideas about transforming the city through infusing culture, she rejected his romanticization of the preindustrial past. With a strong belief in social progress, Addams did not desire a return to the past. She felt that society should grow and adapt to its conditions, even in regard to morality.

If Addams appropriated aspects of Ruskin's and Carlyle's sense of moral heroism, if not their elitism, to her own ethical motivation, Leo Tolstoy (1828–1910) was another type of hero to Addams—an antihero. Her wide intellectual curiosity made such extremes possible. Addams read Tolstoy's works from the time that she graduated from college until the last years of her life, and she often praised his writing in articles and book reviews. Tolstoy's emphasis on working for and with the oppressed while simultaneously writing novels and essays that influence a wider audience was in tune with Addams's work at Hull House. However, Tolstoy was a moral idealist. In *What Then Must We Do?* Tolstoy observes his own failure at charitable work and concludes that property in the face of poverty is hypocritical and that charity work in big cities is ineffective. He leaves everything behind to take up the plow and work as a common farm laborer. Addams was moved by Tolstoy's account, and, typical of her self-critical, thoughtful approach, she began to question Hull House and her role in the social settlement. Motivated by his troubling moral challenge, Addams sought him out while she was on vacation (and recovering from typhoid) in Europe in 1896. The story of the meeting, which she recounts in *Twenty Years at Hull-House,* left a lasting impression on Addams.[30]

Tolstoy comes in from working the fields to be introduced to Addams and her partner, Mary Rozet Smith. The meeting begins with Tolstoy questioning Addams's fashion choice because her sleeves, consistent with contemporary styles, had "enough stuff on one arm to make a frock for the girl."[31] He is concerned that the trappings of material wealth alienate Addams from those she purports to help. This criticism expands when Tolstoy learns that part of Hull House's funding comes from Addams's estate, which includes a working farm: "So you are an absentee landlord? Do you think you will help the people more by adding yourself to the crowded city than you would by tilling your own soil?"[32] Addams, humbled by Tolstoy's remarks, is determined to engage in direct labor by working in the new Hull House bakery. However, reality quickly demonstrates how Tolstoy's idealism is incompatible with her settlement work: "The half dozen people invariably waiting to see me after breakfast, the piles of letters to be opened and answered, the demand of actual and pressing human wants—were these all to be pushed aside and asked to wait while I saved my soul by two hours' work at baking bread?"[33]

Tolstoy's radical efforts at equality that included no appreciable division of labor were unworkable for Addams. She prized intelligent leadership. Someone had to organize the clubs, arrange for philanthropic support, and chair the meetings. To a certain point, Addams found Tolstoy's labor demand to be self-indulgent: if she engaged in the labor of the poor exclusively, she might alleviate her upper-class guilt, but she no longer could work holistically toward changing the structure of society. Addams's own philosophy of civic activism valued engagement through ongoing presence and listening. Indeed, Hull House had a very flat organizational structure. Nevertheless, Tolstoy's absolutist moral demands failed to take into account context—a hallmark of Addams's approach.

Addams did find Tolstoy's pacifism inspiring. She admired how he sympathized with revolutionaries in the 1870s yet did not compromise his nonviolent convictions. He offered a doctrine of nonresistance that attempted to substitute moral force for physical force. According to Addams, Tolstoy contends that "to oppose one wrong with another is to get away ever further from the teachings of the New Testament in regard to overcoming evil with good."[34] Again, she did not accept Tolstoy's ideas uncritically. For example, she questions the clarity of the categories (moral energy versus physical force) that he creates in his doctrine of nonresistance. Addams also questions whether Tolstoy reduces social issues too simplistically, albeit eloquently. She asks, among other things, "Was Tolstoy more logical than life warrants?"[35] Despite her concerns and her less than congenial meeting with him, Addams referenced Tolstoy as a positive moral example throughout her life. However, like all of her influences, his philosophy was not accepted whole. Addams had to adapt it and infuse her own insight to make it work for society.

Settlement Philosophy:
Samuel Barnett and Arnold Toynbee

Nothing is more important to the development of Addams's philosophy than her settlement work. Although Addams contributed to making American settlements significantly different from British settlements, she was originally inspired by the work of Samuel Barnett (1844–1913) and Arnold Toynbee (1852–83). Barnett shaped the character of Toynbee Hall, the famous settlement in London that

Addams visited in the late 1880s. Barnett served as "warden" of the settlement for more than twenty years. Prior to his service at Toynbee Hall, Barnett worked as vicar of St. Jude's, Whitechapel, where he instituted a number of improvements to the slums surrounding the church, including building educational and recreational programs. St. Jude's was where Oxford students of the time visited and volunteered, while engaging in discussions about how to institute social reforms. One of those students was Andrew Toynbee.[36]

Barnett describes a threefold rationale for the development and growth of settlements. First is a general distrust that institutions can care for the poor. In particular, the government and philanthropy appear to fail the masses. According to Barnett, men and women are compelled to act for the good of society: "They were between two duties. On the one side they were bound to be true to themselves and do their own work. On the other side, they were bound by other means than votes and [charitable] subscriptions to meet the needs of the poor. They welcomed, therefore the proposal for a Settlement where they might live their own lives and also make friends among the poor."[37] The second reason Barnett gives for the rise of settlements is the need for information. Like Addams, he finds a wide-ranging social scientific spirit that seeks to observe and document the circumstances of the oppressed. Finally, Barnett notes a groundswell of fellowship not driven by traditional charities and missions, but by a fundamental humanitarianism. Settlements provide an outlet for these fellow feelings.

Addams, familiar with Barnett's writings, referred to them often. For example, when Addams writes about "A Function of the Social Settlement," Barnett's philosophy plays a prominent role. She agrees with him that settlements should not be missions, because if they become too ideological, they will fail to be responsive to their neighbors.[38] However, despite her acknowledgment that the term *settlement* is borrowed from London, she emphasizes the absence of noblesse oblige in the American version: "The American Settlement, perhaps has not so much a sense of duty of the privileged toward the unprivileged, of the 'haves' to the 'have nots,' to borrow Samuel Barnett's phrase, as a desire to equalize through social effort those results which superior opportunity may have given the possessor."[39]

Addams was concerned about a sense of superiority in settlement work. She always eschewed the notion that she was "lady bountiful." For Addams, Hull House combined epistemological concerns with moral ones. She wanted to learn about others so that she could develop the proper sympathies and strategies for assisting—for example, "sympathetic knowledge." Historian Kathryn Kish Sklar describes American settlements as different from their British counterparts in their predominance of women, their focus on immigrant communities, and their political activism. Prominent British women activists tended to work through philanthropic systems rather than settlements.[40] Of course, Addams cultivated philanthropic support for Hull House, particularly from women's organizations, but charity was not the raison d'être of the settlement.

Occupying the same constellation of influences on Addams as did Barnett was Arnold Toynbee, for whom the famous east London settlement was named. Toynbee's zeal for social change emerged from his Christian convictions, but he had no patience for church dogmatism. Like Addams, Toynbee graduated from college seeking a moral cause.[41] A lecturer at Balliol College, he first desired to reform the Church of England but eventually turned his attention to political economy. A friend of Ruskin and inspired by Samuel Barnett, Toynbee found value in living among the working class. He experimented with such arrangements on several occasions with members of the Oxford community. Shortly prior to his death, Toynbee gave a series of lectures in London that include radical ideas about society: "We—the middle classes, I mean not merely the very rich—we have neglected you [the working class]; instead of justice we have offered you charity, and instead of sympathy, we have offered you hard and unreal advice; but I think we are changing. If you would only believe it and trust us, I think that many of us would spend our lives in your service."[42] Here Toynbee expresses a measure of middle-class guilt that reverberates with Addams's motivation for Hull House. Toynbee's untimely death from "brain fever" galvanized his friends to create a permanent settlement—Toynbee Hall. Reflecting a sense of moral heroism and class consciousness, Addams describes how "it was fortunate for society that every age possessed at least a few minds which, like Arnold Toynbee's were 'perpetually disturbed over the apparent inequalities of mankind.'"[43] Addams maintained Toynbee's positive human ontology—a fundamental belief in the goodness of humanity—throughout her activism and philosophy.

Florence Kelley and the Women of Hull House

Hull House is described in many different ways, reflecting the complexity and multiplicity of its activities. From a philosophical perspective, it was a pragmatist feminist "think tank." Addams was a resident of Hull House for almost a half century, and during that time many skillful women lived and worked there. These educated and accomplished activists influenced Addams's philosophy. Together Hull House residents dined, slept, did domestic chores, and engaged in social work. They also discussed and debated ethics, political theory, feminism, and culture as they went about their daily tasks. The many speakers and visitors to Hull House provided additional stimulation. Prolonged contact, shared gender oppression, and a common mission made for a unique intellectual atmosphere, and a sense of community.

Ostensibly, Hull House was the first coeducational settlement. Addams recognized the need for male residents so that men in the neighborhood could better connect to Hull House endeavors. However, it was quite clear to visitors and residents that Hull House was a woman's space. The residents included some of the era's great minds and agents of change. Alice Hamilton (1869–1970), a physician trained in Germany and the United States who founded the field of industrial medicine, lived at Hull House for twenty-two years. She went on to teach at Harvard, where she became a nationally recognized social reformer and peace activist. Longtime resident, and the subject of a book by Addams, Julia Lathrop (1858–1932) was a Vassar graduate. In 1912, she became the first woman to head a federal agency, the Children's Bureau, which she modeled after Hull House. The Children's Bureau gathered research on children and disseminated information on child raising and motherhood while advocating child-friendly policies. Rachel Yarros (1869–1946), a twenty-year resident at Hull House, was also a physician as well as a birth control activist who later taught at the University of Illinois. The university created a position for Yarros in recognition of her tremendous contribution to social hygiene and sex education.

Author and feminist theorist Charlotte Perkins Gilman (1860–1935) was a resident for a short period of time. Gilman thought highly of Addams but had no stomach for the challenging settlement existence among the oppressed. Her groundbreaking work on gender and economics likely influenced Addams, while the communal existence at Hull House likely influenced Gilman's feminist utopian vision. Hull House resident Sophonisba Breckinridge (1866–1948) graduated from Wellesley and went on to obtain both a Ph.D. in political science and a J.D. from the University of Chicago. Her greatest contribution was in social work education. Edith Abbott (1876–1957) and her sister Grace Abbott (1878–1939) joined Hull House about the time Breckinridge did (1907). Edith obtained a Ph.D. in political economy from the University of Chicago while Grace earned a Ph.D. from Grand Island College in Nebraska. Edith had an academic career at the University of Chicago prior to her appointment as chief of the Children's Bureau after Julia Lathrop's departure. Another resident, Mary Kenney (1864–1943), became an important labor organizer for Samuel Gompers's American Federation of Labor and influenced Addams's sensitivity to the plight of organized labor, something that not all progressives shared. I have only mentioned a few of the well-known residents, but numerous women used their Hull House experience as a springboard to careers in social reform or professions of various sorts.

Men were also present at Hull House. Beatrice Webb describes the relations of men and women after a visit in 1898: "The residents consist in the main, of strong-minded, energetic women, bustling about their various enterprises and professions, interspersed with earnest-faced, self-subordinating and mild-mannered men who slide from room to room apologetically."[44] In any other context, these "mild-mannered" men might have been the center of attention, given their own skills and accomplishments. Male Hull House residents included MacKenzie King, future prime minister of Canada; Gerard Swope, future president of General Electric; Earnest Carroll Moore, future cofounder of UCLA; and George Hooker, journalist and later director of the Chicago City Club.[45] Despite their abilities, the male residents never influenced the leadership or culture of Jane Addams's Hull House to the extent that the women activists did.

Although Hull House was replete with extraordinary minds, no one was as intellectually challenging to Addams as Florence Kelley (1859–1932). A Cornell graduate, Kelley enrolled at the University of Zurich to study law. She translated Friedrich Engels's *The Condition of the Working Class in England* and Karl Marx's *Free Trade* into English. She was an active member of the Socialist Labor Party, but Kelley's forceful style threatened the leadership and she was expelled. While at Zurich, she met and married Lazare Wischnewtsky, a physician and fellow socialist. They had three children, but their financially troubled marriage turned abusive and fell apart. A single mother with three children, Kelley found a home at Hull House.[46] She opened an employment center there and began conducting research on sweatshops for the Illinois Bureau of Labor Statistics. Kelley later became the general secretary of the new Consumer's League, an organization dedicated to using consumer pressure to ensure the manufacture of safe and quality goods. Kelley was one of the most distinguished social reformers of the early twentieth century.

At Hull House, Kelley altered the dynamics of the resident community. She brought a sense of class consciousness with a great strength of conviction. Her forthright approach rubbed some the wrong way, but her energy was infectious. Alice Hamilton writes of Kelley, "It was impossible for the most sluggish to be with her and not catch fire."[47] Intellectually, Kelley challenged Addams to recognize social class, support labor, and mitigate religious connections.[48] Addams's biographer Allen Davis describes Kelley as someone who "loved to argue with anyone who would take her on, and Julia Lathrop and Jane Addams often waited up for her to listen, to talk, and to debate over a cup of hot chocolate far into the night. Florence Kelley had a great respect and admiration for Jane Addams, like Julia Lathrop, she called her J.A., but she was the only one of the group who could laugh at her, poke fun at her, or even criticize her; and Jane took it from her. More than anyone else Florence Kelley turned Jane Addams from a philanthropist to a reformer."[49] Although Davis overstates the latter point, Kelley did participate in the radicalization of Addams's thought.

After Kelley's arrival, and Mary Kenney's coming a year prior, Hull House became deeply involved in supporting the labor movement, which had been heretofore dominated by men. Kelley also learned from Addams, whom she admired throughout her life. According to Kelley's biographer Sklar, "Both shared a deeply moral commitment to social justice, Addams drawing on her vision of social democracy, Kelley on her understanding of Marxian socialism. Addams's instinct for peacemaking and conciliation made her see every side of social questions and feel compassion for all the actors, while Kelley's aggressive championing of the exploited usually dealt with stark contrasts between good and evil. Kelley expressed anger against the causes of social injustice; Addams demonstrated a tragic appreciation of and sympathy with suffering."[50]

Perhaps the legacy of the many accomplishments of Hull House residents suffered because of the fame of their leader, but given the opportunity, each expressed his or her admiration and gratitude to Addams for making Hull House a hotbed of ideas and action. Addams was the visible and palatable leader of a remarkable group of educated activists whose mutual respect allowed intellectual growth to flourish.

Children

Florence Kelley describes her arrival at Hull House: "On a snowy morning between Christmas 1891 and New Year's 1892, I arrived at Hull House, Chicago, a little before breakfast time, and found there Henry Standing Bear, a Kickapoo Indian, waiting for the front door to be opened. It was Miss Addams who opened it, holding on her left arm a singularly unattractive, fat, pudgy baby belonging to the cook who was behindhand with breakfast. Miss Addams was a little hindered in her movements by a super energetic kindergarten child, left by its mother who went to a sweatshop for a bundle of cloaks to be finished."[51]

Perhaps one of the most overlooked of the many influences on Addams's philosophy was the ubiquitous presence of children at Hull House. Philosophers do not often cite children as being philosophically significant. The claim that the presence of children had an intellectual impact on Addams is made more unusual because she never bore or raised any children of her own. Nevertheless, to live at Hull House was to navigate a throng of neighborhood children who participated in its kindergarten, nursery, day care, clubs, programs, and athletics or who simply made use of the gymnasium or playground facilities. Hull House was a "kid friendly" environment before the term was invented.

The daily presence of children is not a trivial philosophical matter. Addams's proximity to children raised her awareness of their needs. As Shannon Jackson describes,

Settlers were surrounded by miniature human beings, and the discursive and social fact of their presence structured everyday life at Hull House. Receiving rooms were often a flurry of diminutive activity, filled with incessant motion punctuated with periodic crying. The lowest places of the rooms often saw the most action, and settlers constantly found themselves crouching on the floor to keep track of its goings-on. Residents composed their thoughts about child welfare while simultaneously attending to children's demands, a conflation of the figural and literal that occurred every time a child peered over a desk to see what a settler was doing. The environment thus percolated with the affect of *littleness*.[52]

Although Addams crafted her educational philosophy from her experiences with Hull House children, she also developed much of the rest of her philosophy amid the frazzled atmosphere of little children. This is not the typical environment for philosophical development, such as that which emanates from university-based scholars. If physical environment has an impact on philosophical work, the ubiquitous presence of children at Hull House cannot be discounted as an influence.

In 1989, writer Barbara Garland Polikoff brought her aunt, Sadie Garland Dreikurs, aged eighty-nine and a longtime Hull House resident, to visit the Jane Addams Hull-House Museum. Dreikurs had avoided such a visit since the bitterly fought destruction of the original Hull House complex to build the campus of the University of Illinois at Chicago in the 1960s. At first, Dreikurs failed to recognize the surroundings at Hull House: they were too quiet and orderly. She recalled, "Every corner of this room was filled with bags of children's clothes, toys, boots."[53] Dreikurs's recollection is a testament to how the presence of children transforms physical space in terms of noise, organization, and the pace of life. Addams's philosophy arose out of such an environment.

Addams's work with adult education overshadowed her efforts with children; however, pioneering work on children's education was initiated at Hull House as well. Numerous pioneering educators influenced Addams's philosophy of education, but she in turn influenced the advancement of the field. She was particularly concerned with engaging students in a variety of pedagogies and activities in an effort to move away from rote memorization. Carmelita Chase Hinton (1891–1983), another significant figure in progressive education reform, credited her time at Hull House and working with Addams for inspiring her educational philosophy.[54] Hinton founded the innovative Putney School in Vermont, a college preparatory school that integrates cooperative endeavors with a wide range of arts and crafts activities into its curriculum.

Addams's dedication to children became evident in her support for the federal Children's Bureau. Although Florence Kelley and Lillian Wald spearheaded the legislative effort to create the agency, Addams addressed the 1909 White House conference on the Care of Dependent Children. In 1912, President William Howard Taft signed the Children's Bureau bill into law. Addams recommended that longtime Hull House resident Julia Lathrop be appointed to head up the agency, and Taft agreed. After swift Senate approval, the appointment of Lathrop gave Addams's feminist pragmatism an even wider range of influence.

Ultimately, the presence of children at Hull House helped ground Addams's development of sympathetic knowledge. Given their lack of communicative sophistication, limited language development, and fluid minds, children require a great deal of attention. This attention requires a disposition of care and trust. Their presence is a constant anchor to lived, embodied existence.

Other Influences

Those who wish to categorize Addams in a particular intellectual stream are challenged by her wide-ranging influences and the resistance to ideology inherent in her pragmatism. Dorothy Ross argues that Addams was a romantic: "Addams's college essays show her to be thoroughly steeped in romantic writers: Goethe, Wordsworth, Coleridge, Scott, Emerson, and Carlyle constantly reappear. I use *romantic* here broadly, to denote the tendency to valorize feeling, subjectivity, individuality, and intuition."[55] On the other hand, Francesca Sawaya claims that Addams was a realist: "Addams's writings depend on important intellectual discourses of the time to compel and convince her audience. What links these discourses together is literary realism . . . a claim to and about reality."[56] So which is it? Was Addams a romantic or a realist? Ross and Sawaya make compelling arguments, but I have presented their positions as a false dichotomy. Addams was a romantic in the manner that she drew human sympathy into her arguments compelling citizens to act in one another's behalf. She was a realist in her thoroughgoing analysis of issues and her use of multiple approaches to address problems. She was a realist in seeking tangible solutions. In many ways, Addams's philosophy defies simple categorization, and this reflects the myriad of influences on her ideas.

Her Christian roots had an effect, as Addams was well versed in the Christian Bible and attended a number of religious courses during her time at Rockford Seminary. Because she used religion in such a particular, instrumental manner, I save this discussion for the latter part of the book, where I address issues and applications of her philosophy. Addams was also well informed about Greek philosophy and on occasion made references to ancient philosophers. In particular, the Greeks moved easily from individual to political concerns, a relation that appealed to her. She was also swayed by August Comte (1798–1857) and the positivists. Comte coined the term *sociology* and believed that science requires a logic drawn from experience rather than the a priori universal rationalism of Descartes. Addams would have been attracted to his ideas about social progress and his development of a religion of humanity.

Finally, Addams also read widely in Western literature, which affected her ideas concerning culture and sometimes seeped into her analysis as it did when she used Shakespeare's *King Lear* to understand labor-management relations. Although she did not believe that reading was a substitute for direct experience, she did suggest more than once that reading great works of fiction is a means of developing a sympathetic understanding.

Addams was shaped by a variety of influences, but she was not a derivative thinker, as many commentators suggest. She drew on a number of great theorists to develop her ideas about social morality but never dogmatically followed in anyone's footsteps. Simultaneously, she influenced many others as she made her unique gift to American and feminist philosophy. The next two chapters explore how Addams fits into the intellectual streams of thought: pragmatism and feminism. Ultimately, her singular contribution to philosophy, sympathetic knowledge, flows from a confluence of these approaches.

CHAPTER 2

Radical Pragmatism

I place Addams's work within two streams of philosophy: American
pragmatism and feminism. These streams coalesce in Addams's notion of sympathetic knowledge. This chapter is dedicated to the tributary of American pragmatist philosophy and has two purposes. The first is to flesh out Addams's position within American philosophy in relation to several key figures in the tradition.
The second is to address Addams's radicalization of pragmatism through her
notion of lateral progress. In the next chapter, I explore Addams's feminism.

The conventional wisdom of American philosophy is that pragmatism
originated in the works of several central figures, usually delineated by some
combination of John Dewey, William James, George Herbert Mead, Charles
Sanders Peirce, Josiah Royce, George Santayana, and Alfred North Whitehead.
Some philosophers deconstruct white male hegemony to create a less exclusive
list of whose work constitutes American pragmatism to include the contributions
of Native Americans, African Americans, women, and nonacademic philosophers (such as Ralph Waldo Emerson and Benjamin Franklin). In anthologies
describing American philosophy, Addams is a minor figure, if she is mentioned

at all.[1] In this chapter, I suggest that Addams engages the ideas of American philosophers in a manner consistent with the tenets of many of its "founding fathers." Furthermore, she contributes a critical dimension to American pragmatism that fleshes out and extends its social and political commitments, particularly as they pertain to pluralism and democracy. Although pragmatists value the integration of theory and practice, Addams's philosophy came from the streets of Chicago, where she lived her theoretical positions.

In what follows, I identify how Addams's work resonates with the definitions of pragmatism offered by various significant figures in the American philosophical tradition. I briefly consider the work of James, Dewey, and Mead from Addams's era, as well as Cornel West and Charlotte Haddock Seigfried from the contemporary resurgence in pragmatist scholarship. The list of pragmatists considered is not exhaustive, but it demonstrates the extent to which Addams's work aligns with this important tradition.

William James: Seeking Cash Value

In 1907, William James (1842–1910) characterized pragmatism as a theoretical approach unlike those of traditional philosophy: "The whole function of philosophy ought to be to find out what definite difference it will make to you and me."[2] For James, pragmatism was concrete, experiential, and eminently relevant. It was a forward-looking philosophy that did not get bogged down by abstract debate at the expense of action. According to him, "the pragmatic method is primarily a method of settling metaphysical disputes that otherwise might be interminable."[3] Relevancy was valued over argument for argument's sake, with little interest in a "pure" or a priori philosophy: "What difference would it practically make to anyone if this notion rather than that notion were true?"[4] James wanted to get past deliberation to address action and power. His philosophy often employed the language of commerce while placing a uniquely American stamp on his approach: "You must bring out of each word its practical cash-value, set it at work with the stream of your experience."[5] James was not against theory. Quite the contrary, he valued theory in relation to what it could accomplish. Theories were instruments not ends.[6] Neither was truth an end. In his view, truth was tenuous, interconnected, and changeable. Truth "worked" for the time being, but could be replaced in the face of new evidence or circumstances. This tenuous truth was founded on experience.

James, never afraid of controversy, emphasized experiential phenomenon to the extent that his philosophical approach was labeled *radical empiricism* (James actually preferred this moniker to that of *pragmatism*). According to James, "everything real must be experienceable somewhere, and every kind of thing experienced must somewhere be real."[7] James distanced himself from rationalism, which he believed all-too-neatly described the universe. Alternatively, he was comfortable with experiences that reflected the messiness and lack of unity in the world, and he claimed that philosophy should embrace pluralism: "philosophy has indeed manifested above all things its interest in unity. But how about the *variety* in things?"[8] James granted the tension between continuity and disparity but criticized philosophy for being obsessed with unity. Certainly such a tension is more consistent with empirical evidence.

For my purposes, James's work reflects a philosophical commitment to concrete experience of a complex and changing existence, which generates working and revisable theories of operant truth. If the words of William James could have conjured into existence a human being who matched his philosophical commitments, Jane Addams would have been the result. Addams and James mutually admired one another and collaborated on a number of endeavors, most notably against war. They both appeared at the Thirteenth Universal Peace Congress held in Boston in 1904. In a 1909 letter to Addams, James states, "The fact is, Madam, that you are not like the rest of us, who seek the truth and try to express it. You inhabit reality."[9] She also inhabited his philosophy of radical empiricism. Addams was the leader of a reflective and engaged community that produced thoughtful social analysis alongside concrete actions in behalf of its neighbors. She was not merely occupied with abstract reflection or singularly mired in social activism.

Addams's valorization of both action and reflection is exemplified in her early comparison of universities and settlements. In 1899, Addams described settlements as having much in common with universities dedicated to pursuing knowledge, except that settlements had the advantage of collective living "to make experience continuous beyond the individual."[10] In many ways, Hull House was an epistemological experiment, and Addams was the resident philosopher. Knowledge was generated through communal experience situated in the neighborhood. Addams thus expressed American pragmatism in action: "The settlement, when it attempts to reveal and apply knowledge, deems its results practicable, when it has made knowledge available which before was abstract, when through use, it has made common that knowledge which was partial before, because it could only be apprehended by the intellect."[11] In this manner, experience was required to make knowledge "practicable." Addams did not merely respond to needs as a charity worker, she allowed intellectual and affective internal changes to seep into her understanding and then thought critically about the experiences, striking a balance: "these experiences [at Hull House] would seem to testify that there is too much analysis in our thought, as there is too much anarchy in our action."[12]

Addams's thematization went beyond the parochial. Almost every time she addressed an issue, whether it was a state, national, or international concern, she drew from Hull House experiences. For example, in one of her better-known articles, "The Revolt against War," Addams discusses group behavior at the local level as consistent with her experience of international belligerence. "Let us say that there are two groups of boys in a boys' club, and I have much experience of that in boys' clubs to draw upon. If one says, 'We did this because the other fellows did that,' you will simply have to say, 'I won't go into the rights and wrongs of this, but this thing must stop, because it leads nowhere and gets nowhere.' And so with larger groups. We all know the strikes that have gone on for weeks, with the original cause quite lost sight of. I submit that something of the same sort is happening in Europe now."[13] Here, Addams asserts epistemological credibility regarding masculine behavior while linking local and international experiences consistent with James's claim about the real as derivative from experience.

Addams's social philosophy is certainly consistent with the pragmatism defined by James, with an important emphasis on integrity. By making this claim, I am not accusing James of being disingenuous to his philosophy. However, James describes a philosophy marked by action and improving society. He is a respected philosopher who has influenced many, but his largest audience is academic in philosophy and psychology. Addams both lived and wrote what James, the eminent Harvard intellectual, only wrote about. Perhaps that is what James referred to when he claimed that she inhabited reality. It is this convergence of thought and action that both places Addams firmly within the pragmatist school and ironically, at the same time, "hides" her in the plain sight of her actions. She was the philosopher that her colleagues could not recognize as a philosopher.

John Dewey: Pragmatism as the Application of Experimental Knowledge

When Addams's philosophy is considered, if at all, her work is quickly associated with John Dewey (1859–1952). This association is appropriate given their friendship and mutual interests. However, her intellectual deference to Dewey is often overstated. Dewey was a most prolific author, though difficult to read. His work appealed to Addams because they shared many of the same commitments, including a belief in the value of a robust democracy as well as the importance of education that engages students' experiences. At Dewey's seventieth birthday celebration, Addams praised his ability to address proximate questions rather than the ultimate ones that philosophers often find themselves wrapped up in: "the problems of social welfare in our time have never been so squarely faced as by the philosopher who deliberately made the study of men and their intelligences a foundation for the study of the problems with which men have to deal."[14]

Dewey's pragmatic method is much like James's, and he also employed terms like "cash value" to emphasize relevancy. Dewey disliked the word *pragmatism* and avoided its use because "the term lends itself to misconception."[15] Like James, Dewey sought to shake up philosophy by envisioning a new approach. In his Gifford Lecture, *The Quest for Certainty,* Dewey accuses philosophy of embracing the security of certitude rather than recognizing the variability of existence: "the predisposition of philosophy toward the universal, invariant and eternal was fixed. It remains the common possession of the entire classic philosophic tradition."[16] One of the criticisms of such philosophic certainty is the separation of the knower from the known in a manner that pragmatists find mistaken. The knower/known split requires a disconnection between action and reflection: "Practical activity is dismissed to a world of low grade reality."[17] The correspondence theory of truth then comes under attack. That is, truth does not correspond to some fact outside the knower but is created in part by the knower. Addams continually challenged what passes for social knowledge. For example, she observed that everyone has ideas about the follies of youth but asked whether people take the time to understand adolescents from their own experience and perspective. In *The Spirit of Youth and the City Streets,* Addams not only demonstrates the significance of perspective but suggests that such knowledge compels certain actions, that is, rethinking municipal configuration and programs.

Dewey endeavored to intertwine means and ends to suggest that action, practice, habits, and experience *do* matter. He wanted philosophers to shift their attention from the ultimate to the proximate: "Knowledge deals with the world in which we live, the world which is experienced, instead of attempting through the intellect to escape to a higher realm. Experimental knowledge is a mode of doing, and like all doing takes place at a time, in a place, and under specifiable conditions in connection with a definite problem."[18] According to Dewey, philosophy should be an ongoing process of truth seeking and revising that values proximate knowledge and experience as well as action for the purpose of positively impacting living issues.

For Dewey, a pragmatist approach to social philosophy begins with common experience. Transactions or exchanges between members of a society are opportunities for educative experiences that can strengthen communal ties. For example, note the high value placed on diversity for stimulating new ideas in the following passage on the democratic conception of education from Dewey's *Democracy and Education,* written in 1916: "Lack of free and equitable intercourse which springs from a variety of shared interests makes intellectual stimulation unbalanced. Diversity of stimulation means novelty, and novelty means challenge to thought. The more activity is restricted to a few definite lines—as it is when there are rigid class lines preventing adequate interplay of experiences—the more action tends to become routine on the part of the class at a disadvantage, and capricious, aimless, and explosive on the part of the class having the materially fortunate position."[19]

Addams made a similar claim in 1893: "Is it possible for men, however far apart in outward circumstances, for the capitalist and the working-man, to use the common phrase, to meet as individuals beneath a friendly roof, open their minds each to each, and not have the 'class theories' insensibly modified by the kindly attrition of personal acquaintance? In the light of our experience, I think not."[20] Addams and Dewey valued interpersonal exchanges in the process of knowledge creation, with particular attention to the limitations of class. They envisioned a socially engaged philosophy grounded in the interplay of theory and action.

Addams and Dewey were intellectual soul mates from the moment they met in 1892. Dewey visited Hull House shortly after it opened, and before he moved to Chicago to teach at the University of Chicago. Following the meeting, Dewey expressed to Addams an appreciation for Hull House's work: "I cannot tell you how much good I got from my stay at Hull House. . . . My indebtedness to you for giving me an insight into matters there is great. . . . Every day I stayed there only added to my conviction that you had taken the right path."[21] Dewey came to the University of Chicago in 1894 and subsequently started an experimental school. There was much intellectual cross-fertilization between Hull House and the University of Chicago. Particularly in the early years of Hull House, Addams acted as a de facto faculty member of the University of Chicago.[22] When Hull House incorporated, Dewey became a board member. He often lectured to the Plato Club at Hull House. He also dedicated *Liberalism and Social Action* to Addams and named one of his daughters in her honor.

Although Dewey and Addams gained celebrity status during their lifetimes, their fame and legacies are characterized much differently. Dewey is the great intellectual—a thinker—and Addams is the woman activist—the doer. In this manner, they are perceived as classic stereotypes of gender: the male as mind generating theory, and the woman as body experiencing and caring. However, there is much evidence that this characterization is inaccurate.

Both John Dewey and his daughter Jane credited Addams with developing many of his important ideas. Dewey chronicled a disagreement he had with Addams over the value of antagonism. She argued that contentiousness was a social error that was never beneficial and often costly. At the time, Dewey disagreed, but he later wrote to his wife that Addams's argument was "the most magnificent exhibition of intellectual and moral faith I ever saw. She converted me internally, but not really, I fear. . . . [W]hen you think that Miss Addams does not think this as a philosophy, but believes it in all her senses & muscles—Great God."[23] The next day he wrote a letter to Addams retracting what he said about antagonism: "Not only is actual antagonism bad, but the assumption that there is or may be antagonism is bad. . . . I'm glad I found out about this before teaching social psychology."[24] This dialogue reveals that not only did Dewey consider Addams his intellectual peer but also that she inspired him.

Scott Pratt carefully documents how Dewey's definition of the purpose of philosophy changed to match that of Addams's active engagement with the world.[25] Charlene Haddock Seigfried makes Addams's influence on Dewey most explicit: "It seems to me that Dewey in his 1916 book, *Democracy and Education,* is drawing on his experiences with Hull House, the story of which was published in 1910 by Addams's *Twenty Years at Hull-House.*"[26] Perhaps one of the factors in the historical oversight of Addams's impact on Dewey is the lack of direct references to Addams in Dewey's philosophy. Writers of the era were less meticulous about attribution than they are today. Nevertheless, sociologist Christopher Lasch recognizes the cross-fertilization: "It is difficult to say whether Dewey influenced Jane Addams or Jane Addams influenced Dewey."[27]

George Herbert Mead

Overshadowed by Addams's relationship with the celebrity philosopher, Dewey, is her friendship and working relationship with George Herbert Mead (1863–1931), who is considered the father of "symbolic interactionism," an approach to social inquiry that emphasizes how symbols create meaning. Mead's work on human development through play and education influenced Addams, but as with Dewey, the influence was mutual.

Mead's intellectual legacy is not altogether settled. His works are recognized as significant by sociologists, but many philosophers overlook them. Mead's academic training was in philosophy, and he was part of the faculty at the University of Michigan when he met Dewey in 1891. After Dewey moved on to the University of Chicago, he successfully invited Mead to join him in 1894. Less gregarious and prolific than Dewey, Mead was considered brilliant by his colleagues and students. His students published a number of his works posthumously; however, Mary Jo Deegan suggests that these publications skew Mead's intellectual legacy toward his work after 1920. Deegan argues that much of his important writing on education and play was completed prior to 1920—the period of greatest cross-fertilization with Addams—and has been ignored.[28]

Addams maintained a long-term, close personal relationship with Mead and his wife, Helen Castle Mead. Addams and Mead often dined together and visited one another's families.[29] Deegan contends that it was Mead's and Dewey's consultations with Addams that helped to create the Chicago pragmatists at the University of Chicago.[30] Mead and Addams collaborated on a number of projects, including pro-labor speeches, peace advocacy, and the Progressive Party. When Addams was publicly attacked for not supporting the U.S. entry into World War I, Mead defended her, even through he did not agree with her position.[31] Like Dewey, Mead was a frequent lecturer at Hull House. Also, like Dewey, Mead was impressed with Addams's intellect. After one of her presentations, Mead wrote to Addams: "I presume that you could not know how deep an impression you made last night by your remarkable paper. My consciousness was, I presume in the same condition as that of the rest of your audience—completely filled with the multitude of impressions which you succeeded in making, and the human responses which you called out from so many unexpected points of view."[32] In 1916, Mead advocated for awarding Addams an honorary doctorate from the University of Chicago. The faculty supported the award, but the administration overturned the decision (then eventually bestowed the award in 1931).[33]

Addams's and Mead's work on the role of "play" in human development is explored in chapter 9 of this book. Although Mead viewed children's play as important in developing imaginative functions that allow them to rehearse a variety of roles in establishing personal identity, Addams construed play as participating in the construction of the sympathetic knowledge necessary for an effective democracy. Like Mead, Addams's philosophy integrates concern for psychological motives and personal development. Addams sought a holistic democracy that facilitates social development as well as personal growth.

Several authors have traced Addams's influence on Mead's social philosophy.[34] Through his long-term interaction with Addams and Hull House, Mead's ideas about human development and social progress evolved. For example, Shannon Jackson observes that Mead's views on social reform shifted from the idealism often associated with the Progressive movement to a more adaptive formulation consistent with the experimentalism and fallibility exhibited in Addams's work at Hull House.[35] As Seigfried observes, Mead and Dewey had a mixed relationship to feminism. Although supportive of many feminist causes, they sometimes fell back on prevailing patriarchal notions. Nevertheless, their pragmatism created a supportive intellectual space open to the possibility of Addams's feminist pursuits.

Cornel West is a major figure in the contemporary resurgence of American philosophy. He develops the notion of "prophetic pragmatism" as an engaging form of public philosophy that emphasizes social criticism and action integrated with reflective work. Although admiring of Dewey, he does not give serious consideration to Addams, who appears to be a good match for what he wishes a philosopher to be.

West, who was influenced by Richard Rorty, writes, "American pragmatism is a diverse and heterogeneous tradition. But its common denominator consists of a future-oriented instrumentalism that tries to deploy thought as a weapon to engage more effective action."[36] In particular, West esteems Deweyan pragmatism: "My focus on John Dewey at the expense of Charles Peirce and William James does not reflect my deep respect for the latter two. Rather, it expresses my sense that the thoroughgoing historical consciousness and emphasis on social and political matters found in Dewey speaks more to my purpose than the preoccupation with logic in Peirce and the obsession with individuality in James. . . . It is with Dewey that pragmatism achieves intellectual maturity, historical scope, and political engagement."[37] West refers to Dewey as the greatest American pragmatist because Dewey's philosophy has a vigorous connection to social life.[38] West views pragmatism as an ongoing cultural commentary that emphasizes morality over epistemology. Accordingly, pragmatism is action-oriented, concerned with consequences, and dynamic so as to meet the moral demands of a fluid society. Pragmatism also favors growth and development over a nostalgic quest for some moral past or a utopian future. West finds the American philosophic tradition rich for structuring present-day discussions of social issues.

In ways that most philosophers have not, West adopts a popular, activist role that goes beyond Dewey's vision of engagement. As a popular speaker and a frequent television and radio guest, West has effectively used the media to get his social message across. Richard Bernstein describes West as "a black John Dewey, in the sense that Dewey was a serious thinker who spoke to the issues of the day—a model that has been sorely missing from the American scene."[39] Given pragmatism's commitment to social engagement, West's public persona is part of the philosopher's task. For West, engaging in private philosophical discourse over abstract disputes is an evasion of the philosopher's responsibility to spur meaningful social dialogue.

Despite West's high regard for Dewey, he is critical of Dewey's actions on a number of fronts. West finds one incident in Dewey's life particularly telling.

In the 1890s, Dewey had the opportunity to edit *Thought News,* a unique blend of philosophy and journalism that he hoped would shake up the staid world of academic philosophy with social and political commentary. However, faced with criticism and perceived threats to his career, Dewey removed himself from the project, and *Thought News* never came into being. West interprets this as a turning point in Dewey's life: "From then on, Dewey practiced professional caution and political reticence. He remained deeply engaged in civic offers, but shunned controversy."[40] For West, Dewey failed to occupy a public, prophetic role and instead embraced middle-class values and concerns.

West also critiques Dewey for parochial thinking: "The major problem with Dewey's project is that his cultural transformation envisions a future Emersonian and democratic way of life that has the flavor of small-scale, homogenous communities."[41] West wants Dewey to break out of a middle-class mindset and come to terms with broader frameworks such as socialism. He is baffled as to why Dewey's political philosophy did not more fully account for Marxist ideas.[42] West proposes "prophetic pragmatism" as a spin-off of Deweyan pragmatism that is responsive to Marxist ideals while recognizing the traditional role of social critique as prophecy in the Christian tradition.

West's *The American Evasion of Philosophy: A Genealogy of Pragmatism* refers to Addams only in passing, and she is not one of the dozen key figures mentioned in the genealogy. Although West acknowledges Alice Chipman's (Dewey's first wife) role in developing Dewey's social consciousness,[43] Addams is referred to as a "bourgeois progressive" who exemplifies Dewey's turn away from radical social reform.[44] However, thorough examination reveals that Addams fits West's definition of a prophetic American pragmatist better than Dewey does. Addams was not beholden to institutional, academic colleagues and therefore was able to maintain a critical perspective and experiential integrity. Like West, she addressed a wide audience while provoking significant discussions of social import. She wrote about women's elective franchise, international peace, labor relations, prostitution, and the needs of young people without the fetters of university norms. Addams couched socially provocative ideas in an ameliorative approach that was widely accessible. For example, she had much exposure to socialism through Florence Kelley and many of the speakers at Hull House. Addams never embraced socialism because she objected to the determinism of endless class antagonism. Nevertheless, she favored socialist analysis, as I explore in chapter 7. Overall, Addams embraced West's call for prophetic pragmatist philosophers to be action- and future-oriented. It is unfortunate that West has heretofore ignored her work.

Charlene Haddock Seigfried: Feminist Pragmatism

A unique yet compelling perspective on pragmatism is found in the work of another contemporary American philosopher, Charlene Haddock Seigfried. What Seigfried recognizes is that feminism and pragmatism have common foundations and that philosophers from each perspective can benefit from greater dialogue. In *Pragmatism and Feminism*, Seigfried begins with the work of the "traditionally designated" classical American philosophers: Peirce, James, Royce, Dewey, and Mead. Her next step is to contrast the classical definition with that of the work of women associated with pragmatism (Addams, Charlotte Perkins Gilman, Elise Ripley Clapp, and Lucy Sprague Mitchell) to reconstruct a pragmatism that acknowledges its feminist influence. Ultimately, Seigfried presents a feminist pragmatist position that recognizes the role of perspective and enriches the classical definition of pragmatism.[45] Addams embodies Seigfried's intersection of pragmatism and feminism.

Seigfried offers a straightforward definition: "Pragmatism, [is] a philosophy that stresses the relation of theory to praxis, [it] takes the continuity of experience and nature [to be] revealed through the outcome of directed action as starting point for reflection. Experience is the ongoing transaction of organism and environment; in other words, both subject and object are constituted in the process."[46] One implication of attending to the relationship between the knower and the known is that the biases and context of the knower are brought into play. One's perspective or standpoint matters. Seigfried also characterizes pragmatism as interdisciplinary and pluralistic. As Seigfried describes, Addams "is undeniably a pragmatist, however, and pragmatism like feminism, cannot be confined to any one discipline. She is an exemplary case of how pragmatism, like feminism, internally disrupts artificial and counterproductive disciplinary boundaries."[47] If experience is the basis for knowledge, then one must account for multiple experiences of the same phenomenon and the differences. No single method of inquiry into experience claims a privileged position of truth. Addams repeatedly demonstrates respect for multiple perspectives and includes those perspectives in public conversation.

Because the knower is intimately involved in knowledge creation, truth becomes instrumental. Why do we want to know something? Because it is useful or beneficial. According to Seigfried, "knowledge is instrumental, not in the sense of merely linking means to predetermined ends, but in the sense of a tool used, along with other tools, for organizing experiences satisfactorily."[48] Addams's notion of sympathetic knowledge, discussed further in chapter 4 of this book, values knowledge of others as instrumental in constructing a vital social democracy. Furthermore, because experience confirms pragmatist truth, that truth is fallible and subject to reconsideration. For Seigfried, feminism adds a kind of perspectival grounding to pragmatism. Although pragmatism recognizes many perspectives, "feminism can help to identify the hidden assumptions of pragmatist analyses and to demonstrate the crucial difference between merely acknowledging other perspectives and coming to terms with the consequences of such recognition."[49] Addams repeatedly asked her audience to consider the standpoint of the other: the immigrant, the laborer, the domestic servant, or the prostitute. She believed that efforts toward sympathetically inhabiting the perspectives of others was the only way for society to make common cause and flourish. In this manner, Addams integrated the pragmatic approach with the experiences of diverse, fleshy bodies to develop a critical social philosophy.

No one has done more to appreciate the contribution of Addams as a philosopher than Seigfried, and no one exemplifies Seigfried's intersection of feminism and pragmatism better than Addams.

Addams's Radical Pragmatism: Lateral Progress

In the first part of this chapter, I claim that the various definitions of classic and modern philosophers reveal Addams to be an American pragmatist, albeit an overlooked one. However, suggesting that Addams's work resonates with that of Dewey, James, Mead, West, and Seigfried does not tell the entire story of her philosophy. Addams made an original intellectual contribution to pragmatism as well. In the second half of this chapter, I suggest that Addams *radicalized* pragmatism by applying a stronger egalitarian approach to social issues, one that was keenly tuned to the impact of class, race, and gender.

It can be difficult to perceive Addams as a radical. At five feet three inches tall, often portrayed in photographs as wearing the puffy dresses of the Victorian era, Addams did not fit the stereotype of a radical. Furthermore, her language and demeanor was not that of a traditional radical. She was soft-spoken and chose her words carefully in order to keep divergent constituencies in the conversation. By contrast, a generation before, Frances Wright (1795–1852) was widely reviled as a radical because of her bombastic rhetorical style, violation of sexual norms, flaunting of nontraditional women's clothing, and active criticism of religion. Wright reveled in public attention because she understood that outlandish behavior generated interest for her speeches, thus facilitating larger audiences to hear her arguments. Wright was a "traditional" radical in ideology, methodology, and demeanor, but Addams was a complex, social radical. If *radical* is defined as challenging existing structures of power, Addams was the least elitist and the most radical of the American philosophers of her era. She consistently took and eloquently supported inclusive positions that sought to benefit society. Rather than defining progress by the achievements of the best and the brightest, Addams advocated the betterment of all in what she calls "lateral progress."[50]

> The man who insists upon consent, who moves with the people, is bound to consult the feasible right as well as the absolute right. He is often obliged to attain only Mr. Lincoln's "best possible," and often have [sic] the sickening sense of compromising with his best convictions. He has to move along with those whom he rules toward a goal that neither he nor they see very clearly till they come to it. He has to discover what people really want, and then "provide the channels in which the growing moral force of their lives shall flow." What he does attain, however, is not the result of his individual striving, as a solitary mountain climber beyond the sight of the valley multitude, but it is underpinned and upheld by the sentiments and aspirations of many others. Progress has been slower perpendicularly, but incomparably greater because lateral.
>
> He has not taught his contemporaries to climb mountains, but he has persuaded the villagers to move up a few feet higher.[51]

Whether one labels them "robber barons" or "captains of industry," those who amassed wealth—the winners of the game—defined the rise of commerce in the United States. The wealthy achieved progress in health care, education, and material well-being. Addams redefined progress by casting a wider net. This inclusive definition eludes us today, as progress continues to be defined by society's privileged.

Addams's notion of lateral progress can be summarized in four points: first, widespread progress is preferred over individual progress. Addams views the solidarity of lateral progress as necessary for effective social philosophy. She says that "the best speculative philosophy sets forth the solidarity of the human race; that the highest moralists have taught that without the advancement and improvement of the whole, no man can hope for any lasting improvement in his own moral or material individual condition."[52] Her philosophy runs counter to social Darwinism, which celebrates the success of individuals as a manifestation of natural selection. Accordingly, the best and brightest receive fame and fortune because they are the most efficient users of social resources. By contrast, lateral progress indicates that all should advance together, but not necessarily in lockstep. Addams was not against social leadership or philanthropy, but believed they must be tempered by widespread social cohesion and participation.

Second, Addams's notion of lateral progress assumes *circumstances* to be the major difference between the haves and have-nots. She employs a positive human ontology that suggests there are not bad people, but that circumstances lead to bad situations. This approach leaves open the possibility for greater interpersonal understanding because good will is shared. Addams assiduously avoided making individuals into "others" through categorical labels that assigned fixed moral status.

Third, because human beings do have much in common, experiences of one another lead to greater understanding, which in turn leads to mechanisms, such as policy change, that create lateral progress. This essentially describes Addams's purpose for the Hull House settlement: establish connective opportunities for people to know one another better. This connected knowledge informs people's collective decision making.

Finally, Addams's lateral progress assumes the possibility that social reform can create widespread improvement. She believed public and private institutions could institute programs that would be the means for social advancement. Hull House incubated numerous public programs, such as the juvenile court system, public parks, and adult education, that represented a means for citizens to be caring and accountable to one another on the path to social progress.

Although her contemporaries did not refer to Addams's philosophy as radical, they recognized how her analysis challenged them to extend their thinking. For example, James admitted to his elitism: "It was not until I read your 'Democracy and Social Ethics' that I was able to understand how wrong I had always been in condemning the masses of the people for what I deemed to be a low moral standard. Your psychology of the minds of the poor has been by far the most helpful aid I have ever known."[53] This is high praise from James, who wrote so much about human psychology. Ironically, Addams is sometimes chastised for expounding middle-class values, which was her point of reference as she started Hull House. Over time, her experiences pushed her to more fully understand and appreciate the oppressed in the neighborhood. Furthermore, Addams was not afraid of pluralism. Hull House exuded a pluralistic existence. Amid dozens of immigrant communities, rampant poverty, and many dire needs, the emergence of philosophy seemed improbable. Yet, Addams thematized within cultural and class diversity, not for the sake of knowledge, but because her theorizing could make a difference to the life of the community. In James's terms, her radical analysis had cash value.

Examples of Addams's use of the notion of lateral progress are numerous. When she discusses the role of labor unions, she argues that they fulfill a function that benefits society as a whole in their attempt to improve working conditions for their constituency: "trade unions are trying to do for themselves what the government should secure for all its citizens; has, in fact, secured in many cases."[54] Addams, who had a track record of supporting labor, made it clear that she did not view collective bargaining as an end. Nor was she interested in improving the lot of one group of workers over another. "Any sense of division and suspicion is fatal in a democratic form of government, for although each side may seem to secure most for itself, when consulting only its own interests, the final test must be the good of the community as a whole."[55] For Addams, unions were important because they improved working conditions, raised wages, reduced hours, and eliminated child labor for all Americans—lateral progress.

Although the first chapter of Addams's *Democracy and Social Ethics* ostensibly is a critique of charity workers and their preconceived notions of the needs of the destitute, it also reveals Addams's disposition toward the poor and oppressed, and supports her notion of lateral progress. She decries the historical position of blaming the victim: "Formerly, when it was believed that poverty was synonymous with vice and laziness, and that the prosperous man was the righteous man, charity was administered harshly with a good conscience; for the charitable agent really blamed the individual for his poverty, and the very fact of his own superior prosperity gave him a certain consciousness of superior morality."[56] Such a judgment served to separate the wealthy from the poor. The rich achieved progress intellectually, materially, and technologically, while the poor were left behind largely because it was their fault. Addams argues that the poor are victims of circumstance and that it is the responsibility of society to first understand the marginalized and then develop means for their increased participation.

Charity, although a good, is not lateral progress. A temporary transfer in wealth, while noble and beneficial in the short term, creates dependence and does not constitute real progress on the part of the poor. Addams never viewed herself as a charity worker, nor did she characterize Hull House as charity: "I am always sorry to have Hull House regarded as philanthropy."[57] Addams sought a lateral progress brought about by the collective will and manifested through social institutions. She believed there would be no need for settlements if "society had been reconstructed to the point of offering equal opportunity for all."[58] She did not advocate a laissez-faire, capitalistic version of equal opportunity that is abstract and rights-based. Her approach to equal opportunity was set in a context of active democracy where citizens and social organizations look out for one another because they all have a stake in lateral progress.

Sociologist Mary Jo Deegan uses the term *critical pragmatism* to describe the "radical extension of the tenets developed by the Chicago School of pragmatism" that informs Addams's idea of lateral progress.[59] Deegan suggests that Addams pushed the philosophers and sociologists at the University of Chicago to extend their ideas further into application than they might otherwise have done. For example, Deegan finds a divergence between Addams and her male counterparts over education delivery: "Education was a central concern to the male Chicago pragmatists, but Addams was more opposed to formal institutions of learning than were the men. Democracy was an underlying theory of the pragmatic program, but for Addams democracy included economic and social equality as well as its political dimensions."[60] Deegan's characterization of Addams's radicalization of pragmatism extends to other areas such as women's rights (the male pragmatists were generally in favor of women's suffrage, but did not put great effort into it), and pacifism (many male pragmatists were antiwar, but equivocated in the face of the U.S. entrance into World War I). Addams's critical pragmatism—her radicalization of pragmatism—stemmed from her commitment to lateral progress: the social advancement of all through inclusive interactive participation. Even on issues such as women's suffrage, lateral progress was a foundational concept. For Addams, women's voting was in the best interest of the entire society, not just for the benefit of women.

Addams's notion of lateral progress exemplifies how she has been misrepresented as an ameliorist. Although Addams was interested in improving social problems, she has not been given credit for her radical edge.[61] Further evidence of this incisiveness is provided in subsequent chapters. Ultimately, her radicalism is indicative of her innovative contribution to American philosophy.[62] At the dawn of the twenty-first century, it is time that American philosophers throw off the mantle of historical prejudice and include Addams among their major theorists. Seigfried laments Addams's exclusion: "Since there are no women acknowledged in the canon of American pragmatists, how could one be a major figure, even a founding member? In the patriarchal records, philosophers relegate Addams to sociology, while sociologists relegate her to amateur reformism, at best to the status of a social worker."[63] This marginalization of Addams, like much prejudice, is not a conspiracy. As mentioned in the introduction, her gender, activism, and writing style contribute to overlooking Addams as a philosopher. However, it is no longer necessary to repeat the errors of earlier intellectuals. Given her influence on Dewey, Mead, and James, her application of pragmatist commitments, and her ability to challenge American philosophy to grow with new ideas such as lateral progress, Addams warrants a respected position among America's great philosophers.

Jane Addams was an articulate cultural feminist who embodied her beliefs. She wrote extensively on the superiority of women's values, worldview, and behavior. She lived her life surrounded by women, and she trusted them more than she did men. Her cultural feminism was actualized in her lifestyle, self-presentation, and epistemology.

—MARY JO DEEGAN

We have not wrecked railroads, nor corrupted legislatures, nor done many unholy things that men have done, but then we must remember that we have not had the chance.

—JANE ADDAMS

CHAPTER 3

Feminist Pioneer

Just as Addams is not included among the fathers of American philosophy, she is overlooked as a mother of American feminism.[1] Nevertheless, examining Addams's corpus of writings reveals not only a concern for women's issues such as suffrage, vocations, education, and violence, but also applications of methodology and theory, foreshadowing feminist analysis of later generations. Initially, this chapter examines contemporary characterizations of Addams's feminism, revealing the difficulty of categorizing her intellectual work. After addressing the nature of her feminism, I explore three areas of Addams's prefigurative engagement with feminist theory—standpoint, care, and proto-lesbian thinking—to highlight her reflective work in feminism. I follow Addams's theoretical analysis by exploring how she addressed specific women's issues of her day. The conclusion examines how her feminist theorizing contributes to the development of her concept of sympathetic knowledge.

Despite the flattening of feminism by contemporary media, those engaged in feminist theory recognize its diverse analytical and political standpoints: liberal, radical, socialist, postmodern, Christian, and so forth. These positions are not mutually exclusive, and, accordingly, Addams does not fit easily into them. One might assume that given her advocacy of women's suffrage and labor rights, Addams was a liberal feminist. That would be partially correct.[2] Liberal feminism has its roots in the classical liberal tradition that stresses autonomy and rationality.[3] Liberal feminists seek the same rights and opportunities for women as other recognized agents in society. Therefore, they are associated with struggles for equal voting rights, equal opportunity to hold political office, and equal job and pay opportunities. Liberal feminists do not necessarily seek to transform or question existing social structures but believe instead that if their individual agency is elevated to that of white men, then their influence, quality of life, and well-being will approximate that of men.

Many of Addams's actions and writings on suffrage and working conditions fall within a liberal feminist framework. For example, writing in 1930, a decade after the passage of the Nineteenth Amendment, Addams reminisces that during the suffrage movement "women had discovered that the unrepresented are always liable to be given what they do not want by legislators who merely wish to placate them," thereby suggesting that without the vote, women's interests were not fully represented.[4] She sought full participation for women within existing political systems because it was in the best interest of society.

The one period in her life during which Addams was regarded as radical was World War I and the time leading up to it. The radical label was applied to marginalize her unpopular position for peace. Although this public label is not what is meant by radical feminism, Addams's critique of war contains an analysis of masculinity consistent with radical feminism. In a 1915 article, she claims that war runs counter to social development: "thousands of men marching to their death are under compulsion, not of this higher type of patriotism, but of a tribal conception, because of an irrational appeal which ought to have left the world long since."[5] She then connects violence to gender: "A state founded upon tribal ideals of patriotism has no place for women within its councils."[6] Here the term *tribal* evokes masculine social competition. Addams lists aspects of society that war is destroying but cautions, "I do not assent that women are better than men . . . but we would all admit that there are things concerning which women are more sensitive than men, and one of those is treasuring of life."[7] She finds masculine ideals particularly prevalent in social beliefs surrounding war.

Addams sometimes employed an analysis reminiscent of socialist feminism. She never explicitly declared an association with socialism, as she resisted ideological positions. In *Twenty Years at Hull-House,* Addams describes social-ists she encountered: "I saw nowhere a more devoted effort to understand and relieve that heavy pressure [of material deprivation] than the socialists were making, and I should have been glad to have had the comradeship of that gallant company had they not firmly insisted that fellowship depends upon identity of creed."[8] Addams became more sympathetic through her exposure to Hull House residents Florence Kelley and Mary Kenney, and visitors such as socialist Eugene Debs and socialist-anarchist Peter Kropotkin. She agreed with socialist feminists' views that women's oppression is integrally enmeshed in class struggle. For example, in *Democracy and Social Ethics,* Addams chal-lenges capitalist presumptions regarding the right to purchase the labor of others (particularly women) for domestic service: "Personal ministrations to a normal, healthy adult, consuming the time and energy of another adult, we find more difficult to reconcile to our theories of democracy."[9] However, she realizes that such a position is too radical for social acceptance, so instead of advocating the elimination of contractual servitude, she outlines a series of reforms that would protect domestic workers from abuse.[10]

Addams never accepted the socialist view that class struggle is definitive of human existence. Her optimistic view of social evolution did not allow this kind of determinism. Although Addams did not directly demand socialism, she called for government intervention and citizen involvement in regulating industry. She has sharp words for capitalists who make large profits while ex-ploiting labor in dangerous and poorly compensated work.[11] Simultaneous with her critique of capitalism and her call for more government control is a belief that women have roles in a more socialized economy: "It is because the govern-ment is constantly concerning itself with these human undertakings which used to lie quite outside of its supposed responsibilities, that some of us feel very strongly that all such undertakings would be infinitely benefited if women were taking a natural and legitimate share in the development and administration of governmental activities."[12] Addams does not use the directness that one might expect from a radical analysis, but the implication of the "infinite benefit" of women's involvement in government is that men have made many mistakes in constructing contemporary capitalism, and another approach is warranted.

Mary Jo Deegan offers another label for Addams's work: "cultural femi-nism." According to Deegan, cultural feminism is a school of thought that prizes those female characteristics that flourished historically in matriarchal societies.[13] Accordingly, "Addams valued the female world and wanted it to be extended throughout society."[14] There is much to support Deegan's claim. For example, Addams suggested that more women in leadership positions would result in greater expression of women's values, thus making society less militaristic and more caring. She argued that if women ran Chicago, different values would emerge, thus altering public policy: "The men of the city have been carelessly indifferent to much of this civic housekeeping, as they have always been indifferent to the details of the household."[15] Here, Addams explicitly connects the personal and the political.

Cultural feminism, like "difference" feminism, highlights and celebrates differences between women and men, making accusations of essentialism possible. Despite occasional assumptions about masculinity and femininity, Addams was not a thoroughgoing essentialist.[16] She understood how historical experiences placed women in their current position. She also recognized the danger of universalizing female character. Although Addams believed women could change society by obtaining the vote, she acknowledged that no one could guarantee how women would vote or how individual women elected officials would act. However, she claimed that the inclusion of women's experience in the political realm could make an important difference.

Addams practiced a unique form of engaged separatism. This was not the strict separatism developed in the women's movement of the 1960s, but recognition that a woman-centered space holds unique power. Marilyn Frye describes separatism as a severance "from men and from institutions, relationships, roles and activities which are male-defined, male-dominated and operating for the benefit of males and the maintenance of male privilege—this separation being initiated or maintained at will, by women."[17] Addams modeled Hull House on the female-centered environment in which she flourished during her college years. Addams thrived in these two environments, but in the decade in between, she suffered from a lack of direction and purpose. Although there were men at Hull House, many of whom went on to great prominence (see chapter 2), they lived in a separate dorm and never held leadership positions during the Addams era. A frequent visitor to Hull House and a friend of Addams, George Herbert Mead went so far as to describe himself as "rather of a feminine cast of mind."[18] Hull House was decidedly women's space. Not all the women residents were lesbians, but it was supportive of strong female bonds. Hull House provided a kind of separatism from the male-centered life choices of wife and mother or religious orders. It also afforded residents physical and mental freedom from the expectations placed on women. Addams or her accomplished cohort would not have likely achieved as much success as activists, writers, and social leaders had they not been able to separate themselves as a community from gender-determined cultural constraints. Hull House was simultaneously separatist, as a strong community for the female residents, and intensely engaged as a public neighborhood agency. Addams and Starr did not start a feminist colony in a desolate, bucolic, or rural setting, but instead chose the heart of densely populated immigrant blight in Chicago. Residents confronted male-dominated social institutions—corporations, city government, and the judiciary—from the safe haven of Hull House. Addams and Hull House residents leveraged the empowerment engendered by their separatism to engage society's problems.

John Craig describes a "separatist paradox" in Addams's era.[19] Addams was part of a generation of women who were gaining the necessary social power to start independent social projects, but that same power allowed women to compete with men in certain arenas. A tension arose over whether women should focus on removing barriers to equality or form separate organizations to coalesce a power base. Addams portrayed some of the ambivalence toward separatism that Craig describes. Clearly, she was comfortable with woman-centered environments and worked effectively in them. However, when it came to organizing a peace movement, her dedication to separatism was less than thoroughgoing. Although some in the peace movement, such as Crystal Eastman, desired a women-only movement, Addams argued against separatism. "I believe that men and women work best together on these public measures," she wrote to Carrie Chapman Catt.[20] She was motivated by political efficacy, believing that a peace campaign populated by men and women would have wider acceptance. Despite these disagreements, Addams became an important figure and chairwoman in the Women's Peace Party, yet her beliefs about gender integration in the peace movement never disappeared. Clearly, Addams was not dogmatic about separatism; she found it useful when appropriate, but not an end in itself.

Liberal? Radical? Socialist? Cultural? Separatist? Postmodernism warns about the limitations of such labels. Each is a subjective attribution applied in retrospect and filtered through modern interpretative frameworks. These categories cannot entirely capture the feminist pragmatist philosophy of Jane Addams, but reviewing their analytic positions reveals the breadth of Addams's reflective capacity. She was willing to use the tools from any of these categories to achieve her end: social improvement.

Feminist Theorizing

Addams's contribution to feminist theory emerged from her inquiry and reflection into social issues of the day. She was the working manager of an active social settlement, met the speaking and writing demands of a public philosopher, assumed leadership roles in national and international organizations, and yet maintained time to think critically about her experiences and their significance. In what follows, I review three of her contributions to feminist theory in the areas of standpoint epistemology, care ethics, and lesbian ethics.

Traditionally, Western philosophy does not problematize the authoritative voice from which it speaks. Extrapolating the Cartesian mind/body split, philosophers often employ theory to develop moral systems that speak to all people for all times. Kant's duties apply to everyone, Mill's consequential calculus works for everyone, and Locke's rights protect everyone—at least if that everyone is a member of the dominant group in society. Accordingly, differences of time, power, and place have little consequence, because abstract theory is not limited by circumstance.

Feminist philosophers, among others, argue vigorously that context does matter. Although debates exist within feminist philosophical circles regarding the nature of objectivity, many, including Lorraine Code, Nancy Hartsock, Sandra Harding, Alison Jaggar, Hilary Rose, and Dorothy Smith, support the idea that knowledge is situated. The standpoint or context of the knower affects the known. No one can escape to an independent objective position of knowledge. According to Harding, standpoint theories explore "'beneath' or 'behind' dominant sexist and androcentric ideologies that shape everyone's lives to relations between, on the one hand, actualities of women's everyday lives and, on the other hand, conceptual practices of powerful social institutions."[21] The concern is that an unencumbered universalization assumes that the author takes an objective view disconnected from entanglements of experience. As part of his categorical imperative, Immanuel Kant (1724–1804) claims that moral maxims can be universalized and offers imperatives such as the duty not to lie. Does it matter that the man considered by many to be the greatest modern philosopher never left his birth city of Konigsberg? Does it matter that he led an obsessively ordered life? Does the social milieu and ideas he was exposed to as well as his social position matter? Standpoint theorists argue "yes," and feminists raise concerns that Kant's philosophy is "abstract, universal, and transcendental."[22] Kant's ideas developed out of his particular experience framed by class, gender, and other aspects of social identity.[23] For those not steeped in philosophical discourse, this may appear to be a trivial point, but many philosophers in the Western tradition treat their work as a priori, that is, prior to experience. Standpoint theorists consider political and social implications of any theory, because theories are always grounded in some context.

In particular, *feminist* standpoint theorists valorize perspectives and theories derived from marginalized positions, such as from women's experience. Harding describes a feminist standpoint as something to be achieved rather than a passive perspective. All women have lived experience in a woman's body and therefore have a woman's perspective, but a feminist standpoint requires an effort at stepping back to gain a holistic picture of power struggles: "To achieve a feminist standpoint one must engage in the intellectual and political struggle necessary to see nature and social life from the point of view of that disclaimed activity which produces women's social experience instead of from the partial and perverse perspective available from the 'ruling gender' experience of men."[24] In this sense, acknowledging standpoint epistemology creates libratory knowledge that can be leveraged to subvert oppressive systems. Lorraine Code concurs with Harding: "Standpoint theorists contend that the minute, detailed, strategic knowledge that the oppressed have had to acquire of the workings of the social order just so as to be able to function within it can be brought to serve as a resource for undermining that very order."[25] One of the challenges of standpoint theory is how to give voice to multiple positions without falling back on hierarchies that favor certain standpoints over others.

Even among feminists, a commitment to standpoint theory is a struggle. In "Have We Got a Theory for You! Feminist Theory, Cultural Imperialism, and the Demand for 'the Woman's Voice,'" Maria Lugones and Elizabeth Spelman, both committed feminist theorists, explore the difficulty in honoring all voices in a conversation about theory. Lugones reveals, "When we are in your world we ourselves feel the discomfort of having our own being Hispanas disfigured or not understood. And yet, we have had to be in your world and learn its ways. . . . We need to think carefully about the relation between the articulation of our own experience, the interpretation of our own experience, and theory making by us and other non-Hispanic women about themselves and other 'women.'"[26] Note that standpoint theory does not posit the incommensurability of voices—Lugones and Spelman do not stop at acknowledging their unique subject positions. They continue the conversation, not to create a hegemonic truth, but to better understand (although never completely owning) the truth of one another's standpoint. We can extrapolate the challenge of standpoint theory even further. Lugones and Spelman participate in academic culture and can articulate their subject positions in the community of ideas, albeit a marginalized one within academia. Many standpoints are dismissed, unrecognized, or unarticulated. In this regard, Addams provides one response to the challenge of multiple voices.

Addams's cosmopolitan philosophy demonstrates resonance with standpoint epistemology. Despite the social position she was born into—white and upper middle class—her settlement avocation immersed her in disempowered communities. Addams poetically describes her moral mandate to recognize her own standpoint (the dominant white, middle-class position) and not to use it to squelch the voice of others: "We know at last, that we can only discover truth by a rational and democratic interest in life, and to give truth complete social expression is the endeavor upon which we are entering. Thus the identification with the common lot which is the essential idea of Democracy becomes the source and expression of social ethics. It is as though we thirsted at the great wells of human experience, because we know that a daintier draught would not carry us to the end of the journey, going forward as we must in the heat of the jostle of the crowd."[27]

Addams links social identification, social expression, and democracy together. Members of a vibrant democracy not only *recognize* diverse standpoints, they must use empathy and effort to *understand* these diverse standpoints. For Addams, standpoint theory was integrated with feminist action and reflection. She took this philosophy to heart, physically undertaking the proximal relations necessary for the insider/outsider border crossing described by Lugones and Spelman. Addams lived the better part of a half century in the diverse immigrant neighborhood of Hull House. She did not go home to the suburbs or return with her data to a university office. She lived her work among crime, civic corruption, garbage, prostitution, sickness, sweatshops, and other ills of the community. Addams and Starr began Hull House as involved outsiders—an oddity that neighbors looked on suspiciously. However, time, proximity, and earnest desire to learn and help won the trust and respect of the neighborhood. The outsiders became insiders.

According to Lugones and Spelman, "only when genuine and reciprocal dialogue takes place between 'outsiders' and 'insiders' can we trust the outsider's account."[28] When Addams wrote or spoke about single women laborers, child laborers, prostitutes, or first- and second-generation immigrants, she employed firsthand knowledge gained from her social interactions. She leveraged her experiences to give voice to standpoints marginalized in society. Simultaneously, she gave the oppressed their own voice in the dominant culture through college extension courses, English language courses, and social clubs that fostered political and social debate. Addams was self-conscious about speaking for others: "I never addressed a Chicago audience on the subject of the Settlement and its vicinity without inviting a neighbor to go with me, that I might curb my hasty generalization by the consciousness that I had an auditor who knew the conditions more intimately than I could hope to do."[29] She did not develop universal moral theories but recognized that the standpoint of Hull House residents was prerequisite for truth that emerges only in some practical context. According to philosopher Kathi Weeks, the recognition of alternative standpoints can be subversive because they "attempt to fashion from our everyday practices a chain of critical levers that can inspire our disloyalty and disobedience to the values of the larger social formation."[30] Addams confronted social misunderstanding about culture, class, and gender by pushing her audience to empathetically inhabit unfamiliar standpoints.

Addams often engaged the standpoint of working-class women. In an 1896 article, she considers the plight of women in domestic labor. These are the most powerless of workers: predominantly women, many of whom are immigrants with limited English language skills, and in jobs affording little legal protection or organizing possibilities. Addams begins the article with a footnote claiming that her knowledge of domestic laborers comes from her experience with the Woman's Labor Bureau, a Hull House project. She addresses the powerlessness of domestic work particularly as it entails isolation and an overwhelming power dynamic: "The household employé has no regular opportunity for meeting other workers of her trade, and of attaining with them the dignity of corporate body."[31] She also identifies the gender dimension of this oppressive work: "Men would all resent the situation and consider it quite impossible if it implied the giving up of their family and social ties, and living under the roof of the household requiring their services."[32] Addams extrapolates her experience of working women to understand their standpoint and give them voice. She explicitly claims as much: "An attempt is made to present this industry [domestic labor] from the point of view of those women who are working in households for wages."[33] Here Addams recognizes the experiences of oppressed people that she knew in an effort to have them participate in the rich democracy she was trying to foster.

Addams's approach to standpoint theory was characteristically pragmatic. She believed that recognizing alternative standpoints was necessary for promoting lateral progress through sympathetic understanding. Accordingly, giving voice to individuals inhabiting marginalized positions in society fostered possibilities for better understanding (although not perfect knowledge) between people as well as mutually beneficial actions. Addams balanced the honoring of standpoints with simultaneously seeking connections and continuities to build on. This dynamic equation is exemplified in her books on young people, *The Spirit of Youth and the City Streets,* and elderly women, *The Long Road of Woman's Memory.* The latter work is an examination of the memories of first-generation immigrant women, markedly atypical of philosophical writing. *The Long Road of Woman's Memory* is about the relationship between traumatic memories and ethical constructions of the present. Rather than writing about women intellectuals, writers, and celebrities—and Addams knew most of the prominent women of her day—she addresses the women who were her neighbors at Hull House. By "addresses," I do not mean that Addams begins by positing a theory about these women. Instead, she retells stories she heard from them and then draws conclusions about the function of memory. For Addams, theory follows experience. Charlene Haddock Seigfried finds this approach to philosophy refreshing and bold. Addams "does not take refuge in abstract universals and safe platitudes that exclude actual conditions and popular understandings. But many of her beliefs and judgments remain fresh and challenging, not least the very invocation of specific memories of actual women as a basis for philosophic reflection and socially transformative action."[34] Out of women's experience, Addams develops a theory of memory as moral reconstruction. Here, she is in the minority among her peers in philosophy or feminism to believe that working-class immigrant women should be given a voice and that they have something important to contribute to the community of ideas.

Addams applies feminist standpoint epistemology in the "Devil Baby" story. Related in the first two chapters of *The Long Road of Woman's Memory,* the story recounts what transpired after three Italian women came to Hull House to view a Devil Baby. One can form a whimsical image from Addams's account: "No amount of denial convinced them that he was not there, for they knew exactly what he was like with his cloven hoofs, his pointed ears and diminutive tail; the Devil Baby had, moreover, been able to speak as soon as he was born and was shockingly profane."[35] This would be just an amusing anecdote if it stopped there, but Addams describes a six-week period of time when Hull House was inundated with stories about the alleged Devil Baby. Visitors even offered Hull House residents money to see the creature, despite adamant responses that there was no such baby. Multiple versions of how the Devil Baby was born arose in the neighborhood, and eventually the hysteria was recounted in the newspapers. One version of the story claimed that the Devil Baby was the offspring of an atheist and a devoted Italian girl. After the husband tore a holy picture from the wall declaring that he would rather have a devil in the house, his wish was granted in the form of his coming child.[36] Although a fascinating social phenomenon, the Devil Baby story appears to have little philosophical importance. Those who perpetuated the story could easily be dismissed as simpletons caught up in hysteria. Not by Jane Addams. She applies sympathetic understanding by refusing to pass judgment and listening carefully. Addams has to actively work and empathize to grasp their subject position.

Although Addams dismisses the "gawkers" who come to see the Devil Baby as a sensation-seeking mob, she wants to understand the older women who perpetuate the myth: "Whenever I heard the high eager voices of old women, I was irresistibly interested and left anything I might be doing in order to listen to them."[37] She discovers women who are serious and highly animated about the Devil Baby using the apparition, and the subsequent excitement, as an opportunity to discuss important and troubling matters. Addams, who never sought simple answers to complex issues, finds a convergence of class, race, and gender dynamics fueling the Devil Baby phenomenon. These immigrant women were in unfamiliar surroundings and had to adjust to foreign ideas and practices. They were alienated from their children, who adapted to the new country more easily, keeping the old ways at arm's length. Many of these women were victims of domestic abuse long before such acts had this label. One of them tells Addams, "My face has this queer twist for now nearly sixty years; I was ten when it got that way, the night after I saw my father do my mother to death with his knife."[38]

For these forgotten and beaten women, the Devil Baby represents a connection to a past that makes sense to them—because it has clear moral imperatives. Another woman tells Addams, "You might say it's a disgrace to have your son beat you up for the sake of a bit of money you've earned by scrubbing—your own man is different—but I haven't the heart to blame the boy for doing what he's seen all his life, his father forever went wild when the drink was in him and struck me to the very day of his death. The ugliness was born in the boy as the marks of the Devil was born in the poor child up-stairs."[39] Addams's recounting of these violent tales provides a depressing view of immigrant women's lives at the turn of the century. For women who lived such a hard life, the Devil Baby provides a momentary opportunity for resistance. Husbands and children listen to them and temporarily stop beating them for fear of divine retribution. Addams describes memory as serving to "make life palatable and at rare moments even beautiful."[40] She finds connections among the personal stories: "When these reminiscences, based upon the diverse experiences of many people unknown to each other, point to one inevitable conclusion, they accumulate into a social protest."[41] Addams proceeds to view the Devil Baby in light of the women's movement and the striking out against oppression. Given the position of the elderly women, the Devil Baby is the vehicle of subversion. Addams takes the time and effort to reflect on the standpoint of these embattled women and is therefore able to find more than superstition.

For Addams, understanding standpoint is a crucial starting point for better understanding of self and others. In this manner, Addams is consistent with what Annette Baier and later Lorraine Code describe as "second persons"—the idea that we are so rooted in relationships that rather than being autonomous first persons, we really obtain our identity through social interaction.[42] Addams begins with humility to imperfectly grasp the standpoint of others instead of approaching others with theories or answers. Such humility allows for listening and learning from others to better understand their position in the world, which in turn sheds light on her position in the world.

CARE ETHICS

Addams's approach to important social issues of her day reflects the relationality and contextualization consistent with contemporary feminist care ethics. Furthermore, although Addams employed caring in response to the needs of others, she contributes an active, even assertive, dimension to care ethics not commonly found among the work of care theorists. Finally, she advocates "socializing care": systemically instantiating habits and practices of care in social institutions.

Although *care* is a simple and widely invoked word, it is invested with particular meaning by feminist ethicists.[43] The original motivation for developing care ethics was an acknowledgment that traditional forms of morality, in particular, principle-based and consequence-based ethics, did not adequately address the richness of the human condition. These approaches typically bracket out emotions, relationships, temporal considerations, reciprocity, and creativity to focus on immediate adjudication of moral conflicts. Accordingly, the use of rules or consequences becomes a reductionist and formulaic response resulting in shortsighted responses to complex and systemic issues. Care ethicists generally find that principles and consequences have significance in moral deliberation, but they seek a more robust sense of morality. For example, the claim that people who spray-paint graffiti on a building ought to be punished because they damage someone else's property (rule/principle violation) likely receives widespread assent. Care ethicists do not deny such an assertion, but they want to know more. The people doing the spray painting are human beings, and their motivations and circumstances may reveal other variables not sufficiently addressed by the mere recognition of rule violations. Systemic issues involving social opportunities or discrimination or lack of voice may contribute to this behavior. Care ethicists shift moral focus from abstract individuals and their actions to concrete, situated people with feelings, friends, and dreams—someone who can be cared about. Standpoint theory and care theory are interrelated in their emphasis on acknowledging and understanding the subject position of others. Care ethics demands effort, experience, knowledge, imagination, and empathy to effectively understand the totality of the moral context. The result is not exoneration of personal responsibility but richer understanding of the human condition where we are all actors and acted upon.

Addams consistently moves beyond formulaic moral accounts of principles or consequences to apply care ethics to her experiences in the Hull House neighborhood. Proximity is crucial, as her direct experience of individuals better provides the resources for caring responses. However, Addams extrapolates her experiences to theorize about others of similar circumstances. In *The Spirit of Youth and the City Streets,* she addresses juvenile delinquency. She recounts charges against young men brought before the Juvenile Court in Chicago (which Hull House helped establish): "These charges were categorized by type such as stealing which included the pilfering of pigeons, blankets, and a bicycle. Another category was disorderly conduct which included picking up coal from railroad tracks, throwing stones at railroad employees, and breaking down a fence. There was also vagrancy, which included loafing, sleeping on the streets all night, and wandering."[44] Addams does not deny the seriousness of some of these infractions, but she does not rush to judgment, instead choosing to investigate the context further. She speaks with the young men and asks them about their motivations. She identifies restlessness and a desire for adventure not quieted by what the city has to offer: "their very demand for excitement is a protest against the dullness of life, to which we ourselves instinctively respond."[45] Addams views the city as built around the possibility of factory production but ignoring the needs of future workers. She finds in the "juvenile delinquents" many young people who simply seek adventure and excitement because their lives lack it. If Addams merely abstracted youth as a category of individuals who are prone to break the law, she could easily find principles to place a negative judgment on them. However, she views them as humans, many of whom she witnessed growing up in the neighborhood, and cares for them beyond the label of troubled youth.

Beyond exhibiting care ethics, Addams infuses a high level of social responsibility into this moral approach, virtually creating a duty to care. Many care ethicists are wary of the notion of duty as it is traditionally formulated. Moral duties historically entail an agreement regarding what actions a person is required to offer in behalf of another. Because the "other" is an abstract other, and the requirements are universalized (I must act in such a way in all cases), duties toward others tend toward moral minimums of obligation. For example, if someone's life is in peril and minimal effort could prevent it, such as an infant drowning in three inches of bath water, there is a moral obligation to act. Although such cases get widespread agreement, it becomes more difficult to ascertain what obligation one has to distant others. For example, does disposable income that can save the life of someone in a poverty-stricken country on a distant continent create a moral obligation to give that person the money? Addams constructs a duty to care differently. Hers is an epistemological demand. She demands that good citizens actively pursue knowledge of others—not just facts, but a deeper understanding of others—for the possibility of caring and acting in their behalf: "if we grow contemptuous of our fellows, and consciously limit our intercourse to certain kinds of people whom we have previously decided to respect, we not only tremendously circumscribe our range of life, but limit our scope of ethics."[46] For Addams, care ethics must be actively pursued, not passively fostered. There can be no lateral progress without care.

Finally, Addams extends care ethics to the public realm. She is not content to compartmentalize personal and social morality. Caring is what she desires for democracy and its various institutions. Addams views the residents of social settlements, for example, as having "an opportunity of seeing institutions from the recipient's standpoint" because they are not distant institutions but neighbors. She views this perspective as significant enough to "find expression in institutional management."[47] Furthermore, she differentiates the epistemological project of the settlement from the university in language that acknowledges a caring element: "The settlement stands for application as opposed to research; for emotion as opposed to abstraction, for universal interest as opposed to specialization."[48] Although social settlements epitomize a democratic endeavor for Addams, she applied the same caring values to other institutions. The creation of the juvenile courts in Chicago represented contextualized regard for young people. The creation of adult education that utilized tangible and contemporary issues also demonstrated a caring regard for the needs of Hull House neighbors. Perhaps most of all, the comportment of Hull House residents manifested care ethics in their willingness to listen, learn, and respond. Addams views socializing care as a way to participate in her rich ideal of democracy.

PROTO-LESBIAN ETHICS?

Perhaps one of the least-explored territories of Addams's theoretical work is the role of her sexual orientation. There are at least two relevant methods of viewing sexual orientation. One is the commonplace social understanding that deals with the facts and history of who is sleeping with whom. The other is a deeper philosophical understanding, which has ontological, metaphysical, and ethical implications stemming from the privilege granted heterosexuality.[49] In regard to Addams, the facts of her sexuality have received more attention than its intellectual implications. The two understandings are not unrelated because, as feminists vigorously argue, the emotional and the rational are not dichotomous opposites as Western philosophy traditionally conceives. For example, Deegan describes the loving correspondence between the women of Hull House as pointing "to a rich emotional world linked to a powerful intellectual and political ideology."[50] Same-sex love cannot be neatly compartmentalized from the activist and reflective work of Addams or her compatriots. I begin with a consideration of Addams's sexuality and then explore the ethical implications.

Deegan describes the writing about the sexuality of the women of Hull House as passing through phases. From 1890 to 1915, the women residents were positively portrayed as transcending sexuality, led by Saint Jane. During World War I, the pacifism of Hull House inspired ridicule, and the residents were characterized as out-of-touch old maids. From the 1920s to the 1970s, the ascendancy of Freudian ideas resulted in an interpretation of the residents of Hull House as pathological women, channeling their frustration into social reform. Since the 1970s, the prevalence of feminist analysis has served to discredit many of the previous interpretations as homophobic.[51] Offering one such feminist analysis, Lillian Faderman observes that many historians present Addams as "asexual."[52] Given widespread homophobia and assumptions implicit in compulsory heterosexuality, it is not unexpected that biographers not broach this subject. Faderman remarks, "Jane Addams lived a personal life that most biographers have attempted to gloss over, since the facts have made them uncomfortable."[53] Perhaps this suppression is owing in part to Addams's Victorian persona. Many women of her era had significant female friendships, some of which, but not all, were physically intimate.

Addams's sexual identity is challenging to clarify. Just as she never admitted to any ideology, or even a label such as "feminist," Addams never announced herself to be a lesbian. Unlike modern lesbian feminists, she had no safe public means for declaring her sexuality, nor did she likely have the inclination, given the growing suspicion of female intimacy in the Freudian era. Leila J. Rupp notes that Addams's adult life corresponds to a transitional period in sexual beliefs: "Before the categorization of the 'female invert' or 'lesbian' at the end of the nineteenth century, women lived in relationships as 'romantic friends' or chose to live out their lives as single women without a diagnosis of abnormality."[54] Accordingly, Addams's relationships with Starr and Smith may have been relatively acceptable and invisible early in her life and less so later. Addams likely may have had her own relationships in mind when in 1930 she expressed concern over Freudian theories bringing "dangers of repression" and profoundly influencing "the attitude of the sexes."[55] Despite renewed social enforcement of heterosexuality in the early twentieth century, there is no evidence that Addams entertained romantic interest in men.[56]

Because of extant letters, we can glimpse into Addams's life at Rockford Seminary (1877–81). The young women formed a close community that included various forms of emotional attachment. This atmosphere created openness and connection among the women, but it also fostered competitiveness for affections. Many of the students participated in "spooning," defined as the pairing off into favorites, with romantic overtones whether the relationship was physical or not.[57] Addams was torn between maintaining a certain emotional distance commensurate with her Victorian sensibilities and the compelling companionship of the close-knit female community. In her correspondence with Ida May Carey, a childhood friend, Carey agrees with Addams that romantic attachments among young women have gotten out of hand: "The girls here are afflicted with the same sentimental 'spooning' malady which, you say, infests Rockford. I heartily agree with you, old fellow that it is both disgusting, horrible, demoralizing to us as women. I have invariably found that 'familiarity breeds contempt.' Indeed, the girls carried the thing so far as to actually *flirt* with *one another,* in a way similar to the different sexes."[58] Editorial comments on the above letter note a pervasive "fascination about female relationships and love" in Addams's early correspondence. The editors conclude, "Perhaps Carey protested too much and may actually have been more interested in schoolgirl relations than she professed."[59] Might the same be said about Addams? Although she maintained a characteristically cool demeanor regarding her college relations, her life and philosophy were affected.

In *Twenty Years at Hull-House,* Addams reminisces about the intellectual environment and hints at the strength of the emotional environment at Rockford, on which she modeled Hull House: "This group of ardent girls . . . discussed everything under the sun with such unabated interest. . . . This early companionship showed me how essentially similar are the various forms of social effort."[60]

She indicates that the atmosphere of "intensity" and "fervor" was in part the result of recognition that these young college women were benefiting from the hard-fought success of the women's movement. Perhaps more important than the intellectual community, Rockford gave Addams Ellen Gates Starr.

Starr and Addams spent only one year together at Rockford. Financial troubles cause Starr to leave for a teaching position, although they remained vital companions. After Starr left Rockford, they corresponded frequently. When Addams fought depression and illness during her postgraduate period, Starr helped her physically and emotionally. They traveled to Europe together and grew closer.[61] According to Faderman,

> Ellen appears to have been Jane's first serious attachment. For years they cel-
> ebrated September 11—even when they were apart—as the anniversary of their
> first meeting. During their separations, Jane stationed Ellen's picture, as she wrote
> her, "where I can see you almost every minute." It was Ellen who prodded Jane
> to leave her family, come to Chicago, and open Hull House together with her.
> On accepting the plan, Jane wrote Ellen, "Let's love each other through thick and
> thin and work out a salvation." It was Ellen's devotion and emotional support that
> permitted Jane to cast off the self-doubt that had been plaguing her as a female
> who wanted to be both socially useful and independent during unsympathetic
> times and to commit herself to action.[62]

Starr and Addams were the backbone of the early Hull House community. Their mutual devotion carried them through some difficult times and set the tone for the environment at the settlement.

Their complementarity made for a dynamic relationship through Hull House's beginning and expansion. As Addams's national stature rose, they drifted apart but remained friends for life. Addams's second long-term relationship was with Mary Rozet Smith, who first came to Hull House in 1890 as a wealthy benefactor of the community. According to Linn, "Mary Smith drifted to the House in the course of its first year to see whether there was anything she could do there. She was barely twenty; tall, shy, fair, and eager. . . . Mary Smith soon became and always remained the highest and clearest note in the music of Jane Addams's personal life."[63] By 1893, Addams and Smith were traveling companions, writing devotional correspondence to one another and taking vacations together. Faderman claims that Addams and Smith shared a double bed and that Hull House residents, although discreet, were aware of their special relationship.[64] Addams and Smith found solace and support in other progressive lesbian couples such as German peace activists Anita Augsburg and Lida Gustava Heymann, whom they meet in 1924, and with whom they maintained an ongoing friendship and correspondence.[65] According to Alan Davis, the relationship between Smith and Addams was "more emotional than intellectual."[66] He describes Smith as deferential to Addams, filling her life with love and devotion.[67] Their relationship kept its intensity for more than forty years, until Smith's death in 1934.

Such evidence suggests that Addams was a lesbian; however, the term *lesbian* requires historical qualification. Faderman concurs: "It is only in the last few years that we can acknowledge, without the fact diminishing her stature, that Jane Addams—whether or not she knew to use the term about herself— was what our day would consider lesbian."[68] Kathryn Kish Sklar correctly points out that the term *lesbian* must be problematized because it achieved wide-spread usage beginning only in the 1960s.[69] Furthermore, social and political implications of the term evolved over time. Sklar prefers the term *homoerotic* to describe Addams and Smith's relationship. Sklar may be too cautious in suggesting that there is only "indirect" evidence of Addams's sexuality, but she is not alone. Gioia Diliberto claims that Addams and Smith's lesbian relationship may not have included sex, given prevalent ideas that women's abstention exemplified their moral superiority over men.[70] Victoria Brown also equivocates over Addams's homosexuality. According to Brown, if *lesbian* is defined as women loving women, as well as nurturing a woman-centered en-vironment and supporting the well-being of women, then Addams was clearly a lesbian. If *lesbian* is defined only by sexual activity, then according to Brown, Addams's sexual identity can never be positively determined. For the purpose of examining her philosophy, I maintain that Addams was a lesbian, given that her identity was so strongly woman-identified, but I think it is important to keep Brown's, Diliberto's, and Sklar's cautions in mind. Nevertheless, even if Addams did not have a robust lesbian identity, as the term is understood from the 1960s to the present, we know that she was perceptive and self-conscious, as exhibited by her personal reflections on religion and morality. She must have recognized that she was living as an "other" in a world where heterosexuality reigned supreme.

The Western philosophic tradition is reluctant to acknowledge that stand-point matters. Accordingly, Addams's sexuality should be a moot point in regard to her theoretical accomplishments. In this section, I address what it means for Addams to have been a lesbian, and why this identity is important to her philosophy. If subject position does matter in theory development as feminists suggest, then Addams's sexuality cannot be ignored.

According to Kathleen Martindale and Martha Saunders, lesbian ethics either defines a moral theory for the lesbian community, or it describes a moral orientation that originates from lesbian identity and experience subsequently extended to others.[71] Given that Addams did not have an explicit lesbian identity or community, her work fits the latter definition. Furthermore, because Addams did not address lesbians per se, it is difficult to argue that she contributes directly to a lesbian standpoint in ethics. However, lesbian experience, it can be argued, contributed to Addams's development of an inclusive social philosophy.

Sarah Hoagland's *Lesbian Ethics: Toward New Value* offers an ethic for the lesbian community commensurate with Martindale and Saunders's first definition. Nevertheless, Hoagland's work sheds light on Addams's theory development. Hoagland describes lesbian ethics as "shifts in perception" that "are meant to be used in lesbian community, among ourselves, as we weave new value, as we try to work out of the habit of dominance and subordination, thereby becoming beings who are not used to it."[72] In an analysis consistent with radical feminist questioning of social systems, Hoagland calls for a moral revolution. She argues that eliminating the oppression lesbians and others have faced requires separating from traditional heterosexist ethics that have created the problem. Otherwise, according to Hoagland, inconsequential reform rather than substantial changes in ethical systems will be made. She declares, "I want a moral revolution. I don't want greater or better conformity to existing values. I want change in value. Our attempts to reform existing institutions merely result in reinforcing the existing order."[73] It is not easy to move beyond an existing moral system. Much like a paradigm shift, moral ideas about rights, duties, and consequences are so ingrained in Western thought that they appear to be natural responses. Hoagland wants to begin ethical consideration from the standpoint of the oppressed—the oppression of lesbians—and move beyond the individualism that permeates traditional morality. Her lesbian ethics "starts with those who have a sense of desiring connection, who move toward each other. It starts with those who have many differences and who also have a ground on which to learn from those differences."[74] Connection, growth, and integrity rather than rules or calculations of right behavior are key ingredients of Hoagland's moral approach. Although lacking a specific lesbian analysis, Addams's feminist pragmatist values resonate strongly with those of Hoagland.

Addams's lack of attention to lesbian oppression makes it difficult to characterize her as a lesbian ethicist. However, it seems equally problematic to ignore her women-identified experience of oppression, given that she put so much emphasis on the role of experience. The question remains, how did Addams's sexual orientation influence her philosophy? First, in terms of content, Addams's social philosophy carves a special place for women from young to old. Addams's loving attachment to women is demonstrated, for example, when she so carefully attends to the stories of older immigrant women who retell the Devil Baby story. The content of her work is never explicitly lesbian, but it does reveal an affection for women. Second, methodologically, Addams does address and advocate for the marginalized in society. Her personal life as a woman and a lesbian gave her the imaginative resources to sympathetically understand marginalization.

Addams lived the double life that many lesbians experience. In private, she had long partnerships with Starr and Smith, but in public, she was perceived as a Marian-like figure: an asexual woman devoted to social reform. Although her life was replete with fulfilling experiences, and she was perceived as materially and socially privileged, she encountered something of the identity obliteration that many lesbians endure. She had to keep her relationships quiet or risk losing her ability to influence the public on issues of social reform. Just as Addams was ostracized for advocating peace in the face of a hawkish public, for her to acknowledge or address women loving women would have brought further marginalization. As Julia Penelope suggests, there is no real choice over sexual orientation, because society only offers heterosexuality: "Being a lesbian means living marginally, often in secrecy, often shamefully, but always as different, as the 'deviant.'"[75] For Addams, who emphasized compassionate understanding, her own deviance provided internal resources to empathize with others who were oppressed. It would be difficult for Addams to fall back on traditional standards and moral approaches, because she stood outside them at a very personal level. Writing in 1930, Addams says that the function of the social settlement is "to bring into the circle of knowledge and fuller life, men and women who might otherwise be left outside."[76] The prevalent assumption about Addams is that she spoke mostly from privilege as a member of white, upper-class America. However, like most people, her identity was layered with complexity, including the social limitations placed on her gender and the marginalization of her sexual orientation.

Rosalind Rosenberg describes Addams as the twentieth-century model of the "New Woman." Technology, affluence, and the need of colleges to fill classrooms created opportunities for women to lead more fulfilling lives. However, this was an unfulfilled opportunity, as women were expected to return to domestic concerns after their education. Addams demonstrated that women need not have careers only as homemakers and live out patriarchal, determined lives. In the autobiographical second chapter of *Democracy and Social Ethics*, Addams writes, "Our democracy is making inroads upon the family, the oldest of human institutions, and a claim is being advanced which in a certain sense is larger than the family claim."[77] Ostensibly, Addams is addressing the career path for women, but the independence spoken of can be extended to sexuality as well. Rosenberg quotes Jessie Taft, a philosopher who was a contemporary of Addams, and who also maintained a lifelong female companion: "The man who comes within [a young woman's] circle of possibilities is too often a man who has no form of self expression beyond his business and who therefore fails to meet her ideal of companionship in marriage."[78] It is no wonder that the deviancy of lesbianism began to be disciplined. Women like Addams were exerting power and independence with little need for men. Women from all over the country with interests in social reform came to Hull House and other settlements. Some were lesbians, but they all wanted an experience of freedom to be women accepted for who they were, joining in common cause.

Addams was muted about her sexuality, but she did make an interesting contribution to the notion of women's community. Hull House was not exclusively a lesbian community because men and heterosexual women lived there. However, it was a woman-identified space. Addams and the other residents created a safe environment for women where romantic relations between women could flourish without fear of retribution. Simultaneously, Hull House directly engaged patriarchal institutions within the city. Men were not systematically rebuked or excluded from Hull House projects. The stated purpose of Hull House was to engage, not separate from, social life. Maintaining physical proximity to, and activist engagement with, male-dominated environments, Hull House was a feminist community that nourished women who thirsted for relief from patriarchy.

Addams on Women's Issues

Elizabeth Cady Stanton (1815–1902) fought for women's right to vote for more than sixty years but died almost two decades prior to the ratification of the Nineteenth Amendment. Addams lived during a period when women's social roles changed drastically. She not only got the opportunity to vote in presidential elections, but she was one of the first women public figures wooed for political endorsement. Suffrage was an important issue for Addams and was the dominant symbol of first-wave feminism. She was convinced that excluding women's standpoints from the political arena was a detriment to social progress. Addams opens a 1912 article by asking readers to make imaginative connections: "The comfortable citizen possessing a vote won for him in a previous generation, who is so often profoundly disturbed by the cry of 'Votes for Women,' seldom connects the present attempt to extend the franchise with those former efforts, as the results of which, he himself became a member of the enfranchised class."[79] Rather than rights-based arguments, she employs care and empathy to remind the reader that many white males had only earned the vote less than 150 years earlier. Furthermore, a healthy society, like a living organism, must grow and evolve in response to new conditions, entailing an ongoing democratization "through the accession of new classes."[80] Addams did not promote women's suffrage only for women's benefit. She avoided pitting one social group against another. In an age when economic efficiency in, for example, the automobile industry had proven to be a powerful force for change and advancement, Addams suggests that society should be no less efficient: "only when all the people become the governing class can the collective resources and organizations of the community be consistently utilized for the common weal."[81] Addams's argument for suffrage is rational and intended to appeal to a wide audience.

On rare occasions, Addams was less guarded in her argument for suffrage. She pokes fun at men in a 1913 *Ladies Home Journal* article, reversing social status and asking what would happen "If Men Were Seeking the Elective Franchise."[82] In this "absurd hypothetical," Addams mentions masculine foibles, such as being "fond of fighting since you were little boys" and thus forgetting that the purpose of the state is to "nurture life." Accordingly, she declares, "out of sheer vainglory you would be voting away huge sums of money for battleships."[83] In a parody of arguments against women's suffrage, she suggests that granting men the franchise would be costly and wasteful: "Can we, the responsible voters, take the risk of wasting our taxes by extending the vote to those who have always been so ready to lose their heads over mere military display?"[84] Another example of Addams's infrequent sarcasm comes when she describes her experience at the Progressive Party's first convention in Chicago: "we were not in the usual position of bringing men around to a new way of thinking."[85]

Perhaps the clearest statement of Addams's views on suffrage appears in a 1915 interview for the *Ladies Home Journal* with an anonymous (or possibly fictional) journalist. Addams responds to a question about women voting with a revealing anecdote:

> The other day in Chicago an Irish woman came to call. Although she was an old woman before she obtained the right to vote, she talked about politics all the time. [Women had obtained the right to vote in municipal elections in Chicago in 1913.] She was very much interested in the two Democratic candidates for Mayor of Chicago. She knew a great deal about both. She said that her younger son wanted her to vote for one candidate and her married son was trying to persuade her to vote for the other. "Do you know," said this woman, "I haven't talked to my boys so much for five years?" So, you see, it gave mother and sons a mutual interest, and it gave her an entirely new interest. Such a woman would not be interested in abstractions, but if she was to make up her mind to vote, and if men, her sons and other people talk about her vote as of consequence, she wakes up and feels herself to be a factor in life as she never did before.[86]

Addams habitually engaged social issues with arguments grounded in her feminist pragmatist philosophy, and suffrage was no exception. Here she makes a unique suggestion employing care ethics: women's suffrage will improve the quality of interpersonal relationships. Traditionally alienated from the public sphere, women who engage in democratic processes will make more interesting intellectual partners for men and will therefore have more meaningful relationships. This was not Addams's only argument for women's winning the vote, but this story demonstrates how important individual relationships were to her. She next turns to the theme of social progress. The interviewer asks Addams whether women naively believe that obtaining the vote will result in ending all economic problems. She responds: "The vote is simply an instrument; a means toward securing a better social order through self-government."[87] Addams believed that women would use their experience and perspective to bring attention to issues not addressed by men.

In some ways, Addams's best-known article on suffrage, "Why Women Should Vote," originally published in the *Ladies Home Journal* and then made into a pamphlet, is the most conservative of her appeals for women's enfranchisement. In this essay, she claims that social circumstances necessitate that a woman "extend her sense of responsibility to many things outside of her own home."[88] Addams created a foundation for transgressing the public/private sphere divide by contending that voting was a means for fulfilling traditional responsibilities of women to their families and children. Dictated by population growth, demographic changes, and technological advances, society, and specifically government agencies, were engaging in activities traditionally conducted at home under the purview of women (i.e., education, child care, food preparation, garment making). According to Addams, a woman could only influence these institutions if she brought "herself to the use of the ballot—that latest implement of self-government."[89] The exact motivation for political rhetoric is difficult to know with certainty. Addams ostensibly wrote this piece to encourage women to vote, but the message seems to appeal to traditional roles in a manner stronger than some of her other suffrage pieces.

Addams leveraged her public position to support women's right to vote, but she also wrote and worked in behalf of women's interests in other areas, such as prostitution, labor organization, career choices, and gender-related violence.

Feminist and Pragmatist

In the previous chapter, I addressed Addams's pragmatist commitments. This chapter has focused on her feminist identity, theorizing, and activism. The two aspects of her thinking are intertwined in her writing. Addams's feminism is pragmatic. She does not treat her life and work in behalf of women as political advocacy or dogmatic ideology. For Addams, the advancement of women is an important component of social progress. She collects data on the lives of women to form tenuous notions of truth upon which to act, revising her understanding as new experience and information warrant it. Similarly, Addams's feminism effects her pragmatism. Her position outside the dominant masculine standpoint makes her sensitive to alternative subject positions, resulting in a radical appreciation for diverse voices. Furthermore, she extends socially constructed stereotypes of women's role as nurturer to develop the idea of socializing care ethics. Whether Addams was a feminist first and a pragmatist second, or vice versa, is less important than the dialectic of the two approaches in her philosophy.

Although I suggest that Addams makes contributions to both feminist and pragmatist philosophy, I further contend that the two philosophies coalesce in her concept of sympathetic knowledge. Positing that knowledge can be transformative, disruptive, and inseparable from morality, sympathetic knowledge is Addams's consistent approach to social issues and the subject of the next chapter.

Sympathetic knowledge is the only way of
approach to any human problem, and the line
of least resistance into the jungle of human
wretchedness must always be through that
region which is most thoroughly explored, not
only by the information of the statistician, but by
sympathetic understanding. — JANE ADDAMS

CHAPTER 4

Sympathetic Knowledge

Evolving from Addams's pragmatism and feminism is her notion of *sympathetic knowledge:* an inclusive approach to morality that reassesses the relationship between knowledge and ethics. Sympathetic knowledge emphasizes actively knowing other people for the purpose of understanding them with some degree of depth. For Addams, social knowledge entails openness to the possibility of caring for others and a willingness to act when the new knowledge warrants it. Sympathetic knowledge is imaginative in its empathetic response and consistent with contemporary feminist care ethics.[1] In my reading of Addams's work, sympathetic knowledge is her most significant contribution to philosophy as well as the moral approach that she brings to every social issue. Addams's sympathetic understanding exhibits American pragmatist commitments to experience and democracy as well as a nascent feminist ethic of care.

Addams's sympathetic knowledge rests on four interrelated claims that are addressed further in succeeding sections: (1) Human existence is ontologically defined by social interconnection funded by an ability to find common cause (but not at the price of eliding diversity). (2) If individuals take the time and effort to obtain a deep understanding of others, that knowledge has the potential to disrupt their lives with the possibility of empathetic caring. (3) Empathy leads to action: people who care enough act in behalf of others so that they may flourish and grow. (4) An effective democratic society depends on caring responses. Accordingly, for Addams, socializing care is emphasized over the application of moral systems such as rights-based ethics that locate morality in individual agency. For example, rights are morally, politically, and symbolically useful, but they are no substitute for the widespread anchoring of morality found in a society grounded in the practice of sympathetic knowledge.

Human Interconnection

Addams and her fellow progressives are often criticized for being utopian in their belief that social ills can be eradicated. An alternative reading of Addams finds her work rooted in an ontology grounded in human goodness and connection rather than a fixed utopian vision. Addams believed that despite powerfully constructed social barriers to knowledge of interdependence, reinvigorating understanding of human interconnection makes solving moral challenges a greater possibility. For example, in *The Spirit of Youth and the City Streets,* she posits that generational differences are exaggerated and surmountable: "Perhaps never before have the pleasures of the young and mature become so definitively separated as in the modern city."[2] Addams does not condemn young people or their morality: "The mass of these young people are possessed of good intentions and they are equipped with a certain understanding of city life."[3] She never presumes that people are "wholly other": defined by an essentialist concept of evil. For Addams, young people, like all humans, cannot be marginalized or discarded. Rich, poor, young, old, oppressed and oppressor—we share much in our humanity, including the capability of caring and being cared for.

In *Democracy and Social Ethics,* Addams demonstrates the nuances of sympathetic understanding by drawing some surprising conclusions about Chicago aldermen and their ability to connect to their constituents. These aldermen epitomized corruption in government given their use of bribery and cronyism. Rather than moralize and castigate aldermen for their violation of social principles, Addams attempts to understand these local politicians from the perspective of the people who support them. After the women of Hull House had repeatedly attempted to unseat Alderman Johnny Powers, Addams reflects on the phenomenon of Powers's success (without ever naming him). She does not condone the extortion and graft of the aldermen, but she admires their social interaction and the relationships they formed.

Addams dispassionately considers the emotive elements of the aldermen's success. The aldermen knew how to make a connection to their constituents at a basic human level: "They [aldermen] are often politically corrupt but in spite of this they are proceeding upon a sounder theory. . . . Men living near to the masses of voters, and knowing them intimately, recognize this and act upon it; they minister directly to life and to social needs."[4] For Addams, the popular attraction of these corrupt politicians stemmed from their connected knowledge: they understood their community and its needs. Addams sympathetically understands why the community has an emotional attachment to the aldermen without condoning the aldermen's behavior. These politicians knew their communities but used that knowledge for the purpose of exploitation. The aldermen lacked a commitment to the social growth of the community. Addams approaches this, and other moral issues, by attending to contexts, people, experiences, and relationships as enmeshed. She refuses to treat people as isolated moral automatons moving from compartmentalized transaction to transaction.

Addams suggests that given our common humanity, if we know one another better, we will care. This interpersonal understanding was the basis for the settlement movement: the knowledge that comes from living in proximity. Addams finds continuity between knowing and caring: if someone who is foreign, misunderstood, or made to be "other" can be brought into the light of familiarity, the potential for care is greater. For example, in *A New Conscience and an Ancient Evil*, Addams does not offer an abstract condemnation of the morality of prostitution that employs principles and duties. Rather than moralizing about the ethical weakness of young women, the lesson of this book is that harm comes to people when they lose social, economic, and cultural connection. Moreover, it highlights how women are defined by social, economic, and cultural dynamics that lead to acute vulnerability. In this manner, prostitution is a sad metaphor for the plight of many women.

In *A New Conscience and an Ancient Evil,* Addams describes how the rise of big cities creates greater potential for disconnection between sectors of society. For example, middle-class suburban women are disconnected from, and thus lack understanding of, urban workingwomen. To counteract this disconnection for her audience, Addams provides stories of individuals, not as prostitutes, but rather as human beings, like the reader. Addams describes Olga as "a tall, handsome girl, a little passive and slow, yet with that touch of dignity which a continued mood of introspection so often lends to the young."[5] She confronts the reader with flesh-and-blood examples, demonstrating that the women who enter prostitution (or, in the case of Olga, barely avoid it) are very much like us in their humanity. Addams wants us to care about Olga and in turn see prostitution as populated by women like Olga, with lives, families, and dreams.

These concrete representations help instantiate sympathetic knowledge. The more vividly we understand the existence of others, the more likely we will care and act in their behalf. Accordingly, for Addams, morality is not wholly determined by poor personal choices. Sympathetic understanding does not negate moral agency. The prostitute is neither entirely blameless nor blameworthy. As a pragmatist, Addams looks forward rather than backward, thus finding heavy-handed moral adjudication a luxury. She endeavors to facilitate social progress, not preach about errors of the past. She seeks a workable theory of social growth. As a feminist, Addams recognizes intersectional forces at work in people's lives. She knows that individual decisions are not made in a vacuum, and that there are levels of coercion, particularly for the vulnerable of society, beyond a gun or a knife. Addams offers compelling moral reflection by attending to the particularities of people's lives because she knows that ethics is incomplete if one forgets about its experiential dimension.

Disruptive Knowledge

Addams's sympathetic knowledge transgresses Western epistemologies traditionally grounded in separations of mind and body, separations of reason and emotion, and separations of ethics from epistemology. Sympathetic knowledge recognizes an embodied existence that entails experiences and emotions. Intriguingly, Addams balances dispassionate reflective analysis with an emotive activist epistemology: she is keenly aware of the power of knowledge to engender caring and action. She wants her audience to understand racism, war, and poverty, not just as facts, but also as inscribed on the lives of fellow humans. When we sympathetically and affectively understand the plight of others, we are more likely to care and act in their behalf.

For Addams, it is a mistake to ignore the affective dimension of ethical dilemmas. Seigfried highlights how Addams employs the notion of "perplexity" to refer to "someone's personal involvement in a situation that baffles and confuses her." Such perplexity engages "the interplay of personal feeling and objective conditions."[6] Seigfried suggests that Addams's use of perplexity differentiates her work from philosophies that endeavor to capture intellectual puzzlement. Personal emotive involvement must be aroused to overcome the puzzlement. Seigfried concludes that for Addams, "moral deliberation is not a dryly intellectual exercise, but rather emotionally pervaded throughout and engages the whole person."[7]

Sympathetic knowledge is not emotivism. Addams does not reduce epistemology or ethics to emotional reactions or personal preference. Furthermore, she was wary of unchecked sentimentalism and was quite critical of how emotions drove the U.S. march into World War I. However, Addams does not strip ethics or epistemology of its emotive elements. She recognizes that social movements find impetus in "emotional incentive" and to ignore their emotional dimension is to lose contact with "a great source of vitality."[8] Sympathetic knowledge responds to our fundamental human connection, and she uses the affective dimension of human relations to connect individuals to issues.

Addams's work on sympathetic knowledge foreshadows contemporary feminist questioning of the dichotomy between emotion and reason. Margaret Urban Walker claims, "Moral competence draws on propositional knowledge—'know that'—but also on perceptive, imaginative, and expressive capacities supported by habits of emotional response."[9] Clearly, propositional knowledge is important. We need to know the facts, relevant statistics, and descriptions of events when addressing moral dilemmas. However, if propositional knowledge constitutes the whole of morality, perhaps a computer could handle ethical controversies as so many variables in a complex algorithm. As Walker suggests, it is emotional knowledge that ignites empathy, draws our attention, and tugs at our heartstrings to act. When we view knowledge in the context of connection to others, it is disruptive because it interrupts our lives and demands a felt response.

Sympathetic knowledge is *disruptive* when it transforms abstract understanding into concrete understanding, thus embedding the circumstances of others in the life of the knower and compelling a response. Addams describes social progress movements as having this transformative power when "intellectual aspects" are "transferred from the region of perception to that of emotion."[10] Such concretization is experienced as affective. The embodied connection allows for a felt understanding with the potential to shake us from the rhythms of our lives and motivate us to take action. For example, I can recount UNICEF reports that one-third of child deaths worldwide are the result of malnourishment.[11] Many might feel this is tragic, but few would be moved to act based on the presentation of propositional knowledge. However, if these people were physically confronted by a child who grew up amid poverty-stricken conditions who describes her experiences, the potential for disruptive knowledge would be increased. The direct experience of her facial expressions, her voice inflection, her hand gestures and body movements is more likely to create a felt response than any statistical presentation. The potential for disruption is greater because malnourishment is concretized in a way that makes an embodied connection, given that we can affectively empathize with hunger, even if we have never starved. Were Addams to confront this issue, she would seek to confront her audience with rational and affective knowledge to engage sympathetic understanding.

Addams declares that "the new social morality, which we so sadly need, will of necessity have its origins in the social affections."[12] Throughout her writing, Addams recognizes the emotive dimension to morality. In *Newer Ideals of Peace*, she describes the role of experience in fostering the moral sentiments of immigrant communities. The common experience of leaving home and trying to make a new life in a foreign land gives rise to compassion, "emotional pity and kindness."[13] According to Addams, "emotion becomes the dominant force in fixing social relations."[14] She gives a "meta history" of social morality when she discusses "tribal man," claiming that today's newer ideals of peace or humanitarianism are an outgrowth of the origins of social relations. The hostile world brought people together to combat the common enemy of their environment. Addams claims "solidarity of emotion and action" is essential to life under siege.[15] Immigrant communities and the poor are also under siege and have similar emotional solidarity. Addams suggests that we must transcend differences to allow that unity of emotion to resurface.

Thus, sympathetic understanding is demanding. Liberalism's tradition of autonomous agents and universal principles offers the safety of emotional detachment and personal distance.[16] The personal connection that can elicit an emotional response shortens that distance. Emotional knowledge implies risk and vulnerability that has the potential to cause us pain and disappointment. Addams asks that we channel that pain into motivation for action. For Addams, sympathetic knowledge is incomplete if it does not lead to action. Her public philosophy is designed to move people to get involved. Caring cannot be passive if it is to be ethical. People who care will act: "the sphere of morals is the sphere of action, that speculation in regard to morality is but observation and must remain in the sphere of intellectual comment, that a situation does not really become moral until we are confronted with the question of what shall be done in a concrete case, and are obliged to act upon our theory."[17] Addams's choice of words is particularly telling here. Morality is actualized by experience. This is not to say that we do not have "theories" about morality, but the true test is the situation and the subsequent action. For Addams, what connects moral epistemology and social epistemology, and what links knowledge and action, is emotion.

Democracy and Sympathetic Knowledge

Addams offers a new definition of democracy as the practice of a social ethic founded on sympathetic knowledge. According to her, the caring actions of individuals coalesce into intelligent collective care. A vital society—one that is making lateral progress in the well-being of its members—includes a robust spirit of care derived from sympathetic knowledge. Hull House is the manifestation of her social philosophy. Addams intertwines epistemology and ethics in her description of social settlements: "The dominating interest in knowledge has become its use, the conditions under which, and ways in which it may be most effectively employed in human conduct. . . . Certain people have consciously formed themselves into groups for the express purpose of effective application. These groups are called settlements."[18] Addams views democracy as a moral manner of living together grounded in sympathetic knowledge.

The settlements are a microcosm of effective democracy whereby meeting and knowing one another leads to care and action. In "A Function of the Social Settlement," Addams connects knowledge and emotion in defining the social settlement: "The ideal and developed settlement would attempt to test the value of human knowledge by action, and realization. . . . The settlement stands for application as opposed to research; for emotion as opposed to abstraction, for universal interest as opposed to specialization."[19] For Addams, emotional knowledge is a key participant in moral deliberation.

Addams can be viewed as a forerunner of contemporary feminist social philosophy. Feminist philosophy has developed a rich corpus of work that engages the full range of philosophical inquiry as rooted in a libratory social theory. Pragmatism is so steeped in concern for relevancy that it too finds its soul in social and political philosophy. Addams develops a robust social philosophy grounded in notions of an engaged democracy with its basis in sympathetic knowledge, a positive human ontology, lateral progress, and evolutionary adaptation. For Addams, human beings are essentially good, but circumstances can limit their ability to exercise their goodness. Accordingly, she views democracy as both a libratory political system and a relational comportment—a way of being—that demands that individuals understand one another so as to act for mutual benefit in a society that progresses by a measure of all its members, improving their collective lot rather than the success of some at the expense of others. Progress entails growth and change, including the evolution and adaptation of moral principles and ideals, in order to adapt to new circumstances.

Democracy and Social Ethics, Addams's first full-length book and her most theoretical piece, establishes the philosophy of sympathetic knowledge that she applies to social issues in her subsequent publications. Like most of her ideas, the material for *Democracy and Social Ethics* went through a testing and distilling process that included lectures and articles prior to coalescing into a manuscript. The book was published in 1902, by which time Addams had been at Hull House for more than ten years and had already achieved celebrity status, including popularity as a public speaker. Her lectures, after revisions, became articles in scholarly periodicals such as the *American Journal of Sociology,*

International Journal of Ethics, and *Annals of the American Academy of Political and Social Science,* as well as popular magazines like the *Atlantic Monthly.* Every chapter of *Democracy and Social Ethics* (with the exception of the introduction) appeared at least in part in previous publications. By the time it was published in 1902, the ideas it expresses had been tested before a variety of audiences.

Like all of Addams's work, *Democracy and Social Ethics* employs experience and personal example in a manner foreign to most political philosophy. According to Seigfried, because Addams "develops her theory contextually and in narrative form rather than systematically or deductively, it is easy to miss the fact that she both argues for and follows an experimental method."[20] Consistent with sympathetic knowledge, each chapter addresses an aspect of social relations and issues rather than abstract concepts of political theory such as personhood, rights, or common good. Addams thematizes her experiences, so they are not presented as disassociated anecdotes, but they do not resemble the abstracted and generalized theoretical positions typical of Western philosophy.

Arguably, the most overtly philosophical piece of *Democracy and Social Ethics* is the brief introduction. Addams begins by positing that righteousness is a normative goal of humanity without which life would be meaningless. The pursuit of morality, then, is a given; however, she quickly reveals her commitment to the notion of social change and development. She declares that "each generation has its own test" of morality.[21] She separates herself from those who contend that morality is distinct from human existence, and thus enduring and unchanging. Specifically, Addams claims that the social morality required in the present age surpasses the individual morality of the past: "To attain individual morality in an age demanding social morality, to pride one's self on the results of personal effort when the time demands social adjustment, is utterly to fail to comprehend the situation."[22] Addams does not dismiss theories of individual morality; she suggests that they are inadequate to the needs of large and diverse societies of the present. She was living in a time when the fruits of the Industrial Revolution had ripened. Big cities, world travel, and industrialization were transforming social life in ways never previously experienced, and Addams lived amid some of the most striking changes in the Hull House neighborhood of Chicago. Given her experience of the burgeoning city, her moral philosophy is rooted in social ethics; she offers no theory of individual ethics apart from the social claim: "the latter day moral ideal is in reality that of social morality."[23]

In the latter part of the introduction to *Democracy and Social Ethics,* Addams equates social ethics with democracy by infusing a normative claim into the political concept. Rather than defining democracy as rule by the majority through free election, her concept of democracy entails caring interpersonal relations and morality: sympathetic understanding. For Addams, democracy "affords a rule of living" that includes a moral mandate to learn about one another.[24] The title of the book could have been "Democracy *Is* Social Ethics," given her equating of the two concepts: "To follow the path of social morality results perforce in the temper if not the practice of the democratic spirit, for it implies that diversified human experience and resultant sympathy which are the foundation and guarantee of Democracy."[25] Addams's feminist pragmatism is evident in the normative claim that we must richly experience one another to participate in an effective democracy marked by lateral social progress. We cannot assume the subject position of others. Her approach requires acknowledging and honoring the diversity of the members in the democratic community.

Addams's introduction to *Democracy and Social Ethics* makes her intended audience quite clear. Unlike Marx, she is not addressing the oppressed and downtrodden while calling for social upheaval. Addams, writing to the middle and upper class, asks them to use their resources wisely, so as to acknowledge their social interdependency. She is well aware that the privileged can leverage their advantage to separate themselves physically and socially from the oppressed. She claims that social segregation is immoral, undemocratic, and unwise because violent class conflict could be the only result—as seen in the Pullman strike. Furthermore, Addams believes that we lose individually and collectively when we fail to experience and learn from those who are different from ourselves: "We realize, too, that social perspective and sanity of judgment come only from contact with social experience; that such contact is the surest corrective of opinions conceiving the social order, and concerning efforts, however humble, for its improvement."[26] Her democracy requires reciprocity between people rather than antagonism between the classes.

In *Democracy and Social Ethics,* Addams engages "various types and groups who are being impelled by the newer conception of Democracy" in a manner not typically found in philosophical analysis.[27] To explore the mismatch of individual ethics to the present condition, she employs the archetype of the charity worker. Addams's fictional charity worker has well-meaning intentions but operates with outdated morality and a lack of experience in her assigned community. According to Addams, a charity worker often confronts those in need with an individualistic morality that claims poverty is the result of personal vice and laziness rather than recognizing the social structures and forces that contribute to poverty and oppression.[28] Addams asks that we not hide behind moral platitudes but seek out the fundamental connection between one another, "the natural outgoing of human love and sympathy, which happily, we all possess in some degree."[29] In order to do this, the charity worker must set aside her moralism, understand and appreciate the plight of the poor, and potentially learn from them.

Addams contrasts the practices and motivations of the charity worker and the settlement worker. The latter lives among the impoverished and works with them rather than imposing a regimen. The settlement is the epitome of a democratic effort of crossing class and cultural boundaries. Although Addams heaps her criticism and analysis on the well-meaning yet ineffective charity worker, the same critique is intended for the reader. As Christopher Lasch notes, this chapter is "exhilarating and disturbing" because she is questioning mainstream morality.[30] The admonishments are made more palatable through the use of the charity worker as foil. Nevertheless, the sentiments are intended to challenge traditional ideas about class relations. Addams is making the radical claim that moral systems must adapt. She is not merely reinterpreting Kantian duties for a new era; she is claiming that moral systems based on the primacy of individual subjectivity must change, given contemporary circumstances demanding a social ethic. Accordingly, the charity worker must be grounded in the context of her clients.

Addams's central thesis that society is changing and our morality must adjust is a far-reaching claim emerging from specific social experiences. Rather than viewing morality as fixed and immutable, Addams views morality as evolving. She recognizes the dilemma of change: "It is quite obvious that the ethics of none of us are clearly defined, and we are continually obliged to act in circles of habit, based upon convictions which we no longer hold."[31] Throughout *Democracy and Social Ethics,* Addams applies the theme that a new context requires a new ethic: one that is social and represented by a richly interactive democracy. After engaging the charitable worker, the book addresses familial morality, privatized domestic labor, business and industry, education, and politics. In each case, individualized morality is shown to be inadequate to the situation, and isolation or compartmentalization is viewed as dangerous. Conversely, Addams finds connection and engagement to be a social good. The final chapter of *Democracy and Social Ethics,* concerning politics, exemplifies her approach. Addams claims that those in power are attracted to individual ethics, while those not in power develop a social morality that she believes is not only superior but evolutionarily appropriate to meet the challenge of the present condition. For society to flourish, its leaders must keep in touch with the lives of their constituents to create an adequate sympathetic understanding. "It is most difficult to hold our political democracy and to make it in any sense a social expression and not a mere governmental contrivance, unless we take pains to keep on common ground in our human experience."[32] For Addams, it is important that political leaders have an engaged relationship with the community that is committed to growth and well-being.

As *Twenty Years at Hull-House* is the most autobiographical of her works, *Democracy and Social Ethics* is the most philosophical; however, for Addams, biography and philosophy are closely associated. Her feminist pragmatism dictates that her philosophy be derived from her experiences. Those experiences indicate that more than rules and rights protect society's members.

Addams suggests that democracy "continually demands new formulation."[33] That reformulation entails moving beyond static notions of isolated individuals endowed with rights to considerations of citizens' responsibilities for others as part of an active and rich notion of public interest: democracy informed by sympathetic knowledge. A revealing approach to understanding Addams's commitment to sympathetic knowledge is to contrast it with a rights-based approach, the dominant theme of contemporary political theory. The 1948 United Nations Universal Declaration of Human Rights transformed the political landscape, and a half century later continues to be the subject of theoretical speculation about the efficacy of rights. Addams did not live to see the declaration, but she would have certainly hailed it. Simultaneously, she would have been wary. Although not disdaining rights-based ethics, she would have found the approach insufficient to the morality required by a dynamic democracy that desperately needs its members to sympathetically understand one another.

On several occasions, Addams takes issue with traditional understandings of democracy that she characterizes as emphasizing autonomy and equality. In *Newer Ideals of Peace*, Addams contends that the founders of the United States operated under a limited notion of personhood:

> Their idealism, after all, was founded upon theories concerning the "natural man," a creature of the sympathetic imagination.
>
> Because their idealism was of the type that is afraid of experience, these founders refused to look at the difficulties and blunders which a self-governing people were sure to encounter, and insisted that, if only the people had freedom they would walk continuously in the paths of justice and righteousness. It was inevitable, therefore, that they should have remained quite untouched by that worldly wisdom which counsels us to know life as it is, by the very modern belief that if the world is ever to go right at all, it must go right its own way.[34]

Addams suggests that the founders conceptualized citizens as abstract, disembodied beings. For classic liberal theory context has no value; human beings exist separately and prior to society. Sympathetic knowledge means context is of vital importance. There is no "natural man"—only flesh-and-blood men and women whose lives are not marked by universal autonomy and contractual relations. In this manner, Addams sees people as fundamentally entangled in one another's lives. In her view, to speak of a natural man, or original position, unfettered by social influences, is an exercise in imagination that can only mislead. Social conditions must be addressed as they are experienced, and therefore the assumptions of traditional liberal democracy cannot be accepted.

In *Democracy and Social Ethics,* Addams refers to John Stuart Mill's concept of an individual in a living society "as one who thinks of himself, not as an isolated individual, but as a part in a social organism."[35] This idea of the social organism is a guiding metaphor for her notion of democracy. The health and happiness of the whole requires that constituencies work toward the benefit of all and not merely for individual benefit. For democracy to be successful, our shared investment in one another has to be cultivated: "surely the demand of an individual for decency and comfort, for a chance to work and obtain the fullness of life may be widened until it gradually embraces all the members of the community, and raises a sense of the common weal."[36] Addams develops an idea of democracy that is inherently social and requires empathy, understanding, and action in behalf of one another. For Addams, newer ideals of peace are grounded in an evolving sense of liberty and freedom, not fixed historical ones.

Most important, Addams is not willing to support the liberal democratic path that is complicit with laissez-faire capitalism. She does not concede that egoism will result in democratic action: "to give [an individual] a sense of conviction that his individual needs must be merged into the needs of the many, and are only important as they are thus merged, the appeal cannot be made along the lines of self-interest."[37] Addams views the basis of democracy to be simultaneously social and ethical. These statements reveal how complex her social morality is: an integration of moral motives, consequences, and caring for others.

Addams is certainly not antithetical to rights. She wrote and spoke often in support of women's suffrage, the labor movement, restrictions on child labor, and other social issues that have an implicit interest in advancing rights. However, she seldom constructs her arguments on these social issues using the language of rights. When she does address rights, and it is often quite indirectly, she frames them as a sign of social progress. Because her approach to democracy is fundamentally social, her theory of rights centers on privileges, which lead to "lateral progress." Addams thus reframes the concept of rights to show their broad social consequences for communal experience. Widespread social experience is the truth test; therefore rights cannot be limited to a privileged few.

When Addams addresses prostitution in *A New Conscience and an Ancient Evil,* she does not confront the issue in the rights-based abstraction of a contractual relationship between two consenting autonomous agents. She provides numerous examples to demonstrate that those involved in prostitution have not freely chosen the vocation. Theoretically, adult women can make a choice to exchange money for sexual acts, but Addams contends that most women are not free at all. She describes a young woman whose ill and elderly family was depending on her to earn money for their sustenance. At first, she attempted a number of "legitimate" jobs, only to be ultimately drawn to the lucrative profession of prostitution.[38] Addams's point is that the experience of freedom can be relativized to one's economic standing. At the conclusion of the book, she lays out a vision for the mitigation of prostitution: "We are safe in predicting that when the solidarity of human interest is actually realized, it will become unthinkable that one class of human beings should be sacrificed to the supposed needs of another; when the rights of human life have successfully asserted themselves in contrast to the rights of property, it will become impossible to sell the young and heedless into degradation."[39] This is one of the few occasions where Addams explicitly addresses rights, but it is not fully developed and appears to be a condemnation of the profit motive more than a treatment of a hierarchy of rights. Notice that she frames this statement on rights by first making reference to human solidarity and to how subordinating one group of people to another then becomes unthinkable. She is more concerned with power relations and the empathetic communication of felt experience than demanding or asserting rights. In *Newer Ideals of Peace*, Addams states that "rights are not 'inalienable,' but hard-won in the tragic processes of experience."[40] Again, she grounds rights in the reality of people's lives, as a tool for social progress given widespread actualization.

Addams generally regards rights as not doing all the work necessary to allow progress toward a social democracy. Three interrelated criticisms of rights-based discourse emerge from her writings: (1) The language of rights fails to comprehensively capture what is necessary to create a moral community. (2) Rights can never be an end; they are merely a means to an end. (3) Rights are static and fail to evolve with changing social conditions and dispositions. In particular, rights-based discourse in the United States is too fixed on eighteenth-century assumptions that include an elitist standpoint and a fear of diverse experience.

For Addams, constructing and invoking rights, while not without merit, cannot supplant eliciting broad-based understanding and action. When she writes about mitigating prostitution, she calls for a thorough analysis of the "resources that may at length be massed against it."[41] These resources include legal measures, but law alone does not solve the social problem as far as Addams is concerned. Instead, she suggests that "sympathetic knowledge is the only way of approach to any human problem."[42] Accordingly, if we want to reduce prostitution, we should engage in social inquiry and carefully communicate the issue to the community who, after attaining a degree of sympathetic understanding and participating in deliberation, may undertake measures such as a living-wage system, education programs, and providing social opportunities to alleviate the problem.

Addams addresses women's suffrage in a similar fashion, never seeing it as an end in itself. She characterizes voting as a means to achieve wider social advancement. She does not directly address the rights to elective franchise or the equal rights of men and women, but rather chooses to address the good derived from women's voting. For example, Addams recognized that society was in flux and that domestic responsibilities such as education, housekeeping, and maintaining the safety of family members were no longer the exclusive purview of the household. Increasingly, social institutions were taking on vital domestic activities. Addams argues that because these areas historically have been women's responsibility, women should be given the opportunity to influence decisions that affect these spheres.

Because Addams views a democratic community as a social organism held together by sympathetic knowledge, an assumption of natural rights based on a fixed human nature is unworkable. She quotes Josiah Royce in her concern about the static nature of rights: "A man of this generation easily discerns the crudeness of that eighteenth-century conception of essentially unprogressive human nature in all the empty dignity of 'inborn rights.' Because he has grown familiar with a more passionate human creed, with the modern evolutionary conception of the slowly advancing race."[43] Like many intellectuals of her day, Addams embraced evolutionary theory and applied it widely. The idea that a right, once established, resolves a social ethical need is incompatible with her understanding of a growing and changing society.

Addams, steeped in the experience and lives of her Hull House neighbors, recognizes the situated nature of thinking and theory. She is critical of eighteenth-century political ideas that she regards as outmoded in the late nineteenth and early twentieth centuries. The reification of eighteenth-century rights-based discourse is particularly problematic because it derives from privileged authors who are suspicious of diverse experience. For Addams, democracy is a living collective of diversified experience strengthened by its multivariate exchanges. She wrote an article in 1930 titled "Widening the Circle of Enlightenment," where she places the highest value on exchanges with immigrant peoples. Addams describes such exchanges as having a "revivifying effect" that can be obtained "in no other way." She contrasts this standpoint with the work of Thomas Jefferson and others who eschewed heterogeneous experience.[44]

For Addams, the language of rights does not provide a sufficient social morality, perhaps because she invests a greater ethical stake in democracy than most. Rights provide a theoretical baseline but are inadequate to carry the full weight of her social democracy. Sympathetic knowledge is the imaginative baseline needed to fund the empathetic resources that a democratic society needs to sustain itself.

Sympathetic Understanding and Contemporary Philosophy

In 1993, M. Regina Leffers published an article describing how resources found in Addams's and Dewey's work could facilitate contemporary discussions of care ethics by offering theoretical clues as to how it is possible to care for strangers and unknown "others."[45] It is unfortunate that no one took up Leffers's theme. Very few attempts have been made to bridge American pragmatist thought and feminist care ethics, although the potential for fruitful interaction is apparent in common concern for connections, experience, and diversity.[46] Care ethics has gone unnoticed by American pragmatists, and feminist ethicists have ignored Addams's social morality. Given the opportunity, Addams can serve as a significant bridge figure in contemporary ethical thinking. Her notion of sympathetic understanding has much to offer contemporary discussions of relational approaches to morality. Susan Hekman describes present moral thinking as undergoing an intellectual "sea change" that is moving away from absolutism and universalism toward particularism and concreteness.[47] Addams's work seems well positioned to contribute to this new direction.

PART II

Theory, Action, Reflection

Portrait of Jane Addams with flower arrangement, ca. 1883.

> My temperament and habit had always kept
> me rather in the middle of the road; in politics
> as well as in social reform I had been for "the
> best possible." But now I was pushed far toward
> the left on the subject of the war and I became
> gradually convinced that in order to make the
> position of the pacifist clear it was necessary that
> at least a small number of us should be forced
> into an unequivocal position. — JANE ADDAMS

CHAPTER 5

Ultimate Social Progress: Peace

July 9, 1915, was a pivotal day in Addams's career. She delivered an address titled "Revolt against War" at New York's Carnegie Hall that altered the public's perception of her. The speech came at a tumultuous time. One year earlier, war had broken out in Europe, and casualties were numerous and came quickly. In only three months of fighting, the equivalent of the entire original contingent of the British army was killed.[1] At the end of the Great War, more than nine million soldiers were dead. Although this death toll is a tragedy of great proportion, World War I was also a crucial turning point for collective consciousness about violence in western Europe and the United States. The Industrial Revolution had brought humanity so much progress that, coupled with a decline in social stratification in terms of colonialism and slavery, one might ask whether human progress had advanced beyond violent geopolitical confrontations. At this pivotal moment, Addams desperately tried to shape the direction of the collective consciousness toward peace—and failed.

After the Great War began in Europe in 1914, debate raged in the United States regarding whether to join the battle. The sinking of the British ocean liner *Lusitania* on May 7, 1915, killing 1,198 people, including 124 Americans, made U.S. involvement appear inevitable. Addams's response to war in Europe parallels her response to problems that arose in the Hull House neighborhood: mobilize sympathetic knowledge and a community of activists to search for rational and caring solutions leading to lateral progress. When Addams rose to speak at Carnegie Hall, she had already traveled to Europe to meet with other peace activists at the first International Congress of Women at The Hague. With Alice Hamilton and Emily Greene Balch, Addams had visited heads of state in Europe (as well as troops in the field), attempting to stop the war and to learn about conditions and motivations of belligerents. Although the delegation was unsuccessful in obtaining a cease-fire, Addams was elevated to an international peace figure. Domestically, however, her stature was about to drop.

Prior to the Carnegie speech, Addams was a national treasure. By 1915, she was a successful author and a highly sought-after speaker. Just short of her fifty-fifth birthday, Addams was at the height of her public acclaim, but her position unraveled in the weeks following that evening at Carnegie Hall as she faithfully applied her public philosophy. She began by recounting her experience at The Hague and her subsequent efforts to persuade heads of state to turn to peace. Had her speech been limited to anecdotes, it would have reinforced her public image as a woman committed to caring. However, Addams was a public philosopher who perceived her responsibility to place events in the context of social democracy. In this and many other speeches, Addams shared her critical reflections on the motivations and folly of war, including debunking the popular belief in the nobility of war, as well as her concerns about unbridled nationalism. In particular, she discussed the disconnection between decision makers and those who suffered the horrible consequences of war. She challenged the idea of national solidarity around war patriotism. Addams viewed the war as spearheaded by men of a different age: "This war was an old man's war; that the young men who were dying, were not the men who wanted the war, and were not the men who believed in the war; that somewhere in church and state, somewhere in the high places of society, the elderly people, the middle-aged people, had established themselves and convinced themselves that this was a righteous war, that this war must be fought out, and the young men must do the fighting."[2]

Journalists jumped on Addams's claims that many soldiers were not interested in fighting the war. Even worse, she went on to reveal that sometimes troops fought under the influence of drugs. Though these remarks were only a fragment of her speech, the press focused on them. Her fame did not protect her from the backlash. She subsequently received severe hate mail and numerous newspaper editorial rebukes. Addams had dared to counter popular discourse, and perhaps even more galling, she had entered a realm of male hegemony: war.

In this chapter, I explore the nature of Addams's pacifist philosophy, including its inherent feminist aspects, its connection to social progress, and its reliance on cultural diversity. For Addams, peace is much more than the absence of war. Her "newer ideals of peace" view social democracy as working toward peace in all social relations, but because she lived at a time when world war broke out, she faced it head on. This chapter closes with an examination of Addams's pacifist realism, particularly as compared with the work of Kant on peace. Given the ongoing worldwide bellicosity in the twentieth and early twenty-first century, Addams's philosophy of peace remains relevant.

War as Wasteful and Regressive

Addams amasses a number of arguments to support her pacifist stance. Two of her pivotal claims are that war is a waste of resources—human and otherwise—and that warfare represents a step backward for society. Sociologist Christopher Lasch, who found Addams's work on peace to be her most brilliant writing, characterizes her stance as finding war "inexcusably inefficient."[3] For Addams, war is an unneeded expenditure of effort and human life: "Many of us . . . have become convinced that the sacrifice of life in warfare is unnecessary and wasteful."[4] For those opposed to war, the wastefulness appears obvious, given the lives and resources lost. However, no one advocates war in the abstract; rather, contextual moral or political imperatives often make it appear inevitable at the time. To those calling for battle, Addams contends that war accomplishes little, satisfying a human need that can be satiated otherwise, and represents an opportunity cost for social progress. In her view, the insidious nature of war is that even in its aftermath, it remains wasteful. Long before the term "permanent war economy" was coined to describe the diversion of resources to preparation for war in peacetime, Addams identified the trend.[5] In 1930, she noted that the previous decade witnessed an increase in worldwide defense spending and conscription.[6] She considered this expenditure of resources to be based on the false assumption that "safety depends upon military defense"[7] and wondered whether as many resources would have had to have been funneled to defense if more effort had gone into communication, understanding, and developing relationships. This question remains pertinent.

Addams was perpetually concerned with solving social problems and working toward achievable goals or ends-in-view. For her, war was an ineffectual and regressive means of accomplishing social goals, but this became a lonely position against the rising tide of support for World War I. Many of her colleagues believed the Great War could precipitate a more stable international social organization. Dewey supported U.S. involvement in the war, as did Julia

Gulliver (1856–1940), president of Rockford College and one of the few professional women philosophers of the era. Gulliver, sharing the sentiments of many intellectuals of the time, thought that the World War would be a triumph for democracy: "I believe in this war with all my heart and soul and mind and strength."[8] Addams never agreed with this proposition: "war . . . affords no solution for vexed international problems; and . . . moreover after war has been resorted to, its very existence, in spite of its superb heroisms and sacrifices which we also greatly admire, tends to obscure and confuse those faculties which might otherwise find a solution."[9] Here Addams is asking a sociological question about the function of war: Is war meant to resolve disputes over resources, treaty violations, or threats? Warfare, because it entails the large-scale destruction of property and human life, seems to be an inefficient means for achieving such resolutions. For Addams, war is emotionally motivated under the cover of a rational attempt to resolve political conflict. Although she had been discredited as an idealistic pacifist, in fact she calls for rational discussion of the true aims of war. Peace is her crucial goal because it provides the foundation for the hope of all other forms of social progress.

One of the criticisms of American pragmatism is that in the absence of absolute principles, it lacks the resources to categorically declare certain activities immoral. Although pragmatists have values and commitments in the spirit of experimentalism, they are also open to adapting new information while accepting a plurality of perspectives. Such openness lends itself to concerns over relativism. In regard to war, Addams comes closest among American philosophers to finding an absolute moral position. Although she never flatly stated that war is morally wrong under any and all circumstances, she persistently resisted violent antagonism, even as the nation enthusiastically endorsed the U.S. entry into World War I. Addams wrote dozens of articles and made numerous pacifist speeches. She authored a trilogy of books on peace: *Newer Ideals of Peace* in 1907, *Women at The Hague* in 1915, and *Peace and Bread in Time of War* in 1922. *Newer Ideals of Peace* was written in the period following the Spanish-American War (1898–1902). It has a peacetime perspective and speculates how a lasting peace might be achieved. *Women at The Hague* is a coedited volume with Emily G. Balch and Alice Hamilton, written in the midst of World War I. It describes the efforts of the Women's Congress in 1915, spearheaded by Addams, to bring an end to the war. Addams contributed three of the book's seven chapters. Finally, *Peace and Bread in Time of War* gives Addams an opportunity to look back on the Great War and its aftermath. She also addresses peace issues in other books, such as *The Second Twenty Years at Hull-House* and *The Long Road of Woman's Memory*, but the aforementioned trilogy represents the most sustained pacifist discussions in her published works.

Her vociferous and persistent stance in behalf of peace transformed Addams into a public radical and the object of ridicule. The following excerpt from a 1917 editorial is not atypical of the journalistic response: "If Miss Addams does not have the intelligence to appreciate the fact that her maunderings . . . give aid and comfort to the enemy then the position she has occupied in the public life of this country has been wrongly bestowed. . . . America is fighting because she was forced to fight or become a nation of Jane Addamses, and the sooner the Chicago pacifist lets that fact infiltrate into her brain the sooner will she understand why this nation is going to fight for a righteous peace."[10] Addams was not accustomed to such attacks. Her social work, though perhaps widely misunderstood as charity, was considered publicly praiseworthy and acceptable. Had she never entered the realm of geopolitical conflict, she would likely have died unscathed by widespread social criticism. However, Addams did not compartmentalize social progress in her philosophy. She believed that her social transactions at Hull House were pacifist projects. Peace was an idea that transcended war. Peace was an end-in-view: a challenging yet obtainable vision achievable through education, social progress, and the improvement of relations. Helping oppressed immigrants, therefore, was an act of bringing forth peace. International and domestic relations had bidirectional equilibrium for Addams. The outbreak of war in the world not only meant international violence, it threatened domestic harmony as well. As historian Kathryn Kish Sklar explains, for Addams, war "was the greatest enemy of her work."[11] Note that Addams wrote about peace early in her public career, prior to the specter of war, and she remained committed to its flourishing domestically and internationally until her death. However, prior to 1915, few saw the implications of Addams's pacifist inclinations. It took war for the public to realize how radical Addams had been all along.

Feminist Pacifism

There is a gendered dimension to the invective leveled at Addams's pacifism. For example, in 1917, an editorial in the *Cleveland News* addressed the pacifism of Addams and Jeanette Rankin (1880–1973), the first woman elected to the United States House of Representatives and one of a small minority to vote against the U.S. entrance into the Great War (later she would be the only member of the House to vote against entering World War II): "To accept a couple of foolish virgins as accurately typifying the attitude of a whole sex toward war would be to do hideous injustice to thousands of noble women who, in this as in other wars, were quick to perceive what it was all about and to lend their aid with splendid discrimination and devotion."[12] The gendered nature of this ad hominem attack is striking. Addams undermined public/private sphere divisions through conducting what was considered "social housekeeping" in her work at Hull House. As such, her previous endeavors ran largely under the radar of patriarchal control. When she publicly denounced war, Addams more overtly crossed over into masculine political territory. In response, her peace activism and rhetoric took on an increasingly feminist consciousness.

As a feminist pragmatist, Addams recognizes that experience matters. Women continue to be socialized as the caregivers who knit together the fabric of society. Because their role and experience are drastically different from that of men, women bring an alternative perspective to issues of war and peace. Addams claims that women can "bring a distinct factor into the peace of the world. We ought to make it clear that bodies of people can act together without fight spirit, without the spirit of competition, without the spirit of rivalry."[13] She is making a distinction between traditional masculine and feminine modes of interaction. Her use of the term "bodies of people" is intriguing in light of feminist theorizing about the body and how the Hull House community brought peace to its neighborhood.

Beyond communication style, Addams often reiterates the theme that women stand in a different subject position to issues of life than men: "We would all admit that there are things concerning which women are more sensitive than men, and that one of these is the treasuring of life."[14] Addams claims a position of epistemic privilege for women grounded in the "basic human experiences ever perpetuating and cherishing the human race, and courageously to set them over against the superficial and hot impulses which so often lead to warfare."[15]

Addams also views the furthering of violence in war as a direct threat to the progress women have made in society. If the world becomes a more violent place, women will surely suffer disproportionately: "Women have a right to protest against the destruction of that larger ideal of the state in which they have won a place . . . and to deprecate a world put back upon a basis of brute force—a world in which they can play no part."[16] Part of the regressive nature of war is that it retards the advance of feminism. Addams views an important part of social progress as entailing the equality of men and women. She describes war as a gender wedge that fosters asymmetrical relations and constitutes an outbreak of patriarchal power. In a 1916 article, Addams presents what she describes as the composite voice of women who consider themselves patriotic yet recognize the folly of war:

> "It would be absurd for women even to suggest equal rights in a world governed solely by physical force, and feminism must necessarily assert the ultimate supremacy of moral agencies. Inevitably, the two are in eternal opposition.

I have always agreed with the feminists that, so far as force plays a great part in the maintenance of an actual social order, it is due to the presence of those elements which are in a steady process of elimination; and, of course, as society progresses the difficulty arising from woman's inferiority in physical strength must become proportionately less. One of the most wretched consequences of war is that it arrests these beneficent [sic] social processes and throws everything back into a coarser mold."[17]

Despite the obfuscation of Addams's "composite voice," this passage suggests her identification with feminist ideals. During the Cold War, Australian feminist theorist Lynne Segal asked "Is the Future Female?," championing feminist sensibilities while simultaneously warning that essentialist claims will always reinforce dangerous hierarchies. This is a position that Addams shares. Segal suggests that "women can and must reject the type of 'protection' they have been told they need—whether from men or the state" while also seeking male allies in antimilitarism efforts.[18] Although Addams's work on peace has a gendered dimension, her claims are not grounded in essentialism: "The belief that a woman is against war simply because she is a woman and not a man cannot of course be substantiated."[19] Addams consistently sought male allies and worked for the advancement of society as a whole. However, for Addams the growth of society and the advancement of women went hand in hand. Her assessment appears accurate. War retarded women's social, political, and economic advancement in the United States through the middle of the twentieth century. Although many middle-class women benefited from the experience of entering the workforce, the gains would take years to come to fruition. In the meantime, the specter of war instantiated notions of a gender hierarchy where strong men must protect weak women.

Newer Ideals

Some might assume Addams became concerned with peace later in her career, given her renowned social activism. However, within a decade of starting Hull House, Addams addressed peace in her speeches and writings. In an 1899 talk reprinted in *Unity,* she explains "What Peace Means." She begins with a theme consistent with her ethical philosophy: new times demand new moral thinking. She is concerned that "we may make a mistake in politics as well as in morals by forgetting that new conditions are ever demanding the evolution of a new morality."[20] Ever progressive, Addams is not content to simply map old moral systems onto new issues. When it comes to peace, her "newer ideals" mean enlarging what constitutes peace: "We must also remember that peace has come to mean a larger thing. It is no longer merely absence of war, but the unfolding of life processes, which are making for a common development. Peace is not merely something to hold congresses about and to discuss as an abstract dogma. It has come to be a rising tide of moral feeling, which is slowly engulfing all pride of conquest and making war impossible."[21] Her notion of the "the unfolding of life processes" is reminiscent of the work of G. W. F. Hegel (1770–1831). For Hegel, history is fundamentally teleological as it progresses toward greater human freedom, but for Addams, the progression of society can only be brought about by collective effort. Romanticism links the writings of Hegel and Addams. However, Hegel's view of history has been criticized for providing theoretical underpinnings for totalitarian governments, whereas Addams viewed progress leading to a better-interconnected society, characterized by democracy and sustained by peace. Addams's definition of peace demonstrates her valorization of action and experience over abstraction. In addition, her allusion to a "rising tide of moral feeling" is indicative of lateral progress in ethical thinking. Just as real progress can only be obtained if there is widespread participation, peace can only be obtained through a general will. She senses a growing wellspring of desire for peace.

In "What Peace Means," Addams maintains populist themes by claiming that common laborers are appropriately rallying for peace because militarism demands the most sacrifices of them. Again, Addams, more so than other progressive philosophers, places a class consciousness on her pacifist theorizing. She argues that working people "have borne the heaviest burden of privation and suffering imposed on the world by the military spirit."[22] Employing a consequentialist claim, Addams views the working class as bearing the brunt of casualties, economic suffering, and increased acceptance of violence.

It is the last of the above points that Addams eventually develops into the need for moral substitutes for war. She finds compartmentalization of social life is unacceptable. Not only are individual lives caught up in one another's, thus creating the need for democracy as a social ethic, but social activities cannot easily be isolated: "National events determine our ideals, as much as our ideals determine national events."[23] Addams views U.S. involvement in warfare as impacting social life. She recounts children playing at war games and "killing Spaniards," thus replicating what was being said about fighting in the Spanish-American War. She makes this observation in an era without violent video games or action movies. She also notes with horror that legislation for reestablishing the practice of whipping children in prison had been introduced in the face of international belligerence. Much as Michael Moore suggests in the documentary *Bowling for Columbine*, Addams views violent social behaviors as not coincidental to U.S. engagement in war. Violence fosters further violence, and war is sanctioned violence. As early as 1899, Addams warns, "The appeal to the fight instinct does not end in mere warfare, but arouses the brutal instincts latent in every human being."[24] Accordingly, she would not have been surprised by the abuse of prisoners by U.S. soldiers at the Abu Grahib prison in 2004.

Addams calls for careful thinking about political conflict that leads to war. War is such an awful last resort that she wants to isolate it and keep it at arm's length: "Let us not make the mistake of confusing moral issues sometimes involved in warfare with warfare itself. Let us not glorify the brutality."[25] Her concern for the impact of violence echoes those worried about the impact of widespread exposure to bloodshed today. Addams seldom offered criticism without investigating root causes and then devising plans to deal with the problem. Sympathetic understanding showed her that warfare allows expression of a fundamental need: to act heroically. This was something she had experienced through Carlyle's heroes, and Addams was swayed, for a time, by the seductive call of individual heroism.

In 1906, Addams already had been at Hull House for more than fifteen years and had written *Democracy and Social Ethics*. In her second book, she connects her Hull House experience to a robust concept of peace. *Democracy and Social Ethics* allowed Addams to put forth a comprehensive understanding of democracy. In *Newer Ideals of Peace*, she articulates a concept of peace that is more than a vacuum of war, and that pertains to aspects of society other than military defense. Addams makes her intent quite clear from the opening of the introduction: "The following pages present the claims of the newer, more aggressive ideals of peace, as over against the older dovelike ideal."[26] The use of the word *aggressive* is unusual for Addams and emphasizes her conviction that peace is not a passive state of being; rather it is found in moral substitutes for war through a variety of social actions. Addams views peace as motivated by "newer humanitarianism." *Newer Ideals of Peace* includes chapters on government, immigration, the labor movement, industry, child labor, women in government, and several chapters on militarism. The book represents her most comprehensive explanation of interconnected notions of peace. A peaceful democracy can only be brought about by equilibrium between domestic peace and international peace.

Moral Substitutes for War

In 1971, Daniel Levine described Addams's peace writings as lacking originality and largely recapitulating the work of William James. According to Levine, Addams was "simply absorbing currents of thought around her, not originating anything."[27] To be fair, Levine's conclusions are not uncommon, particularly in regard to her pacifism. In 1910, James published a well-known essay titled "Moral Equivalents of War," which was the culmination of years of developing his ideas in lectures and writings. In the essay, he admits that the desire for war goes beyond logical argumentation: "Showing war's irrationality and horror is of no effect upon [modern man]."[28] James recounts how history is replete with war and notes that although humanity has advanced in many ways, bellicosity remains pervasive. He laments that there is a persistent unwillingness to imagine a world without war.[29] Not content with accepting the ongoing existence of war, James suggests that pacifists take a new tack, because rational arguments against war are ineffectual against its affective attractiveness. Specifically, James proposes a military-like conscription of young men to perform a wide variety of public service activities that require hard labor and discipline: a moral equivalent to war.

Because Addams's concept of moral substitutes for war is similar, and given that she references James often (while James never cites Addams), the assumption has been that her ideas on pacifism are derivative of James. Historical evidence suggests a different story. Both Addams and James spoke at the Thirteenth Universal Peace Conference in October 1904, but they had known one another since 1898. Addams had addressed the concept of the moral substitute for war publicly since at least 1899. In personal communication, James acknowledged her unique contribution: "Yours is a deeply original mind and all so quiet and harmless! Yet revolutionary in the extreme."[30] He found *Newer Ideals of Peace* so stimulating that he wanted to make sure H. G. Wells and George Bernard Shaw received copies.[31]

Nevertheless, James did not publicly credit Addams with influencing his thoughts on the subject. Katherine Joslin finds a gendered rationale for James's omission: "In fashioning his pacifism, James left out Jane Addams, the very woman he had been talking with in conversations, speeches, lectures, and letters. Could it be that on the topic of war and in discussion of manly activity a female voice would strike a wrong note?"[32] The point of this foray into the origins of the concept of "moral substitutes" is not to claim Addams's primacy on the subject, because that cannot be categorically proven, nor is it ultimately important. Both James and Addams used their considerable skills to develop this compelling idea, and did so in consultation with one another. However, dismissing Addams's work as derivative or overlooking her discussions should no longer be acceptable when discussing pacifist theories. Addams was clearly on the cutting edge of this important idea.

Furthermore, Addams's notion of moral substitutes for war has some marked differences from James's moral equivalents.[33] James is content with traditional gender roles and views the moral equivalent for war as something needed only by men: "We must make new energies and hardihoods continue the manliness to which the military mind so faithfully clings."[34] Although trying to redirect combat energies, and viewing war as irrational, his language reveals respect for militarism and masculine virtues: "militarism is the great preserver of our ideals of hardihood, and human life with no use of hardihood would be contemptible."[35] James's solution is a national service program that would allow men to expend their inherently militaristic energies on good works projects such as road building or mining. Ultimately, men who participated in such a program would be highly valued by women because their irrational tendencies would be "knocked out of them."[36]

Addams shifts the emphasis away from essentialist understandings of human nature and gender. Rather than separate spheres of endeavor, she calls for men and women to share in the great cause of social improvement as a moral substitute for war. Although James succinctly lays out his moral equivalents for war as a philosophical concept peppered with concrete examples, Addams draws richly and vividly from her experience in Chicago to make her gender analysis clear: "The men of the city have been carelessly indifferent to much of this civic housekeeping."[37] James invites men to redirect their energies; Addams invites men to join women in making the country a better place to live through local engagement.

For Addams, alternatives to war are a matter of imagination: "When we once surround human life with the same kind of heroism and admiration that we have surrounded war, we can say that this sense is having such an outlet that war will become impossible."[38] Addams finds a misplaced sense of purpose and self-sacrifice in war efforts that are imaginatively intoxicating: "Let us not glorify the brutality. The same strenuous endeavor, the same heroic self-sacrifice, the same fine courage and readiness to meet death, may be displayed without the accompaniment of killing our fellow man."[39] War encourages heightened emotional states that fire certain forms of imagination. Why not redirect the imagination and emotions of citizens with an endeavor less socially detrimental? Consistent with her robust understanding of peace, war can only be mitigated if men's interests and women's interests are aligned toward civic improvement. Addams laments, "We fail to bring about the end of war simply because our imaginations are feeble."[40] Moreover, militarism is not inevitable for Addams. Just because human history is replete with war does not mean we are destined to repeat it. Are human beings so lacking in imagination that we cannot foresee anything besides endless warfare? "We continue to defend war on the ground that it stirs the nobler blood and the higher imagination of the nation, and thus frees it from moral stagnation and the bonds of commercialism. We do not see that this is to borrow our virtues from a former age and to fail to utilize our own."[41] She is not satisfied with ethical answers from the past and wishes to find new moral responses.

Addams and James may have been singing a duet on alternatives for war, but they were singing in different keys. Perhaps the biggest difference between their approaches to moral substitutes is Addams's emphasis on pluralism. Other than gender, diversity plays no role in James's concept of moral equivalents to war. For Addams, pacifism is not fully understandable outside of an appreciation for the power of diverse peoples.

Overcoming War through Diversity

Not only did Addams tie her community experience to pacifism, she recognized that the pluralism in a cosmopolitan city has the potential to lead the way in mitigating war: "I believe the diversity of immigrants is a source of great strength to this country in regard to keeping peace and averting war."[42] The community around Hull House demonstrated the ability of immigrant peoples from all over the world to cooperate, given proper conditions. Addams is not Pollyannaish about social tolerance: social harmony requires hard work and perseverance. She claims, "It is possible that we shall be saved from warfare by the 'fighting rabble' itself, by the 'quarrelsome mob' turned into kindly citizens of the world through the pressure of a cosmopolitan neighborhood. It is not that they are shouting for peace—on the contrary, if they shout at all, they will continue to shout for war—but that they are really attaining cosmopolitan relations through daily experience."[43]

Addams describes a manifestation of sympathetic knowledge through embodied care. Understanding begins with proximal transactions: people with very different cultures and worldviews living in neighborhoods that require daily interaction. Everyone harbors stereotypes of unknown others, not for nefarious purposes, but as uninformed coping behavior. Through regular contact, these stereotypes are challenged: "Because of their difference in all external matters, in all of the non-essentials of life, the people in a cosmopolitan city are forced to found their community of interests upon the basic and essential likenesses of their common human nature; for, after all, the things that make men alike are stronger and more primitive than the things that separate them."[44] Proximity forces people to see others not as reductionist caricatures, but as fellow human beings sharing in the struggle to survive. History and differences are not erased but are transformed into resources for informing shared understanding of human conditions: tragedy, joy, triumph, and defeat.

Dewey felt that the message of flourishing amid diversity in *Peace and Bread in Time of War* continued to be relevant years after Addams's death because of "its sense of the positive values contributed by our immigrant populations. The pattern of American life, composed of multiple and diversified peoples, hostile in the countries from which they came but living in reasonable amity here, can and should provide the pattern of international organization."[45] Addams advocated the power and benefits of diversity because of her experiences at Hull House. This was a lived philosophy.

Sympathetic knowledge of others becomes the basis for actualizing natural human tendencies toward care and connection. Addams does not accept militarism as a determined human state. There are other human impulses that require fostering and attention, such as care and connection. However, there is a long history of literature ennobling the pursuit of battle. Addams views the role of the philosopher (herself included) as thematizing what city residents already understand: "At the present moment it requires the philosopher to unify these spiritual efforts of the common man into the internationalism of good will, as in the past it was natural that the philosophers, the men who looked at life as a whole, would have been the first to sigh for negative peace which they declared would be eternal."[46] She took this role seriously as she made a moral appeal to various sectors of society. She actively sought out African American club leaders to pursue the course of peace, including Mary Church Terrell, Mary B. Talbert, Charlotte Atwood, Mary F. Waring, and Addie Hunton.[47] Addams addressed peace arguments to immigrants who learned to live with one another in the city, to women who stood to lose so much of their social progress in war, and to workingmen and women who would bear the brunt of the increased production in wartime. As she saw it, the road to peace was paved by the sympathetic understanding among diverse people.

Peace and Patriotism

A commonplace understanding today, as well as in 1914, is that patriotism is loyal nationalism. To be a patriot is to be demonstrative in support of one's country and the policies of its leadership. The loyalty of patriotism makes war possible. Because war is such a gruesome undertaking with inevitable casualties, destruction, separation, and uncertainty, few humans would participate without powerful emotive impetus. Patriotism, like religion, has the potential to provide the requisite motivation to move people to take on difficult tasks. As Addams observes, "[Patriotism] has long connoted courage and candid loyalty to the highest achievement of which one's country is capable."[48] She values patriotism, not as it is traditionally understood, but as allowing honest and free speech about the country's foibles. She is concerned about an emotionally driven and repressive patriotism that she experienced firsthand.

Sissela Bok describes the partisanship of war as fostering "a pathology all its own. When this happens, partisanship goes beyond the emphasis on loyalty and cohesion needed for the well-being of any community and leads people to become obsessive and heedless of their group's long-range self-interest, even its survival."[49] Bok describes war patriotism as irrational: to be pathological is to abandon logical consequence. Similarly, Addams finds patriotism defined in single-minded terms: "A good patriot of differing opinion finds it almost impossible to reach his fellow countrymen with that opinion, because he would not for the world print anything which might confuse the popular mind, for war belongs to that state of society in which right and wrong must be absolute."[50] Addams advocates group cohesion through care and connection, which she frames in inclusive and rational terms rather than exclusive and emotional terms of national patriotism. She recognizes that the exclusive nature of nationalism transforms persons in foreign countries into "others."

This "othering" perpetuates disconnection and prejudice and enhances the possibility of violence: "An absolutely uncritical opinion of one's own nationalism is inevitable when nation is arrayed against nation with the virtues of one constantly contrasted with the villainies of the other by every device of able propaganda."[51] Yet, although she disagreed with the hawks who advocated U.S. entrance into the war, she refused to treat them as distant "others." Historian John Farrell describes Addams as unique because "unlike many pacifists, she strove to understand those who supported war."[52] Consistent with her philosophy of sympathetic knowledge, Addams was not a passive pacifist; she vigorously entertained discussion in an earnest attempt to understand those who disagreed with her. In this case, sympathetic understanding not only helped her to maintain bonds with those who differed with her on war (such as Dewey and Mead), it also made Addams a formidable opponent. Not tied to ideology, she opposed war with a variety of moral approaches, including the invocation of principles, consequences, and virtues.

For example, although personally not deeply religious, she maintained a positive relationship with religious organizations such that when she felt it was necessary, Addams cajoled them without rancor. In 1923, she recalled that a number of representatives of Christian organizations indicated to her that only religion has within its power to repair the social damage wrought by war. She replied using a formulation familiar to her Christian audience that religions must first "declare that war is a sin."[53] Such use of theological language was rare for Addams, but she knew how to effectively engage others. She applied no wholesale criticism of religion, yet she challenged the churches to use their resources for social progress. Addams was a peculiar pacifist—thoroughgoing yet ever-rational, responsive, and caring. Her staunch pacifism ought not be confused with dogmatism or a lack of patriotism.

Addams refers to national pride patriotism as "old patriotism." Just as she contends that modern society requires modern morality, which she names "democracy," modernity also mandates a new form of patriotism not limited by geographic borders: "There arises the hope that when this newer patriotism becomes large enough, it will overcome arbitrary boundaries and soak up the notion of nationalism. We may then give up war, because we shall find it as difficult to make war upon a nation at the other side of the globe as upon our next-door neighbor."[54] She suggests that nationality, determined by "arbitrary boundaries," is the result of moral luck. Furthermore, patriotism excludes as it fosters allegiances, whereas Addams's philosophy of inclusion and widespread participation cannot.

She views society as capable of moving past old notions of nationalistic patriotism to human patriotism (she sometimes used the term "cosmic patriotism"): a loyalty to the well-being of all. She envisions the possibility of a new patriotism tied to a spirit of democracy that is capable of moving "masses of men out of their narrow national considerations and cautions to new reaches of human effort and affection."[55] Addams finds war to be a conservative force, destroying newer ideals of patriotism in favor of older, primitive forms of national partisanship. Old patriotism is dangerous because it exudes self-righteousness: a feeling of superiority that prevents us from understanding and learning from others.[56] Just as Addams sees the possibility of moral substitutes for war, she views patriotism as entailing a virtue that can achieved through alternative means: "A people united as one is an imposing spectacle, but we can get these virtues in other ways."[57]

The Realism of Peace

Because of her pacifism, Addams is sometimes dismissed as naive, idealistic, and wrong. In some ways, hindsight appears to vindicate Addams's detractors. The rest of the twentieth century was replete with international conflict, civil war, and terrorism. Her faith in humanity seems misplaced. Of course, this observation is based on the false assumption that what occurred in the past necessitates that it will happen again in the future. Political realism is rooted in a deterministic claim that war will always exist. Why is Addams considered naive? Naïveté is a relative assessment. The claim of Addams's lack of sophistication is partially grounded in the choices made by international leaders during World War I, including Woodrow Wilson, not to heed her arguments. Political paths not taken in the United States—living-wage policy, national health care—are often dismissed as ingenuous and idealistic. Gender likely played a role as well, given that naïveté is often attributed to women because of their alleged lack of experience in the public sphere.

Dewey, when given the opportunity to write a revised introduction to *Newer Ideals of Peace* for an edition published a decade after Addams's death, realized the opportunity that the world had missed in not taking her seriously: "It has become customary to give the name 'realistic' to the kind of organization that is based upon opposition to an enemy and that relies upon armed force to maintain itself. In contrast, the road indicated by Miss Addams is, I submit, infinitely more 'realistic.'"[58] Dewey, Mead, and most of the other men of the Chicago school were swept up in the idea that World War I had the potential to set the world right. They believed the resulting treaties, organizations, and social forces would allow democracy to flourish. It was "the war to end all wars." They were wrong. World War I ushered in a new era of bloody international conflicts that arguably has lasted until the present.

Modern analysis supports Dewey's claim about Addams's realism. Historian Alan Dawley describes the work of Addams and the Women's International League for Peace and Freedom as underwritten by moral realism. Describing WILPF's comprehensive approach, which integrated social justice with international peace, Dawley characterizes its ideals as "grounded in realistic analysis and tough-minded activism."[59] In philosophy, realism is associated with questions of the nature of existence. In politics, realism is the idea that obtainable goals be sought. Wars are often described as fought to make the world a safer place. Given such a goal and the experience of recent history, one might ask whether war is more realistic than peace. For Addams, the answer is no.

Kant and Addams on Plans for Peace

Although Addams's philosophy is sometimes described as idealistic and derivative, few level the same criticism at Immanuel Kant (1724–1804), who is considered among the greatest of modern philosophers. Kant's reliance on rationality and the abstract subject position has made him the target of criticism from feminist philosophers,[60] although recent attempts have been made to reconcile Kant's philosophy with feminism.[61] In 1795, Kant wrote an intriguing essay, "Perpetual Peace: A Philosophical Sketch."[62] Philosopher, A. C. Armstrong describes Kant's article as "hailed with enthusiasm upon its first appearance" and "one of the most celebrated of Kant's shorter works."[63] Many of the ideas that Kant outlines resonate with Addams's understanding of peace and her plan for international action. This comparison between Kant and Addams is offered to challenge the idea that Addams's approach to peace is naive.

Before addressing Kant, let me review the specific plans that Addams and her colleagues at the International Congress of Women developed at The Hague from April 28 to May 1, 1915. This was a meeting of more than one thousand women from twelve countries who believed that they could make a difference in ending not only the Great War, but also perhaps all future war. Addams was selected president and led the assemblage. The final document developed by the congress closely reflects Addams's philosophy. The resolutions include a call for respect for national sovereignty and the will of the people of all nations—an idea consistent with her valorization of democracy. They also suggest a level of unparalleled international cooperation and communication. Accordingly, the congress envisioned an international organization or "Society of Nations" and an "International Court of Justice." With these structures in place, countries would engage in "continuous mediation" to resolve disputes before they developed into armed conflict. The resolutions' emphasis on communication and cooperation is consistent with Addams's philosophy of sympathetic knowledge.

The congress also called for international control over arms sales and international pressure to be placed on any country that resorted to violence against another. Addressing the systemic aspects of peace, other resolutions call for the worldwide education of children and the enfranchisement of women.[64] These provisions echo Addams's view that peace is a comprehensive social goal actuated through lateral progress. The women at The Hague anticipated much of what became the United Nations and the World Court. Addams viewed the possibility of international efforts toward peace and overcoming disasters as a possible moral equivalent for war that would bring countries together in the name of peace. She hoped for a new era of international relations "founded not so much upon arbitration treaties, to be used in time of disturbance, as upon governmental devices designed to protect and enhance the fruitful processes of cooperation in the great experiment of living together in a world become conscious of itself."[65] In a 1932 radio interview, Addams provided an overview for her program of world peace:

1. The establishment of machinery for the arbitration and adjudication of all differences between nations.
2. A sense of security which would result from the use of this machinery.
3. Disarmament gradually occurring because arms were no longer essential for security—but a deadly menace to it.[66]

With the work of Addams and the International Congress of Women as a backdrop, let me examine what Kant calls for in his plan for "perpetual peace." He begins by offering an expansive notion of peace. Although he does not integrate a social justice component, as does Addams, he proposes that peace is more than a truce; it should also provide for ongoing cessation of hostilities.[67] Kant claims that nations cannot be treated as possessions to be acquired. Consistent with his second formulation of the categorical imperative, he views the human collectivity of nationhood as irreducible to the status of object to be manipulated.[68] Kant proposes that "standing armies be gradually abolished."[69] He provides a threefold rationale for eliminating military forces: First, they threaten other nations, and their mere presence goads others into contemplating the possibility of war. This is a claim that Addams often expressed. For example, as part of the Women's Peace Party, she discouraged U.S. preparation for the possibility of entering World War I because it would compel international imitation, as well as foster mistrust and fear.[70] Second, Kant is concerned that armies incur inordinate cost. Third, they represent a rights violation: "Moreover, paying men to kill or be killed appears to use them as mere machines and tools in the hands of another (the nation), which is inconsistent with the rights of humanity."[71] The proposition to eliminate armies is as radical as anything that Addams called for. Addams longed for international disarmament, but was only cautiously optimistic that it could be achieved: "I would have disarmament come about through international agreement, and would be very proud if the United States—perhaps the most secure and powerful of all the nations—would lead the movement as rapidly as possible."[72]

Like Addams, Kant calls for cooperation among nation-states to insure perpetual peace. He describes a federation of countries in which "each nation can and should demand that the others enter into a contract resembling the civil one and guaranteeing the rights of each."[73] Also, like Addams, Kant challenges the idea that war is somehow an ennobling endeavor.[74] Where Kant and Addams differ is in ontology. Kant accepts the Hobbesian notion that the state of nature is a state of war. Accordingly, for Kant, peace is a rational response to the state of nature. For Addams, peace is a rational response, but it also reflects the cooperative potential of human nature. In *Peace and Bread in Time of War,* Addams refers to texts that claim "cooperation among men is older and more primitive than mass combat."[75] Like Kant, Addams believes that international peace is possible. However, she thinks that treaties and international organizations can only be a start and are ultimately insufficient to make for lasting peace. These structures are an outward manifestation of the internal transformation required: the widespread acceptance of newer ideals of peace, including human patriotism. In an article coauthored with Emily Greene Balch, Addams states, "One essential part of the creation of a warless world is the growth of general and genuine peace-mindedness and a new outlook on world affairs."[76]

Because Kant accepted Hobbesian suppositions about human nature, he views the rise of populated city-states as exacerbating warlike tendencies: "The state of peace among men living in close proximity is not the natural state; instead, the natural state is one of war, which does not just consist in open hostilities, but also in the constant and enduring threat of them. . . . As nations, peoples can be regarded as single individuals who injure one another through their close proximity."[77] Ironically, it is through living in close proximity that Addams believes diverse people will develop the sympathetic knowledge to live in peace with one another. Kant and Addams see rationality as playing a role in bringing about peace, but for Addams, rationality is tied to affective knowledge of the other.

Kant encourages an expanded notion of citizenship that assumes humans have moral duties beyond national borders. He describes world citizenship, under which people would have a right to travel to other nations and furthermore could expect to be treated hospitably.[78] Kant shares Addams's desire to understand citizenship as shaped by more than national borders, although her ideas of citizenship entailing sympathetic understanding toward others are absent. Kant's advocacy of democracy is less than absolute. He views representative forms of government as advantageous because the alignment of disposition between the government and the people is much stronger in a democracy than in a monarchy.[79] However, he accuses democracies of being despotic at times because the will of the majority can hold sway over the minority.[80] Addams understands democracy as social morality that entails both the structure of government as well as a disposition shared by citizens.

Kant's proposals appeared one hundred years prior to Addams's and were written in a different social context. Nevertheless, the commonalities are as intriguing as the differences, and both are worthy of further study. A comparison of the two sets of ideas, particularly given the status accorded to Kant in the philosophic canon, suggests that Addams's social philosophy of peace should not be easily dismissed. Her work on peace can be read as a realistic alternative to living with militarism that resonates with ideas offered by other great philosophers in history.

A Missed Opportunity

History is always subject to interpretation. A number of historians provide compelling evidence that the world was at a crossroads on the eve of the Great War. Although not universal, a spirit of social progress and optimism was hijacked by the onset of war. Attention and resources were diverted to the war, and progressivism never fully recovered. Perhaps more important, war became a familiar international companion during the twentieth century. Gone was the consensus that humans could progress beyond war. Without hope for something different, political realism took on the character of a self-fulfilling prophecy. Is war inevitable because of human nature, or because of what we currently believe about human nature? In *14–18: Understanding the Great War,* Stéphane Audoin-Rouzeau and Annette Becker suggest that many of Addams's fears were realized in the advent of World War I. First, it was a regressive force because "the sustained violence of the Great War, particularly in its first weeks, the fact that it was widely approved and accepted by millions of people in every part of the European continent and every social group, is certainly a màjor rebuttal to the thesis of 'civilizing progress' in modern history."[81] Moreover, as Addams warned, the violence of that war altered the psyche of society. George L. Mosse describes brutalization as the most significant impact of World War I.[82] It was the first of the world wars, and its casualties were of enormous proportions, but it led to a century of brutal wars unlike the world has ever witnessed. Audoin-Rouzeau and Becker claim that we too easily overlook the specter of violence unleashed by the Great War. To borrow Kuhn's overused term, a paradigm shift occurred in which we are still mired. The concept of "going to war," as serious as it is, remains intelligible, even acceptable, to society because we fail to imagine that we have a choice not to go to war. Addams wanted to demonstrate the reality of war as an unacceptable, irrational, unthinkable choice—a horrific tragedy rather than a noble and compelling decision.

Addams's work on war and peace is arguably the most enduring aspect of her intellectual legacy. Replace some of the dated language and historical references, and much of what she addresses remains relevant. For example, finding moral substitutes for war is still worthy of exploration a century after it was proposed. Philosopher Chris Cuomo offers that "war makes evident the need for real alternatives to war, and can therefore draw the imagination towards dreams of peace."[83] However, Cuomo continues, such dreams are usually abandoned, as few have the pacifist moral courage to work toward peace. Addams was a realistic dreamer whose lifelong efforts for peace were partially vindicated by receiving the Nobel Prize in 1931. Her work remains a model of moral courage that the world needs more than ever, given that the stakes today are significantly higher than in 1914.

CHAPTER 6

Widening the Circle

Cornel West finds that the root of race issues in the United States is
the perception that people of color are "problems." For West, characterizing
a person's race as a problem is a form of objectification that keeps African
Americans alienated from the social mainstream. Accordingly, African Americans continue to be "others" and therefore not treated as full agents or citizens:
"Hence, for liberals, black people are to be 'included' and 'integrated' into 'our'
society and culture, while for conservatives they are to be 'well behaved' and
'worthy of acceptance' by 'our' way of life. Both fail to see that the presence
and predicaments of black people are neither additions to nor defections from
American life, but rather *constitutive elements of that life*."[1] Ever hopeful, West
finds a solution to the current crisis by recognizing common histories, finding
common language, and reenergizing discussions of the common good.

Although Jane Addams did not have the modern analytical tools or the benefit of the past century of experience with race relations, she did not view members of different races or cultures as problems. In a 1930 article titled "Widening
the Circle of Enlightenment," Addams makes the case that diversity should be

a strength of American democracy: "In all our work with the foreign born we have found that our own attitude toward them as aliens is most important. We may make their foreign birth a handicap to them and to us, or we may make it a very interesting and stimulating factor in their development and ours."[2] She seeks sympathetic understanding that entails knowing others for the purpose of caring and action. This process transforms unfamiliar others from abstract objects of speculation to interconnected neighbors.

Addams lived at an opportune time and place to formulate a philosophy of diversity. In 1888, the year prior to the opening of Hull House, an astounding 78 percent of the one million residents of Chicago were foreign born or first-generation Americans.[3] In 1895, *Hull-House Maps and Papers* reported the accumulated data collected by Addams and her colleagues in the first full-scale sociological study of an urban neighborhood. The depth of local diversity was clear: "Eighteen nations are thus represented in this small section of Chicago. . . . The Italians, the Russian and Polish Jews, and the Bohemians lead in numbers while the Germans, although they make up more than a third of Chicago's population, are not very numerous in this neighborhood; and the Scandinavians, who fill north-west Chicago, are a mere handful. Several Chinese in basement laundries, a dozen Arabians, about as many Greeks, a few Syrians and seven Turks engaged in various occupations at the World's Fair, give a cosmopolitan flavor to the region."[4]

Addams and Starr intentionally chose to live among immigrants; however, Addams had limited experience with diverse peoples prior to founding Hull House. Nevertheless, her idealistic beginnings and privileged preconceptions gave way to one of the most sophisticated positions of pluralistic advocacy among American theorists of the time. As philosopher Judith Green describes, Addams and the women of Hull House moved from one-sided notions of hospitality, characterized by one-sided philanthropy, to a mutual form of hospitality governed by humility and vulnerability that led to growth by the host and the guest.[5] At first, Addams was concerned with what she was going to bring to her immigrant neighbors, but she learned that they brought much to be gained from as well.

Addams was not beyond reproach when it came to matters of race, but it can be argued that, aside from peace, widening the circle of democratic participation became her most significant concern during the latter part of her career. In this chapter, I explore her writings on race and culture as well as what some of her critics claim. The chapter concludes with a study of a public exchange between Addams and anti-lynching pioneer Ida B. Wells that demonstrates Addams's shortcomings and strengths in regard to race.

Addams's historical context contributes to obfuscating her philosophy on issues of racial diversity. Much has transpired in race relations in the century since she lived. "Race theory" and "postcolonial studies" did not exist during her time. Although racism remains virulent, its manifestations have evolved, and the responses to racism have become more complex. At the dawn of the twentieth century, racist language and practices were more explicit and widely accepted than today. Many of Addams's feminist contemporaries exhibited racist tendencies despite their ardent stands on gender issues. Charlotte Perkins Gilman, who although at times argued against racism, also made statements indicative of a racial hierarchy, such as "the savage is incapable of large relation because his mental area is not big enough."[6] Carrie Chapman Catt (1859–1947) delivered two lectures, "America for Americans" and "The American Sovereign," and also wrote an article, "A True Story," that criticized immigrants as perverting American society and its institutions.[7] Catt later became more tolerant and accepting of immigrants. Although Addams made occasional remarks indicative of implicit cultural superiority, such statements were infrequent, brief, and largely early in her public career.

Addams's devotion to advancing the causes of African Americans is surprising, given that much of her work at Hull House was concerned with issues of "culture" as opposed to race. Her early activism was in behalf of Italians, Irish, Greeks, Poles, and Jews who inhabited the Hull House neighborhood. These groups do not constitute separate "races," yet the concepts of race and culture are not unrelated. For example, at the turn of the nineteenth century, Italians in the United States were not considered "white," and although not a separate race, they faced many of the discriminations and stereotypes typical of racism. The definition of "race" as a distinct biological type has been eclipsed in favor of viewing it as a social construction of reality that has served to separate and organize peoples.[8] Nevertheless, socially constructed realities are experienced as a form of truth, and to deny the existence of race carries the potential danger of ignoring the history of injustice that it has engendered. To inclusively define this project, this chapter pursues Addams's philosophy of diversity rather than race.

Addams wrote and worked for social progress that included women, immigrants, and people of color. She led numerous efforts to advance the plight of African Americans, including playing a leading role in the founding of the National Association for the Advancement of Colored People (NAACP).[9] Addams had limited exposure to a black community at Hull House. Only one black resident is documented during its first decade, physician Harriet Rice.[10] The immediate vicinity of Hull House did not have a large black population during the early years of Addams's tenure. Despite these experiential shortcomings, she befriended influential African American leaders such as Ida B. Wells (1862–1931), Mary Church Terrell (1863–1954), and W. E. B. DuBois (1868–1963) and became a significant champion of their causes.[11] Addams took a number of actions to support African American leadership. She backed the nomination of Fanny Barrier Williams as the first African American woman member of the Chicago Woman's Club; she hosted the National Council of Colored Women at Hull House; she attempted to have the National Convention of Women's Clubs admit African American clubs, but failed; and she was a member of the Chicago Urban League.[12] The women of Hull House assisted in the formation of several black social settlements. Addams's commitment to sympathetic knowledge would have been vitiated if she had not sought to learn about other cultures and races. Her feminist pragmatist predilection for risk and fallibility not only permitted the vulnerability necessary to earn the trust of others but also allowed her to grow in her personal understanding and appreciation of diverse peoples. The spirit of sympathetic knowledge supported her philosophy of diversity beyond the limitations of her social standpoint and her era.

Risk and Fallibility

Addams brought critical reflection to her activism. Her books, lectures, and speeches leave a legacy of feminist pragmatist analysis of social issues. Her thematization of experience is what sets her apart as a social activist and as a philosopher. Addams does not separate theory from practice. Part of that practice is a personal challenge to move out of contexts of comfort to confront social experience. Risk and fallibility are essential parts of her social philosophy and are particularly pertinent to her work on race and diversity. Addams came from a social position of relative power and security. She was a college-educated white woman with a sizable inheritance who had traveled to Europe and understood high society prior to starting Hull House. Although she had nagging progressive values that made her troubled about the inequality in society, she was certainly capable of finding a suitable outlet for her largesse that would have afforded her social distance and personal comfort. Addams instead started Hull House, turning her whole life over to achieving lateral progress and the risks that settlement living entailed.

Addams readily admitted that in the early days of the settlement, she and the Hull House community made many blunders in establishing reciprocal relations with the larger community. The diversity of the neighborhood meant that there was much to learn and experience. One such failed project was the Hull House Coffee House and Public Kitchen. Some Hull House residents were concerned about the nutritional intake of their neighbors. According to Addams,

"An investigation of the sweatshops had disclosed the fact that sewing women during the busy season paid little attention to the feeding of their families."[13] Addams wanted to improve the quality of life for her neighborhood. At the time, Ellen Swallow Richards was popularizing "Oekology," a precursor to the ecology movement that purported to be a science of healthy and happy homes existing in equilibrium with the environment. Among its aims, Oekology sought to provide nutritious food at reduced cost, energy usage, and effort.[14] Richards exhibited a kitchen at the Chicago World's Colombian Exhibition in 1893 attended by Addams and the women of Hull House. Addams wanted to bring the latest knowledge of food production and nutrition to her neighborhood in the form of a coffee house and public kitchen. The settlement was relatively new, and latent racist misunderstandings about immigrant cuisine were operant.

In hindsight, Addams admitted that the residents were acting paternalistically when they brought the latest domestic practices to the neighborhood. Addams purchased kitchen equipment, and space underneath the gymnasium was renovated for the new restaurant. A Hull House menu read, "Food is cooked after scientific prepared recipes and on sale in quantities for home consumption."[15] As one might guess from this appealing slogan, the Coffee House and Public Kitchen soon became a culinary, economic, and social failure. The residents were not happy with the fare offered, the coffee house lost money, and the community stayed away. Instead of responding to the needs of the immigrant community in a process of reciprocal dialogue, the settlement members had acted out of a sense of ethnocentric superiority in deciding that they knew better what the dietary needs of the community were.

Significantly, the nature of the error was not lost on Addams: "the experience of the coffeehouse taught us not to hold to preconceived ideas of what the neighborhood ought to have, but to keep ourselves in readiness to modify and adapt our undertakings as we discovered those things which the neighborhood was ready to accept."[16] Note that she does not take the posture of blaming the neighborhood, nor does she abandon lateral progress. Admitting failure and allowing the project to adapt, Addams oversaw the evolution of the coffeehouse to better meet the needs of the neighborhood, and to fill an important niche, although not the one originally intended. This incident exemplifies how Addams and Hull House residents risked themselves, sometimes made mistakes (including some that resulted from cultural insensitivity), reflected on the experience, learned from their errors, and moved on. Such experiences allowed Addams to hone her pragmatist philosophy, particularly as it pertained to the close relationship of theory and practice.

Addams's admitted fallibility and humility in the face of learning about diverse others exemplifies a methodology necessary for sympathetic knowledge. She recognized that it was a mistake to try to understand others through her own preconceived notions of prescriptive moral responses. Addams observed that people reject the ability to know one another by keeping unknown others at a psychosocial distance. Accordingly, lateral progress cannot be achieved without difficulty and self-reflection, but neither can it be accomplished without widespread social participation or widening the circle.

Racism as Waste

Consistent with pragmatic concerns about outcomes, Addams's philosophy sometimes reveals elements of consequentialism. When she supported a particular position, she employed a variety of arguments. Lateral progress inevitably dealt with the consequences of choices, and in an era where progress was valued, positive social benefits were a significant component of the public articulation of her philosophy. One of the ways that Addams made combating racism tenable to society was by appealing to the numerous painful outcomes of its existence.

Addams sought a democracy of individuals engaged in one another's lives, achieving lateral progress through education and growth. Her premise is that everyone can and should contribute to society for mutual benefit. Anything that prevents individuals from full participation is inefficiency. Racism is one such waste. On the fiftieth anniversary of the issuance of the Emancipation Proclamation, Addams questioned whether the country had stagnated in its efforts to assist African Americans. The theme of waste permeates her assessment: "What has been and is being lost by the denial of opportunity and of free expression on the part of the Negro, it is now very difficult to estimate; only faint suggestions of the waste can be perceived."[17] A democracy working toward the improvement of the common lot can ill afford the luxury of underemploying the talents of any group of people.

For Addams, one of the dangers of racial stereotypes and segregation is that the emotivism it engenders contributes to antagonism that has the potential to lead to lawlessness and chaos. Nothing is more emotion-laden than lynching. In 1911, a year when sixty African Americans were lynched,[18] Addams wrote in an article for DuBois's *Crisis*, "Everywhere in America, a strong race antagonism is asserting itself, which has various modes of lawlessness and insolent expression."[19] Lynching is the ultimate example of racially charged antagonistic emotions raging out of control and resulting in a needless waste of human life through the abuse of power.

Another aspect of the waste of racism is all the time and energy expended on the enmity between blacks and whites. Addams's feminist pragmatism comes to the fore as she argues against racism, not because it violates principles of fairness or rights, but because it is unworthy of the expenditure of resources it demands. However, this argument also reveals Addams's faith in human nature. She calls for a renewed effort to fight racism, and one of her principal arguments is the social cost of failing to do so: "It means an enormous loss of capacity to the nation when great ranges of human life are hedged about with antagonism."[20] She believes in the power of humans to settle differences without resorting to personal attacks.

Addams's pragmatism motivated her to use whatever serviceable tools were available to help her accomplish social progress. Although comfortable with care ethics generated from sympathetic knowledge, as a shrewd observer of her audience, Addams knew that in light of booming industrial development, many in society concerned about building a strong economy would respond favorably to concerns about waste. Progressives were predisposed to concur with inclusive arguments, so language that enlarged interest in the subject to other groups was a potent tool.

Addams on Cultural Aesthetics

Just as Addams entertained a robust notion of democracy, she also had a rich and evolving notion of culture. Her Hull House experience included many transactions with culturally diverse peoples of the neighborhood, which served to expand her understanding. When Addams first arrived at Hull House, her concept of culture was derived from her education, travel, and reading. Over time, and numerous proximal experiences among many cultures, she gained an appreciation for a wide variety of aesthetic experiences. She came to view culture as both a source of moral knowledge and as source of social energy.

Culture is a system of shared meanings, including language, ritual, and symbolism, that requires iterations of expression to unify cultural identity. The performance of a handshake in Western culture as a friendly greeting serves to reinforce the role of this ritual for those involved. The contours or boundaries of culture are clarified when two people from different cultures interact. The experience of a new culture brings one's own cultural practices, which are usually taken for granted, to the foreground. For example, one does not usually contemplate the elements of one's native cuisine until confronted with food from another culture. Culture is socially constructed through interactions, habits, and performance. Hull House's myriad activities (clubs, performances, dances) provided numerous opportunities to explore the contours of culture.

Along with rituals of expression, Addams viewed culture as a transmitter of important social knowledge. History, values, and modes of interaction are bound up in culture and manifested in literature, drama, music, and the plastic arts. Addams valued culture from the beginning, but she initially failed to recognize its class implications. Addams and Starr came to Chicago with the well-meant intention of sharing what they knew of culture with destitute, overworked, and largely forgotten immigrants living in squalor. Thus, Hull House was at first an expression of upper-middle-class, Euro-American, educated culture. As Addams recalled, "We furnished the house as we would have furnished it were it in another part of the city, with the photographs and other impedimenta we had collected in Europe, and with a few bits of family mahogany."[21] Many of the early activities served to replicate Anglo-Saxon cultural tradition: "In the very first weeks of our residence Miss Starr started a reading party in George Eliot's *Romola,* which was attended by a group of young women who followed the wonderful tale with unflagging interest."[22] Addams not only exhibited the received values of Western civilization but also displayed the "high culture" she knew and loved. Her initial use of eighteenth- and nineteenth-century art and furniture at Hull House, combined with the reading of European classical literature, identifies upper-class standing with having culture.

If not for Addams's sympathetic understanding, with its focus on reciprocation, Hull House might have continued as a facility of monocultural upper-middle-class expression. Initially oblivious to class/culture hierarchy, Addams changed her thinking owing to neighborhood reaction to Hull House interiors. Hull House was an inverted home—a private space turned into a public space—where internal furnishings impacted external perceptions of the settlement's project. Addams's relationship with the community was too important to risk aesthetic alienation. She removed brocade curtains and took down her silver because she recognized that "the moral effect of them down here is not good."[23] However, she did not abandon her belief that culture held empowering knowledge, and soon after starting Hull House, she showed greater sensitivity to the potential for cultural estrangement. Charlene Haddock Seigfried describes Addams as "far ahead of her time in her awareness of her own class and ethnic privilege and in her insights into how such privilege subtly undermines the dignity and effectiveness of the poor and working classes and less favored ethnic groups."[24]

Thus, Addams embraced cultural diversity in the Hull House neighborhood and worked at fostering and preserving the social identity of various local cultures. The Labor Museum, discussed further in chapter 8, was one effort at making epistemological connections with cultural practices of the past, not as nostalgia (because, as a progressive, Addams was future-oriented), but to better situate present practices. Hull House efforts toward artistic performance through drama, dance, and music also demonstrated a complex weaving of pluralism and sympathetic understanding fostered by social transactions. Addams encouraged cultural expression through the arts as a means of preserving and invigorating cultural identity. As Shannon Jackson points out, "Settlers found that the process of producing a performance [e.g., plays, choral renditions, orchestral performances] generated unique affective bonds among tentatively formed social groups."[25]

For Addams, one aspect of the social knowledge transferred by culture is morality. She did not distinguish between the moralities of different cultures—one being more desirable than the other. A culture with a long history of development has a cache of moral wisdom to impart. At times, Addams uses the term *social control* to describe the accumulated moral wisdom of a culture. Modern sensibilities bristle at the coercive connotations of this term, but for the late Victorian, it was an expanded notion of "self-control," infused with social moral wisdom. In an article written during the inaugural year of W. E. B. DuBois's *Crisis,* the voice of the newly formed NAACP, Addams describes black families as the "least equipped with social tradition."[26] Ostensibly, this appears to be a racist comment, and one might ask why DuBois agreed to print it; however, it is consistent with Addams's social philosophy. The cultures that came freely to the United States had greater potential for continuity with the culture and traditions of their homelands. Addams recognized that African Americans were forced into generations of slavery and subsequent discrimination, which disconnected them from their cultural resources (e.g., family and religious communities), which in turn held the moral wisdom passed on from generation to generation. She placed the blame squarely on those who robbed African Americans of their cultural heritage.

Moreover, Addams views environmental factors as continuing to pummel African American culture. Class is one such challenge. In discussing young black women as at-risk youth, she cites poverty as intensifying vulnerability. Another factor Addams addresses is segregation. Because sympathetic knowledge relies on people forming connections, isolation is anathema. In her view, segregation contributes to the disconnection of black families from wider social and cultural resources: "the white people in a city are tacitly leagued against colored people within its borders."[27] Segregation limited the interactions and the subsequent sympathetic knowledge between people that is so important to Addams's concept of social democracy.

For Addams, cultures participate in a vibrant social democracy by providing meaning, purpose, and camaraderie. Cultures are an extension of the social nature of human existence that animates her philosophy. For example, in discussing the function of the arts, Addams finds cultural diversity fueling aesthetic imagination: "In the modern city, and especially the cities in America, solidarity cannot depend upon [commonality], for the state is composed of people brought together from all the nations of the earth. The patriotism of the modern state must be based upon a respect for variation, not upon inherited memory but upon trained imagination."[28] As exemplified by so many of the Hull House endeavors, such the Labor Museum, music programs, and drama programs, Addams views the maintenance of cultural heritage as playing a positive role in a vigorous democracy.

The trajectory of Addams's valorization of immigrant cultures appropriately causes her to argue against cultural assimilation. She tells the story of an effort made by a local organization to foster patriotism among immigrants by having lecturers visit city schools and describe Civil War battles. Upon hearing the Civil War stories, one Italian boy described a battle from his homeland. According to Addams, the lecturer rebuked the boy, saying that "he must forget all that, that he was no longer an Italian, but an American." She then comments, "The natural growth of patriotism upon respect for the achievements of one's fathers, the bringing together of the past with the present, the pointing out of the almost world-wide effort at a higher standard of political freedom which swept over all Europe and America between 1848 and 1872 could, of course, have no place in the boy's mind, because it had none in the mind of the instructor, whose patriotism apparently tried to purify itself by the American process of elimination."[29]

In an article titled "Americanization," Addams demonstrates how her convictions regarding immigration and diversity had solidified: "The application of a collective judgment in regard to aliens in the United States is particularly stupid."[30] Less pejoratively, Addams works out her philosophy of diversity in a ten-page article published in *Commons* in 1905 and titled "Immigration: A Field Neglected by the Scholar." Her goal is to counter the popular contention that the influx of immigrants is "blurring those traits and characteristics which we are pleased to call American" and that ultimately, "the national standard of living is in danger of permanent debasement."[31] In a strong response from Addams, these concerns are criticized as arising from "intellectual dearth and apathy; that we are testing our national life by a tradition too provincial and limited to meet its present motly [sic] and cosmopolitan character; that we lack mental energy, adequate knowledge, and a sense of the youth of the earth."[32] She felt that contemporary attitudes toward immigration mirrored conservative and static notions of social morality that had failed to evolve to meet the needs of a changing nation. The failure to learn and grow from immigrant cultures, she says, is to relinquish "one of our most valuable assets."[33]

Typical of Addams's style, "Immigration" interweaves specific concerns about immigration policy, exploitation, and labor practices with social and political philosophy. She repeats a concern that simply granting immigrants their rights is insufficient for guaranteeing lateral progress, in this case, the right to vote: "The philosophers and the statesmen of the eighteenth century believed that the universal franchise would cure all ills; that fraternity and equality rested only upon constitutional rights and privileges."[34] Addams wants to push political theorists to reconceptualize social relations along the lines of sympathetic understanding with its emphasis on care built upon knowledge. She chides, "We still keep to this formalization [rights-based ethics] because the philosophers of this generation give us nothing newer, ignoring the fact that the world-wide problems are no longer abstractly political."[35] Note that Addams chooses "newer" as the operant qualifier. She is committed to the evolution of social morality to meet the times. Addams does not want the pluralism created by immigration to merely fit into old theoretical scaffolding. The older and more removed such philosophic structures are, the more abstract they become. She suggests that new social philosophies should emerge from the present context. Presumably, these social philosophies would reflect sympathetic knowledge and care ethics in a pluralistic context.

Addams demonstrates the radical inclusiveness of lateral progress. American patriotism is warranted to the extent that it participates in cosmic patriotism. For Addams, all such patriotism exists in service of social progress: "Men of all nations are determining upon the abolition of degrading poverty, disease, and intellectual weakness with their resulting industrial inefficiency."[36]

Addams concludes "Immigration" by returning to the theme of broadly defining patriotism, and she uses some strong language to make her point: "It is useless to hypnotize ourselves by unreal talk of colonial ideals and patriotic duty toward immigrants as if it were a question of passing a set of resolutions. The nation must be saved by its lovers, by the patriots who possess adequate and contemporaneous knowledge. A commingling of racial habits and national characteristics in the end must result upon the voluntary balance and concord of many forces."[37] It is notable that Addams chooses the phrase "commingling of racial habits," a formulation that implies an egalitarian approach, rather than employing an additive approach, which would have been conveyed by words such as "other races can contribute to our own." She views assimilation as the enemy of a flourishing social democracy and exhibits an authentic desire to bring the knowledge of the races together.

Criticism

On occasion, Addams's pragmatism makes her ripe for criticism on race, particularly when compared with uncompromising principled positions. For example, Addams faced a showdown on race as a delegate to the Progressive Party in 1912. She was upset that African American delegates from several southern states were not allowed to participate. Not mollified that other delegates had already protested the exclusion of blacks, Addams took stronger action and stood before the Resolution Committee of the party to "point out the inconsistency of pledging relief to the overburdened workingman while leaving the colored man to struggle unaided with his difficult situation."[38] Theodore Roosevelt and the Progressive Party proved intractable, compelling Addams to pragmatically make concessions that left the issue of race unresolved: "I was forced to acknowledge to myself that certainly war on behalf of the political status of colored men was clearly impossible, but that there might emerge from such federal action as the arbitration in interracial difficulties, somewhat analogous to the function of the Hague tribunal in international affairs. . . . The action of the Progressive party had at least taken the color question away from sectionalism and put it in a national setting which might clear the way for a larger perspective."[39]

Addams had hoped that the Progressive Party would lead to women's suffrage, but the emergent racism threw her for a loop. A staunch, principled position on race might have caused her to walk away from the party in a powerful symbolic gesture of moral indignation. Addams, however, balanced various moral concerns and decided that antiracism, although left off the platform in terms of explicit language, was still supported by the overall values of the party. Furthermore, African American males already possessed the vote (at least officially); women did not. Addams reluctantly chose to support Roosevelt while continuing to work for racial justice. Although some African American leaders praised her public stand, others saw her equivocation as a sellout.[40]

The Progressive Party incident is indicative of Addams's work on race. She valued diversity and sought wide inclusion but occasionally misstepped and compromised for what she saw as social progress. As a result, numerous present-day theorists have expressed concerns about her approach to race and culture.[41] Some of the critiques provide useful insights into Addams's thought and failings, although others appear to be underwritten by misconceptions about her project. Perhaps philosopher Shannon Sullivan offers the most balanced assessment of Addams's work.

Sullivan dismisses assimilationist claims about Addams by applying the American pragmatist notion of *transaction* to her relational epistemology. A transactional relationship acknowledges the coconstituitive nature of social interaction, but it neither elides the differences in subject position, nor does it assume mere contractual relationships by unaffected individuals. For Sullivan, the operant metaphor is a "stew," where the constitutive elements have been enhanced by the mingling and interaction, rather than the melting pot, where a unified flavor is produced, or a salad, where each part remains fundamentally independent. Addams sought "stewlike" transactions whereby mainstream and immigrant cultures benefited from their interaction without becoming monocultural or unaffected. The Labor Museum and social clubs were examples of Hull House efforts that celebrated cultural heritage but also afforded opportunities for learning and growth.

Although Sullivan applauds Addams's application of transactional thinking as groundbreaking, she also takes her to task for employing implicit racist language that refers to immigrant cultures as primitive yet energetic. According to Sullivan, this language supports the notion that "white people are seen as fully human and non-white as less than so."[42] In her view, Addams has an ambiguous legacy because she advances "an implicitly racist view of new immigrants to combat white Chicagoans' racist dismissal of them."[43] Sullivan accuses Addams of prizing reciprocity to the detriment of oppressed groups, because underlying racist stereotypes are not challenged. Furthermore, Sullivan believes that segregation and separation may be beneficial for cultural and racial groups in a hostile environment: "Certain groups can be relatively isolated and, moreover, have reasons to desire their isolation. In those cases, it might be beneficial not to try to end their self-enforced segregation, as Addams tried to do with immigrant groups. Or put another way, it can be important for those groups themselves to decide to what degree and when they wish to be brought into a more transactional relationship with other groups."[44] She concludes that although Addams makes some original contributions to race theory, her ideas must be supplemented to avoid making the same mistakes.

Sullivan is correct to identify stereotypical assumptions in Addams's discussions of race. Addams is both rooted in and ahead of her time. She supports intellectual progress and would be pleased that contemporary race analysis has moved beyond what she offered at the turn of the nineteenth century. Furthermore, given her acknowledgment of fallibility, Addams was quick to admit mistakes. Nevertheless, Sullivan's analysis, albeit thoughtful and thorough, rests on several problematic assumptions. First, the notion that Addams somehow ended the "self-enforced segregation" of immigrant groups runs counter to the expressed philosophy of the Hull House settlement. Although Addams encouraged a variety of transactions, Hull House was an open institution that neighbors either chose to participate in, through its many programs, or not. If a group chose to be isolated, Addams had little power to force transaction. Second, and perhaps more important, Sullivan ignores class, or perhaps more accurately, poverty. Immediate physical need determined Addams's day-to-day interaction with Hull House's immigrant neighborhood. The various cultures surrounding Halsted Street existed amid pitiful squalor. Addams did not have the luxury of considering their cultural heritage apart from their dire economic conditions. The transactions she fostered were not merely epistemological; they responded to a moral demand. Given the bias for action gleaned from Carlyle, Addams would have been taken aback for being criticized for doing her best to assist her neighbors. Sullivan is correct to highlight Addams's errors, but the circumstances make her cultural blunders excusable.

Addams and Ida B. Wells worked intermittently with one another for three decades. Despite having dissimilar backgrounds and temperaments, they shared a commitment to social justice. For those who accuse Addams of implicit racism, her relationship with Wells points to the contrary.

Wells's life was filled with tragedy and prejudice that served to motivate her philosophy and activism. She was born a mere two years after Addams, but their upbringing could not have been more different. She was the daughter of slaves in rural Mississippi who were eventually emancipated and became financially independent. When Wells was sixteen years old, her parents died of yellow fever, leaving her to fend for herself. She became determined to be successful and take care of her five surviving siblings. In the face of this misfortune, her religious convictions blossomed. She also found refuge in a thirst for righteousness, developing moral anger as an impetus for her pursuit of justice. Wells was quite aware of her own anger and temper, viewing it as both an asset and a liability.

March 1892 marked a turning point in her life, with the lynching of three shopkeepers who were her acquaintances in Memphis. Wells was the owner of the only black newspaper in the city, the *Memphis Free Speech*. She demanded justice for the lynching in a series of editorials. Another local paper alleged that the shopkeepers were lynched because they raped a white woman. Wells refuted this lie. A mob considered lynching her, but because she was out of town, they instead destroyed the building where her newspaper was housed. The publication ceased operation. From then on, Wells was a fiery anti-lynching activist who wrote articles and books and delivered speeches attempting to discredit the myth that black men were rapists. Her campaign revealed the rape accusation to be a weapon of racism, but it challenged patriarchal notions that white women were the possessions and the protectorate of white men. Wells was probably the most eloquent and determined anti-lynching activist, but her legacy was largely forgotten until modern feminist scholars rediscovered the depth and influence of her work.

Although Addams and Wells differed in personality, temperament, and depth of religious conviction, they worked together on a number of projects.[45] Mary Jo Deegan claims that the earliest work of the Chicago Association for the Advancement of Colored People predated that of the national organization, and it was Wells and Addams who were at the forefront.[46] Addams and Wells were part of a committee planning the 1909 centenary anniversary of Lincoln's birth; however, their relationship predates this collaboration by at least ten years. In 1899, Wells described infighting at the National Association of Colored Women. Mary Church Terrell, who helped form this organization and was president, called for a national convention in Chicago. Wells claimed that she was not invited because Terrell was afraid that she might threaten Terrell's leadership of the organization. Addams, learning of the convention and the rift, invited the organization's leadership and Wells to lunch at Hull House. Wells gratefully used the opportunity to get more involved in the convention.[47]

In 1900, the *Chicago Tribune* ran a series of articles advocating the segregation of Chicago's public schools. The pieces were one-sided and did not include any commentary or interviews with members of the black community. Wells was furious and went to see the editor. After being mistaken for "a colored woman . . . begging for her church," Wells made her plea for balanced reporting. Realizing that she would not get any satisfaction from the paper, she turned to Addams, who immediately organized a group of influential citizens to make the plea. Wells and Addams's successful presentation of their case to this group brought the articles to an end. The *Chicago Tribune* did not return to an editorial position of segregation again.[48]

Interestingly, although Wells relates the above stories in her autobiography, referring to Addams glowingly as "the greatest woman in the United States,"[49] she fails to mention their public disagreement over the issue dearest to her: lynching. In January 1901, Addams wrote "Respect for Law" in the New York *Independent,* where she decried lynching. In her typically balanced manner, she begins by admitting that she is an outsider (not a southerner) and therefore cannot completely understand motivations in the region: "The essence of self-government [is] that it shall be local in administration, in order that special difficulties shall be met by the people who live among them, and who thus understand them better than an outsider possibly could."[50] She is acknowledging the pragmatist valorization of experience and therefore the difficulty of commenting on a social issue about which she has no direct knowledge. This is the essence of the settlement philosophy that Addams so often articulates: the value of local, proximal knowledge.

However, parochial knowledge can still lead to faulty morality, including racism. Addams expresses alarm over "the increasing number of negroe [*sic*] lynchings occurring in the South."[51] She begins her analysis by stating that history is replete with examples of atrocities committed in the name of doing the right thing when "the theory of conduct," as she describes it, is wrong: "One of these time-honored false theories has been that criminality can be suppressed and terrorized by exhibitions of brutal punishments; that crime can be prevented by cruelty."[52] She uses historical examples to indicate that cruel punishment is usually an elitist prerogative manifesting contempt for the oppressed. Addams employs a barrage of arguments to condemn lynching, including that it is ineffectual, degrading, and regressive to the development of society, creating a pattern of violence that spurs more violence.[53] As she sees it, brutal violence such as lynching runs counter to lateral progress. Social progress manifests itself through deliberation and peaceful resolution of differences under the rule of law. Addams concludes the article with a feminist attack on patriarchy, describing violence as a tool of sexism and declaring that "the woman who is protected by violence" is ultimately "the possession of man."[54] In its brevity and force, "Respect for Law" is a thoroughgoing condemnation of lynching that recognizes its racist, classist, and sexist origins. "Respect for Law" also represents a glaring failure of Addams to follow her own philosophical commitments.

In "Lynching and the Excuse for It," Ida B. Wells responded to Addams's attack on lynching with her own article in the *Independent* in May 1901. Wells acknowledges the benefit of "Miss Addams's forceful pen" and does not wish to "lessen the force of the appeal." Yet, she feels compelled to challenge an "unfortunate presumption" in Addams's argument. Addams had suggested that lynching was unlawful and regressive but had failed to make the more direct claim that the accusations, which prompted lynching, were completely fabricated. There was a folk belief among many whites that black men had a predilection for licentiously accosting and violating white women. Accordingly, lynching was believed to be a response to the actions of black men, albeit an inappropriate one. Wells refutes this folk wisdom and appeals to statistics to make her case. Reprinting public records from the *Chicago Tribune* on the allegations that prompted lynching, she demonstrates that only a minority of the total cases were purported to be assaults on white women. The records indicated that hundreds of men, and a few women, had been lynched between 1896 and 1900, but many of the alleged crimes were misdemeanors or no crime at all. She concludes that many well-intentioned individuals (including Addams) were ignoring the facts about lynching. Yet even Wells does not draw the explicit conclusion that lynching is simply a violent racist act; she leaves that inference to the reader.

Addams's arguments about lynching were thoughtful and effective, yet, as Wells pointed out, they had a major lacuna concerning the assumed morality of African American men. This omission may be indicative of implicit racism, but it is definitely a failure of Addams to follow her own feminist pragmatist methodology. As previously discussed, Addams valorized experience in morality as what she described as sympathetic knowledge. Her fully articulated settlement philosophy was based on the proximal knowledge of direct experience. However, Addams did not have a large African American community (at least not up through 1901 when "Respect for Law" was written) from which to draw experiences. This alone is not enough to preclude her from addressing lynching, or any other social evil, but it appears she did not use the resources available to her to develop adequate sympathetic knowledge to fully comprehend the lynching question. Addams meticulously prepared her articles and speeches, often testing ideas before making them public. Apparently, she did not test "Respect for Law" with her friend, Wells, or she might have constructed a different argument. Another explanation for Addams's oversight might be her keen sense of audience. As a pragmatist, Addams may have felt that it was more important to make headway with her southern audience than to be morally "correct" or victorious. What Wells views as an "unfortunate presumption" may have been a calculated effort to engage southern audiences that might not have listened if they were summarily condemned.

Complex Issue, Complex Response

In *Race Matters,* Cornel West sets out the pernicious character of racism. Simple solutions such as economic programs, although helpful, are insufficient in the face of such a pervasive and entrenched disposition. An effective response to racism requires a collective will, diverse resources, and imagination, as well as a change of heart. West muses, "Let us hope and pray that the vast intelligence, imagination, humor, and courage of Americans will not fail us. Either we learn a new language of empathy and compassion, or the fire this time will consume us all."[55] Addams spoke the language of intelligent compassion that West alludes to. She simultaneously worked for changes in exclusionary and discriminatory laws and practices while writing social philosophy that emphasized changes in personal disposition.

Philosopher Lucious T. Outlaw pointedly places the lens of racist analysis squarely on the field of philosophy: "Modern philosophy, in important instances, is implicated in the formation and legitimation of modern racism."[56] He justifiably asks why African American voices are not included among those who speak for American philosophy. Outlaw suggests that the time has come to reconsider who can be counted as an American philosopher. Certainly, if Addams's philosophy of diversity that reinvigorates social democracy and international peace in terms of genuine valuation of cultural and racial pluralism is taken seriously, a more robust multicultural tradition might develop within American philosophy. Outlaw calls for the kind of transformation of scholarship that Addams sought for through the settlement movement: "We philosophers may well be called on to revise our professional identities with regard to the intellectual traditions and figures in terms of which we define ourselves and that we mediate to our students and colleagues. Were we to do so, perhaps we might be able to speak to others in our nation about the prospects for resolving problems involving raciality and ethnicity in just ways that are demonstrated by our own profession life and in our philosophizing. And we may do so while meeting one of our major responsibilities: namely, contributing to social reproduction through our teaching of subsequent generations of young men and women of various races and ethnicities."[57] Addams's efforts were sometimes flawed, but she theorized about and practiced the kind of social opportunities that Outlaw refers to. She took personal responsibility for improving race relations in a manner that few of her contemporaries did.

> This dream that men shall cease to waste strength
> in competition and shall come to pool their powers
> of production is coming to pass all over the earth.
> —JANE ADDAMS

CHAPTER 7

The Reluctant Socialist

It may come as a surprise to many that Addams offers a good deal of economic analysis. It is not as prominent a feature of her work as peace or race, but economic discussions are usually a part of every subject she engages. What is not surprising is that Addams emphasizes market policies and practices that support her vision of social democracy based in sympathetic connections between individuals. Her analysis remains intriguing, given the widespread acceptance of free market forces since her time.

Statements like "Government is not the solution to our problem; government is the problem" made former President Ronald Reagan a hero of the free market movement. The early twentieth century, when U.S. commerce was bound by few regulations, provides a case study in the ramifications of free markets.[1] Although states passed labor legislation and the federal government eventually caught up, the markets could not have been freer. Given the influx of immigrant workers, these markets had an abundant labor supply. From the standpoint of the quality of one's work life, the results of unfettered markets were less than inspiring. Discrimination, injustice, and dangerous labor were part of what factory work in big cities brought. In 1907, deaths on the job numbered twenty-seven thousand. In 1911, the Triangle Shirtwaist Company in New York caught fire, killing 146 workers trapped behind locked doors and beyond reach of firefighters' ladders. In 1914, thirty-five thousand workers were killed in industrial accidents in the United States while another seven hundred thousand laborers were injured. To compound these tragic numbers, businesses were not legally compelled to assist families of those killed or hurt. As a result, few victims of industrial accidents received compensation.[2]

In addition to the dangers of factory work, employment was tenuous. Workers were hired on an at-will basis by employers who could therefore fire them without warrant. Racist and sexist discriminatory hiring and compensation practices were widespread and legal. Some businesses posted differential wage rates based on national origin or ethnicity. Children of working-class families routinely found jobs, including dangerous factory labor, to keep their families financially afloat.[3] Laborers also bore the brunt of an unstable economy. The Great Depression of 1929 is deemed "Great" because it was preceded by numerous depressions and economic swings (such as the panic of 1907) that resulted in bouts of widespread unemployment and lowered wages. Although warranted concerns about employment, working conditions, discrimination, and economic vicissitudes persist in the twenty-first century, their magnitude pales by comparison to dangers faced by workers during Addams's era, who labored for corporations unconstrained by government regulations.

Chicago exemplified the nation's worst economic problems. In the 1890s, Chicago was home to two hundred millionaires who coexisted with the blighted poverty of overcrowded immigrant neighborhoods. Some of the country's worst industrial violence, strikes, and working conditions transpired in Chicago. The Haymarket Riot of 1886 exemplified how close to the surface racial and labor tensions resided. Hull House was no stranger to economic strife. The surrounding area was the center of the garment industry's sweatshop system.[4] Sweatshops eliminated the need for manufacturers to maintain equipment or rent space. They simply contracted work out and turned a blind eye to the conditions under which garments were produced. Addams is uncharacteristically blunt in her description: "An unscrupulous contractor regards no basement as too dark, no stable loft too foul, no rear shanty too provisional, no tenement room too small for his workroom."[5] Work was treacherous in Chicago, but these conditions fostered resistance.

Class inequities, the economic instability of capitalism, and dangerous factory labor drove some intellectuals to favor socialism. For many, the popularity of socialism arose not so much from admiration of Marx and his ideals, but from fear that free market capitalism had failed everyone but the "robber barons"—the wealthy capitalists such as John D. Rockefeller, J. P. Morgan, and Andrew Carnegie, who had taken advantage of anarchic markets. Writers, activists, and intellectuals such as Upton Sinclair, Jack London, Eugene Debs, Margaret Sanger, Helen Keller, and H. G. Wells openly advocated socialism as a cure for the country's economic ills. Jane Addams did not.

Addams on Capitalism

Addams was often exasperated by commercialism: "We have a way of believing that if any great thing is to be done, it must be done by means of a commercial activity."[6] Not surprisingly, she came to her economic philosophy as an outgrowth of her experience with workers and their families in the Hull House neighborhood. She knew their financial struggles and the wounds of factory labor. She discussed economics with local laborers through the Working People Social Science Club, which Addams described as one of Hull House's most popular social organizations. The club met weekly for two hours and held open forums on economic and political issues including anarchism, socialism, single-tax theories, and even the works of Arthur Schopenhauer. According to Addams, the club "convinced the residents that no one so poignantly realizes the failures in the social structures as the man at the bottom."[7] This realization is consistent with her advocacy of lateral progress—advancing the interests of all members of society. Addams wanted economics to do what she wanted philosophy to do: help society move forward to a more engaged social democracy.

In *Democracy and Social Ethics,* Addams presents a twofold concern about the plight of labor. Her critique primarily addresses industrialized labor, and specifically, the assembly line worker, although she does mention other job categories. Her two major concerns are worker *disconnection* and the dearth of workplace *participation.* Addams views industrialization as being responsible for disconnecting workers from important relations, as well as for reinforcing a lack of significant worker participation. The major culprit in creating worker disconnection is what she refers to as the division of labor, or specialization. The following sections address Addams's claims about capitalism.

INDUSTRIAL DISCONNECTION AND EDUCATIVE RECONNECTION

In *The Wealth of Nations,* Adam Smith (1723–90) puts forth well-known arguments for the advantages of dividing the labor necessary for manufacturing products into discrete and limited functions so as to facilitate skill development into expertise: "The division of labour, however, so far as it can be introduced, occasions in every art, a proportionable increase of the productive powers of Labour."[8] Two hundred years later, the output advantages of specialization continue to be an axiom of commerce. Addams, like Marx, does not disagree with the truth of Smith's claim, but, beyond productivity, she finds negative implications for specialization: "We are still childishly pleased when we see the further subdivision of labor going on, because the quantity of the output is increased thereby, and we apparently are unable to take our attention away from the product long enough to really focus it upon the producer."[9] Addams, ever concerned about people, their relationship to one another, and to society, was quite anxious that capitalism had shifted concern from workers to production— from process to its outputs. Specialization was the overt manifestation of human transformation into objects of productivity. Today, the public generally has no qualms with terms such as *human resources* because of internalized capitalist ideals that equate workers with factors of production. Addams was not willing to accept this language.

Addams suggests that specialization has two negative impacts on workers: it estranges them from what they produce and extinguishes morality. She describes assembly line work: "Feeding a machine with a material of which he has no knowledge, producing a product, totally unrelated to the rest of his life, without in the least knowing what becomes of it, or its connection with the community, is of course, unquestionably deadening to his intellectual and moral life."[10] These are severe criticisms for Addams. Because her philosophy emphasizes comprehensive individual and social growth, "deadening" work stifles that growth and inhibits social democracy. Her cure for intellectual numbness is education.

Addams suggests that if workers gain understanding of how valuable their work is, they may embrace the division of labor as liberating: it frees workers to do what they do well, and they can unite in common cause to accomplish tasks.[11] She claims that traditional education cannot accomplish necessary connections. Memorizing names, dates, and places is too abstract and removed from the experience of factory laborers to empower them. What she proposes is an education whereby workers can find their identity and voice as contextual: "If a working man is to have a conception of his value at all, he must see industry in its unity and entirety; he must have a conception that will include not only himself and his immediate family and community, but the industrial organization as a whole."[12] Addams does not want to see workers evolve a morality separate from the rest of the community. Education has the power to keep commerce and society connected, for example, by highlighting the history of industrial development: "Every factory filled with complicated machines has in it the possibilities of enormous cultural value if educators have the ability to bring out the long history, the human as well as the mechanical development, which it represents."[13] She asserts that employees must understand the place of their work historically, economically, politically, and socially in order to be in a position to master it. For Addams, labor education should "teach the child to dominate the machine."[14] The Hull House Labor Museum was one effort to historically contextualize the relationship of workers to their industry and tools.

Addams's approach to worker education can appear assimilationist. Although educating workers may have a subversive dimension, given, for example, knowledge of labor unrest, it might also placate them to accept their existence. If some of her statements on educating workers are taken out of context, Addams does appear to be an agent of industrial conservatism. However, her second concern—that specialization deadens the moral life—invigorates a more radical edge. On the face of it, to suggest that a division of labor extinguishes the moral life appears to be an odd claim. We recognize that assembly line work can be excruciatingly dull and repetitive, but how could it ruin a person's morality? For Addams, developing a sense of morality requires education, time for reflection, and social connections found in social exchanges: "We would all agree that only when men have education, a margin of leisure, and a decent home can they find room to develop the moral life. Before that there are too many chances that it will be crushed out by ignorance, by grinding weariness, and by indecency."[15] Specialized laborers are cut off from all but essential and efficient associations during work hours. These are relationships, but they are superficial and truncated. The sympathetic understandings necessary for moral development and action require relationships with rich and meaningful transactions. The need for advancing connectedness is one reason why Addams advocates collective worker associations or labor unions.

WORKER PARTICIPATION

Hull House was a labor-organizing dynamo. By the second year of the settlement's operation, obvious community need for collective resistance by workers drew Addams and the residents into the task of organizing, supporting, and defending collective labor organizations. Labor organizing was a treacherous affair, but Addams did not shy away from her neighbors' needs. In 1891, she wrote to an associate, "We find ourselves almost forced into the trade unions."[16] Union advocates Mary Kenney and Alinza Stevens as well as socialist Florence Kelley, early participants at Hull House, ensured that the community became a center of labor activism. Many local labor organizations were given their start at Hull House prior to finding permanent facilities for themselves.

Although all labor unions were welcome at Hull House, women's organizations were particularly favored. Addams writes, "In the first years of Hull House we came across no trades-unions among the women workers. . . . The women shirtmakers and the women cloakmakers were both organized at Hull House as was the Dorcas Federal Labor Union, which had been founded through the efforts of a working woman, then one of the residents. The latter union met once a month in our drawing-room. It was composed of representatives from all the unions in the city which included women in their membership and also received other women in sympathy with unionism."[17] Addams's feminist consciousness was ever present in her reflection on the needs of the community.

Addams views unions as an expression of social democracy. She writes, "For many years I have been impressed with the noble purposes of trade unions, and the desirability of the ends which they seek; and at the same time I have been amazed at the harshness with which their failures are judged by the public."[18] Addams's democracy demands robust transactions in the building of sympathetic knowledge. She describes unions as facilitating such transactions through worker participation: "The trades-unions say to each workingman, 'Associate yourself with the fellow-workers in your trade. Let your trade organization federate with the allied trades and they in turn, with the National and International Federation, until working-people become a solid body, ready for concerted action.'"[19] She claims that unions support lateral progress, advancing the well-being of all members of society by "expressing moral striving in political action" through "a desire to secure some degree of improvement in the material condition of working people."[20] For Addams, unions engage in the ethical work of social democracy—collectively deliberating policies and actions that have the potential to bring about social benefit.

Addams's advocacy of labor unions was nuanced and not without restrictions. She was unwilling to support partisan efforts that advanced one group over another, as witnessed by her analysis of the Pullman strike, discussed in the next section.[21] Furthermore, Addams remained firmly against unnecessary antagonism. She did not support verbal or physical assaults from labor or management. She was not naive about power and politics, but she viewed dialogue and connection between groups of people as most efficacious. Addams balanced the competing interests of various constituencies to foster cooperation. This was a difficult position, given the high passions associated with labor organizing. She claims, "Any sense of division and suspicion is fatal in a democratic form of government, for although each side may seem to secure most for itself, when consulting only its own interests, the final test must be the good of the community."[22] Addams defended unions, yet refused them uncritical loyalty.

Addams's guarded support for unions is also demonstrated by her embrace of technological advancement. Unlike Ruskin, her opposition to industrialization has nothing to do with returning to simpler times without technology. Addams's criticism of modern capitalism targets its negative impact on humanity, but she remains forward-looking. When labor unions oppose new machinery that has the potential to displace workers, she is less than sympathetic, describing the "disgraceful attitude which [trade unionists] have from time to time taken against the introduction of improved machinery—a small group blindly attempting to defend what they consider their only chance to work."[23] However, even here her remarks are not without qualification. She recognizes that if society had a more "equitable distribution of the leisure" then labor concerns about technology would not erupt, given the potential benefits from increased production.[24] Addams's actions and philosophy indicate her pro-union stance, but her support is always framed as in service of social improvement.

Labor–Management Relations: A Modern Lear

Addams's most intriguing work on the problems of economic relationships is "A Modern Lear," her analysis of the Pullman strike of 1894. Only five years after the opening of Hull House, the strike crippled the nation's economy and drew Addams into a new role as public mediator. The Pullman strike was a watershed moment for fledgling labor unions and for their leader, Eugene Debs (a Hull House speaker), who was catapulted to national prominence. Debs later ran for president on the Communist ticket. The Pullman strike was also an opportunity for the nation to reflect on its rapid industrialization and the resultant impact on social relations.

Even at this early stage in her career, Addams was an experienced labor activist. The Pullman strike was a unique opportunity for her to put her public philosophy to the test. Her process of sympathetic knowledge demanded that she demonstrate understanding for all parties without creating heroes and villains, while her concern for lateral progress meant that she was compelled to seek the best path for advancing all members of society. As with her peace efforts, Addams's philosophy failed to change events, but she left a legacy of reflective analysis that portrays unique insight into economic relations.

For Addams, the key player in the tragedy of the Pullman strike was George Pullman (1831–97), the president and founder of the Pullman Palace Car Company, the dominant producer of luxury railroad passenger sleeping cars. Pullman was one of the richest men in the United States. In 1893, his company was estimated to be worth $62 million.[25] Like other "robber barons" or "captains of industry" of his era, Pullman had a reputation as a ruthless businessperson who manipulated politics and coerced workers for his financial benefit. Also, like his wealthy colleagues, he was concerned with his public image and at one time made a donation to support Hull House.

Because of the rapid growth of his business, Pullman decided to build a company town near a new production facility located south of Chicago. In 1880, he purchased 4,500 acres for $800,000, and by 1892, the developed land was valued at $5 million. The buildings, streets, and parks that Pullman constructed were modern and aesthetically pleasing. He received philanthropic praise for his efforts. However, his ultimate objective was profit. The venture was intended to earn a 6 percent annual return as workers leased homes and purchased food and utilities from Pullman.[26] At its peak population, twelve thousand people lived at the company town. Pullman ran the city with an iron fist, preventing unsavory business such as saloons from opening, and using coercive measures on residents to ensure complicity with his policies. Collective bargaining was bitterly fought in Pullman's company and was anathema in the town. One of Pullman's policies was that community members who lost their jobs or who could no longer pay rent were expected to leave.[27] Like employment, community membership was strictly a contractual relationship, and if the contract was breached, the relationship was terminated.

Although some citizens were disgruntled over paternalistic policies, the town of Pullman functioned until the economic panic of 1893. The roller-coaster ride of early industrial capitalism took another sudden dip, and the demand for luxury rail cars plummeted. Nevertheless, the fiscal year ending in July 1893 witnessed healthy Pullman profits of $6 million.[28] Despite these profits, the company met the economic downturn by slashing wages and employment, but Pullman rents were not reduced. The community was threatened with the prospect of becoming a ghost town, given the economic conditions. Residents and workers appealed to Pullman for ameliorative measures to no avail.

The events of the Pullman strike unfolded in short order. On May 10, 1894, Pullman workers presented a grievance. The next day, three of the workers who put forth the petition were fired, and the local American Railway Union (organized and led by Debs) struck. In June, the ARU called for a general strike of all railroads with Pullman cars. The company town was shut down, and railways from the Mississippi to the Pacific were no longer operating.[29] Only six days after the ARU walkout, President Grover Cleveland ordered in the military over the objections of the Illinois governor. Tension mounted and violence erupted, resulting in the death of twelve people in the Chicago area from clashes between mobs and either the police or the military. Chicago, a railway hub, was particularly hurt by the strike. Ironically, Chicago may have also been the intellectual crucible for the strike, because the city was a hotbed of radical thought and activism.[30] In particular, Hull House, which facilitated union organization and welcomed anarchists and Marxist speakers, supported the atmosphere of resistance. Throughout the unrest, George Pullman remained intransigent, refusing to agree to arbitration or talks. His stubbornness succeeded, as social institutional support opposed the workers' efforts. Court injunctions got the railroads rolling again by July 9. The American Federation of Labor failed to join a sympathy strike, and by August 2, the strike ended, but its impact was not over. Addams's analysis provided part of the Pullman strike's legacy.

Addams was drawn into the Pullman strike because she was a member of the newly formed Civic Federation of Chicago and its Board of Conciliation of the Industrial Committee. This organization formed to create harmony between workers and employers. In May 1894, Addams visited the company town, and, consistent with the social habits of embodied care, dined with some of the women who worked for Pullman. She also met with Debs and other representatives of the ARU. Out of a sense of duty, and some cautious optimism, Addams set out to arbitrate the dispute. Much like her international peace efforts, she was under no illusions that her arbitration efforts would be successful, but given the stakes, she felt a moral obligation to try. The residents of Hull House had recently arbitrated a strike of the Star Knitting Workers in 1892, so Addams had some collective bargaining experience, but nothing matching the scale of the Pullman strike.[31] Nevertheless, Addams was pulled in two directions. Labor wanted her to support their position, and her philanthropist associates wanted her to get workers back on the job. Brown describes how Addams refused partisan advocacy, taking "an independent position on the labor question precisely because she was the 'impassioned advocate' of a cause: the cause of mediated conflict through democratic process."[32] Ultimately, Addams's tactics were ineffective. Pullman refused to meet with her, and company representatives, although cordial, were uncooperative. She made the most out of the experience by developing an eloquent analysis describing her philosophy of organizational leadership in the controversial article "A Modern Lear."

Addams wrote "A Modern Lear" in 1896 for an address she gave to women's clubs in Chicago and Boston, but almost twenty years passed before its publication because numerous journals rejected the contentious piece. Addams compares George Pullman to Shakespeare's tragic King Lear, who failed to understand his youngest daughter, Cordelia, and felt unappreciated, just as Pullman felt unappreciated for what he provided for his workers. Cordelia attempted to be honest with Lear when he was expecting unremitting praise, just as the workers attempted to be honest with Pullman. Addams describes the analogy: "The relation of the British King to his family is very like the relation of the president of the Pullman Company to his town; the denouement of a daughter's break with her father suggests the break of the employes [sic] with their benefactor. If we call one an example of the domestic tragedy, the other of the industrial tragedy, it is possible to make them illuminate each other."[33]

This is a fascinating approach for Addams: confronting asymmetrical power relationships by framing her analysis in terms of a traditional patriarchal understanding of a father-daughter relationship. Pullman is the patriarch. Patriarchy places power squarely with the father, and the power of corporate presidents far exceeds that of employees. Her critique is not based on principles of social equality, but on experiential consequences of inequality. Power differentials can alienate and disconnect people. Addams claims that Lear "forgets [Cordelia's] royal inheritance of magnanimity, and also the power of obstinacy which he shared with her."[34] Similarly, power causes Pullman to forget "the common stock of experience which he held with his men."[35] Both men act paternalistically as a consequence of their disengagement. For Addams, tragedy can result when people become disconnected. In this case, Pullman forgets or lacks the resources to understand what it is like to be a laborer on the edge of subsistence. Addams was not asking for charity or perfect economic equality. She wanted Pullman to enact policies that allowed workers and employees to make common cause in dialogue with management. She sought reciprocal relations and sympathetic understanding.

Addams's analysis of the Pullman strike is indicative of an ethic of care. Her focus on relationships is clear when she asks the reader "to consider this great social disaster, not alone in its legal aspect nor in its sociological bearings, but from those deep human motives, which after all, determine events."[36] In her view, a traditional analysis of principles or consequences is not instructive. By going beyond the analogy between King Lear as George Pullman and Cordelia as the laborers, she cajoles readers to engage their ethical sensibilities and imagination by working from the familiar to the less familiar: from family relations to business relations. "In the midst of these discussions the writer found her mind dwelling upon a comparison which modified and softened all her judgments. Her attention was caught by the similarity of ingratitude suffered by an indulgent employer and an indulgent parent. King Lear came often to her mind. We have all shared the family relationship and our code of ethics concerning it is somewhat settled. We also bear a part in the industrial relationship, but our ethics concerning that are still uncertain. A comparative study of these two relationships presents an advantage, in that it enables us to consider the situation from the known experience toward the unknown."[37] Addams characterizes corporations as a system of relationships that include personal, emotional, and ethical dimensions. Although her approach is to shift focus from production to laborers, she is not overtly taking sides. Employing a method of rational detachment, despite her own ties to labor, she is not directly condemning the management of the Pullman Company.

Addams provides a phenomenology of the Pullman crisis. She praises Pullman in a guarded way, describing him as being philanthropic in a manner consistent with current understandings of philanthropy: "The sense of duty held by the president of the Pullman company doubtless represents the ideal in the minds of the best of the present employers as to their obligations toward their employees, but he projected this ideal more magnificently than the others."[38] Pullman's intentions are reasonable given the economic climate of the time; even his company town can be viewed as praiseworthy. Addams is not naive, as she recognizes that the company town is profitable for Pullman, but overall Pullman went further than other employers in acting in behalf of his employees. Nonetheless, his good intentions, like Lear's, are vitiated when they lack reflection and connection to the experience of others:

> It shocks our ideal of family life that a man should fail to know his daughter's heart because she awkwardly expressed her love, that he should refuse to comfort and advise her through all difference of opinion and clashing of will. That a man should be so absorbed in his own indignation as to fail to apprehend his child's thought; that he should lose his affection in his anger, is really no more unnatural than that the man who spent a million of dollars on a swamp to make it sanitary for his employees, should refuse to speak to them for ten minutes, whether they were in the right or wrong; or that a man who had given them his time and thought for twenty years should withdraw from them his guidance when he believed them misled by ill-advisers and wandering in a mental fog; or that he should grow hard and angry when they needed tenderness and help.[39]

Pullman was so indignant at the workers' strike that he refused to meet with them or any of their representatives. Addams viewed Pullman as practicing autocratic, disconnected leadership, thus failing to make "common cause" with his workers. Because Pullman was out of touch, he insisted on treating his employees paternally. Addams's critique of Pullman is consistent with her observations about politicians in *Democracy and Social Ethics* when she describes corrupt Chicago aldermen as successful. Aldermen were connected and therefore effective, yet corrupt. Pullman was disconnected and therefore ineffective, despite some good intentions. For Addams, effective ethical leadership in business or politics entails listening and responding. Nevertheless, she frames the Pullman strike as a tragedy, refusing absolute condemnation or approval. Pullman only shares the blame. One of his mistakes was to apply old notions of philanthropy.[40] Addams views the virtues of one generation as "not sufficient for the next, any more than the accumulations of knowledge possessed by one age are adequate to another."[41] Modern morality involves social ethics, which she describes as democracy, whereas Pullman's philanthropy is strictly autocratic.

In "A Modern Lear," Addams repeats many of her ethical themes. One is the progress of morality: "Of the virtues received from our fathers we can afford to lose none. We accept as a precious trust those principles and precepts that the race has worked out for its highest safeguards and protection. But merely to preserve is not enough. A task is laid to each generation to enlarge their application, to ennoble their conception, and, above all, to apply and adapt them to the peculiar problems presented to it for solution."[42] The Pullman strike was a modern problem born out of new collective forces, including big cities and big industry. For Addams, morality has to adapt to confront new social organizations. Individual morality is insufficient to handle social problems. Sympathetic understandings are necessary to foster an engaged social democracy that accounts for both laborers and business owners. Her ultimate point is that corporate harmony or disharmony is a product of an organization's social relations. Just as democracy is a way of being in the world dictated by the disposition of citizens to one another, corporate harmony is dictated by the cooperation and connection among all the constituencies of the corporation.

Child Labor

Although Addams insisted that "the settlement should not be primarily for the children,"[43] the sea of youth that permeated Hull House indicated otherwise. She devotes a chapter of her autobiographical *Twenty Years at Hull-House* to child labor issues, replete with anecdotes from her experiences: "Our very first Christmas at Hull House, when we as yet knew nothing of child labor, a number of little girls refused the candy which was offered them as part of the Christmas good cheer, saying simply that they 'worked in a candy factory and could not bear the sight of it.' We discovered that for six weeks they had worked from seven in the morning until nine at night and they were exhausted as well as satiated. The sharp consciousness of stern economic conditions was thus thrust upon us in the midst of the season of good will." Addams's proximity to poor, working families with children engaged in factory labor revealed the prevalence of child exploitation. She also describes the death of a young boy injured in a factory. She is not only aghast over the injury, she is shocked that the employer makes no reparations to the boy's family.[44] During her first decades at Hull House, Addams's writing and activism were often animated by concern for working children.

Addams considered child labor to be detrimental to the developmental process of youth and thus, subsequently, to the future of the nation. She describes working children as suffering "unwarranted nervous strain" when they are "still in the stage of family and group dependence."[45] In this era, childhood, and particularly adolescence, was just coming to be understood as a separate period of psychosocial development (see the next chapter on Addams's philosophy of education). Addams viewed child's play to be a crucial part of moral development because it exercised imaginative habits that fueled sympathetic understanding of others. Accordingly, "play in youth is the guarantee of adult culture" and the rich sense of democracy that Addams valued.[46] Factory labor was the antithesis of play. The dull, repetitive activity performed under the threat of discipline stifled imagination. Furthermore, she claimed that many children became alienated from the idea of labor because of discouraging early experiences, thereby developing "a dull distaste for work."[47] She believed that child laborers became disaffected toward work and had underdeveloped imaginative habits that boded poorly for society's future.

Given her thematizing of child labor experiences, combined with the lack of movement by corporate institutions, Addams undertook a campaign to pass labor laws limiting the employment of working children. In 1904, she helped to establish the National Child Labor Committee to lobby in behalf of compulsory education and federal child labor laws. Child labor laws did not receive resounding support from poverty-stricken families who faced the prospect of losing an income source. Addams characteristically sympathized with and engaged these people: "I addressed as many mother's meetings and clubs among working women as I could."[48] She reported that given an opportunity to fully consider the matter, most women agreed with the idea of regulating child labor.

Addams's social philosophy requires labor that promotes maturity and growth. She wanted workers to enter employment with their eyes wide open, fully understanding the meaning of their work and their relation to their chosen occupation. She understood the need to earn money, given the squalor she witnessed in and around Hull House. Nevertheless, she believed that experiences of work should be integrated into one's life, not merely coerced by material needs because society sharply limited opportunities. Therefore, she actively sought a labor market that was open to women but that limited children's labor until they were ready. For Addams, the economic system, whether capitalism or socialism, was not as crucial as that of work experiences that provided opportunities for growth and happiness. Issues of price and productivity took a back seat to a comprehensive sense of the quality of working life: "We may in time be justly proud, if we can say that no American product enters into foreign or domestic commerce which does not represent the free labor quality of an educated producer who is exercising his adult powers."[49] Because capitalism was the operant economic system, and it failed workers, Addams found many of the socialist claims compelling.

Philanthropy

Addams maintained a steady drumbeat of concern about philanthropy, beginning with her first book, *Democracy and Social Ethics*. She devotes a great deal of "A Modern Lear" to criticizing Pullman's philanthropy as a manifestation of individual morality: an act of an individual in behalf of another. For Addams, philanthropy went astray in at least two ways. First, because charity is unidirectional—that is, does not require reciprocity and is thus disconnected—it might not meet intended needs. Second, philanthropy can be a public demonstration of egotistical largesse that may promote the giver but not serve society's best interests.

Hull House depended on philanthropy. Addams was friends with many wealthy people, including the architect Allen B. Pond, philanthropist William

Kent, and Chicago socialite Louise de Koven Bowen. After the incorporation of Hull House in 1894, a board of trustees was created, composed mostly of prosperous men and women who made important resource contributions to Hull House and kept the settlement connected to the power brokers of Chicago. Addams's partner, Mary Rozet Smith, the daughter of two affluent parents, willingly shared her wealth with Addams and Hull House. Addams inherited a sizable estate upon her father's death, much of which went to Hull House. As Louise Knight describes, "For Addams, as an inheritor of wealth rather than a creator of it, the question was how to merit the wealth her father had earned."[50]

Because Addams was familiar with wealth, she could suggest sympathetic understanding to an elite class that might not otherwise be disposed to hear it. Given her iconic association with the oppressed, some might find her social mobility surprising. Nevertheless, Addams finds no hypocrisy in her transactions with the well-to-do. Unlike Marx or Tolstoy, Addams was not an ideologue and was willing to meet and work with whoever advanced the cause of lateral progress in society. She challenged her rich associates to acknowledge the responsibilities that came with their wealth.

Just as she advocated connected leadership in her analysis of the Pullman strike, Addams advocated connected philanthropy. In her view, the philanthropist who operates from an individual morality not grounded in the social experience of others is misguided. Philanthropists, like all good democratic citizens, have an obligation to develop sympathetic understandings of others. Wealth brings additional responsibility to use resources in behalf of others, but it does not negate the requirement of knowing others. Addams brought her philanthropist acquaintances in touch with the oppressed. This was one of the principal purposes of Hull House: to create immediate social connections. Often, charitable contributions have the opposite effect of what Addams's philosophy attempts to achieve. Mailing a check to a worthy cause may assuage the guilt of disparate wealth but also quiet any desire for new knowledge beyond one's class, thus sustaining barriers between people. Addams demanded richer transactions that left all parties more knowledgeable of the other. Hull House needed philanthropists to fund the myriad projects it supported, but Addams also used philanthropy to draw the upper class into greater participation in Hull House's operation.

Louise de Koven Bowen was Addams's greatest success in bringing an affluent and well-known Chicago socialite into reciprocal, affective transactions with the community of Hull House. Born into wealth, Bowen married into further wealth. She became involved at Hull House in 1893. Over the course of the decades during which she was associated with Hull House, Bowen made donations totaling over half a million dollars.[51] Her largesse was sufficient to leave an important legacy in the buildings and programs it supported, but monetary generosity was not enough for Addams. Bowen was asked to get involved with the Hull House women's club, otherwise composed of members of the neighborhood. She was later elected president and served the women's club for seventeen years in one official capacity or another. At Addams's beckoning, Bowen allowed her life and consciousness to be disrupted by her experiences at the settlement. Sympathetic understandings were formed that provided motivation for Bowen to give of her financial and political resources. Reflecting on the women's club, Bowen identified the epistemological purpose of the social transactions at Hull House: "I often felt at this Hull House club that not even in church did I ever get the inspiration or the desire for service, so much as when I was presiding at a meeting of the club and sat on the platform and looked down on the faces of 800 or 900 women gathered together, all intensely in earnest and all most anxious perhaps to put over some project in which they were interested. The club also proved to be a liberal education for me."[52]

Her internalization of Addams's philosophy was thorough. When Bowen was informed that workers at the Pullman Palace Car Company were being exposed to lead poisoning, she used her influence to have Pullman build a hospital. She also used her influence to obtain minimum wage standards for women at the International Harvester Company.[53] Yet, Bowen was not merely a power broker. She worked at Hull House for decades, and, like Addams, applied what she learned to issues beyond the neighborhood. Her autobiography is replete with anecdotes of service to the community alongside Addams. She eloquently captures the spirit of sympathetic knowledge:

> Miss Addams in these early days was really an interpreter between working men and women and the people who lived in luxury on the other side of the city and she also gave the people of her own neighborhood quite a different idea about the men and women who were ordinarily called "capitalists."
>
> To come in contact constantly with the people of that neighborhood certainly gave one a new impression of life in a great city and I began to feel that what was needed more than anything was an acquaintance between the well-to-do and those less well off. Until an acquaintance of this kind can be effected, there will always be difficulties and there never will be that sympathy which should exist.
>
> ... Although the people I met at Hull House lived a life far removed from the kind I led, yet, after all we are all cast in the same mold, all with the same emotions, the same feelings, the same sense of right and wrong, but alas, not with the same opportunities.[54]

Addams's philosophy of philanthropy infused class-consciousness with sympathetic understanding.

Addams's economic commentary includes both genders in pursuit of holistic social advancement. Nevertheless, she recognizes the vulnerability of women workers and directs much of her effort toward understanding and empowering this new segment of paid labor. Three areas that receive considerable attention from Addams are women in unions, domestic labor, and prostitution.

UNION WOMEN

As mentioned earlier, Addams advocated the full participation of women in society, not as ideology, but as the consequence of reasoning: it was in the best interest of society that women be integrated into all aspects of public life. Of course, this full participation extended to labor as well. Through Hull House, Addams supported working women in many ways, perhaps the most important of which was in providing child care. In a country that has never developed a national child-care policy, Hull House freed women who desperately needed an opportunity to work with the knowledge that their children were well cared for. Addams did not stop there.

The creation of the "Jane Club" is an example of the responsiveness and listening skills of Hull House residents. At a meeting of working women from a local shoe factory attended by Addams, it became clear that these laborers lacked clout because they were incapable of amassing effective strike efforts. Single women were particularly vulnerable to intimidation because, with only one income, they lost their apartments if they could not make monthly rent payments. Addams helped start a housing cooperative so that single workers could assist with one another's rent and responsibilities during times of need. The cooperative was named the Jane Club, and it was organized as self-sufficient and independent from Hull House operations. The Jane Club eventually grew to occupy an entire building filled by fifty tenants, including stenographers, dressmakers, printers, teachers, and bookkeepers of both immigrant and non-immigrant origins. In creating the Jane Club, Addams demonstrated how care could be socialized through an institutional structure. She provided the seed money for this cooperative, and then the workers managed the organization on their own. There was no paternalistic oversight. The Jane Club afforded an opportunity for growth and empowerment but was not fettered by rules typically placed on single women of the time: no curfew or limitation on the movement of residents. According to Addams, "Any girl who can come into the city and earn an honest living knows enough to run her own evenings."[55] Despite the potential for asymmetrical power relations, Addams treated these working women as full moral agents.

In *Democracy and Social Ethics,* Addams devotes a chapter to domestic labor. Although men or women can engage in household work, her analysis primarily addresses women who worked as live-in servants. Interestingly, Addams began Hull House apparently with the intent of including a domestic worker: "On the 18th of September 1889, Miss Starr and I moved into [Hull House], with Miss Mary Keyser, who began by performing the housework, but who quickly developed into a very important factor in the life of the vicinity as well as in that of the household."[56] In later economic analysis, Addams questions the need for household help: "In our increasing democracy the notion of personal service is constantly becoming more distasteful, conflicting, as it does, with the more modern notion of personal dignity. . . . Personal ministrations to a normal, healthy adult, consuming the time and energy of another adult, we find more difficult to reconcile to our theories of democracy."[57] Addams does not oppose domestic service workers tending to children, the sick, or the elderly, but her class-consciousness makes it difficult for her to reconcile adults serving one another. Yet, as witnessed in her confrontation with Tolstoy, Addams recognized that effective managers cannot always lead and simultaneously engage in the activities of those who work for them. She accepted a certain amount of specialization, but domestic service struck her as putting too much power in one person over another.

Addams delineates many concerns about domestic labor. First, she is concerned with isolation. Although factory work creates a certain kind of isolation in its truncated relationships, domestic work entails a physical isolation, as live-in servants have little regular contact with others in the same profession and therefore no opportunity of "attaining with them the dignity of a corporate body."[58] On several occasions, she describes the extreme control that the employer has as "undemocratic"—a strong moral indictment for Addams. She suggests that the isolation and social estrangement of live-in working women can lead to sexual impropriety: "Certain hospitals in London have contributed statistics showing that seventy-eight per cent of illegitimate children born there are the children of girls working in households."[59] Although Addams has concerns about factory labor, at least such work allowed for social contact. Factory workers go home at the end of the day, and there are opportunities for personal advancement. Domestic labor has the potential to trap workers outside public view.

As a public philosopher, Addams not only raises questions but provides solutions as well. She is a pragmatist, so although her criticisms indicate that she might advocate eliminating domestic labor altogether, or at least for some able-bodied families, Addams instead offers ideas that reconnect domestic laborers with one another. First, simply enough, she indicates that household servants should be allowed to go home in the evening and live with their families to make their lives more consistent with factory workers. Second, she suggests creating "residence clubs" where workers can meet and socialize.[60] Such organizations would advance professional skills, but more important, they would facilitate the associations so important to Addams's sympathetic understanding. Residence clubs would also provide women the opportunity to help one another and perhaps even collectively bargain.

PROSTITUTION

In *A New Conscience and an Ancient Evil,* Addams describes the plight of Marie, a young French woman who at the age of twelve was forced by her poor father to work in Paris as "a little household drudge and nurse-maid, working from six in the morning until eight at night."[61] After three years of this work, a young man enticed the poor girl with pictures of young women in fine clothing who were allegedly part of an acting troupe. Marie "joined" the troupe and was snuck into the United States, ending up as a prostitute in Chicago earning $250 a week. She was not allowed to retain her earnings, and, furthermore, was physically abused. While in a hospital after contracting typhus, she confessed her situation and revealed her exploiters. Addams reports that despite her subsequent marriage, Marie continued to work in the sex industry because she was demoralized and "powerless now to save herself from her subjective temptations."[62] For Addams, Marie's story was part of a pattern of exploitation in the trafficking of young women that could not be ignored.

A decade after writing her general ethical theory in *Democracy and Social Ethics* (1902), Addams addressed prostitution in *A New Conscience and an Ancient Evil* (1913). Less lurid and more analytical than many other pieces written in the exposé genre common during this period, *A New Conscience* also provides a forum for Addams to apply her pragmatist philosophy. According to Addams, the book "endeavors to present the contributory causes [of prostitution] as they have become registered in my consciousness through a long residence in a crowded city quarter."[63] To reach a wider audience, she also published her work on prostitution in women's magazines such as *McClure's Magazine* and *Women's Journal.*

Prostitution is not an easy subject for Addams. A product of Victorian morality and uncomfortable with explicit discussions of carnal issues, she employs euphemistic language to describe sex and prostitution. For example, her definition of prostitution is not only euphemistic (describing sex as "the great human dynamic") but betrays a valorization of virginity not shared by many modern feminists: "Throughout this volume the phrase 'social evil' is used to designate the sexual commerce permitted to exist in every large city, usually in a segregated district, wherein the chastity of women is bought and sold."[64] The discomfort with sexual language is indicative of the challenge that prostitution posed for settlement residents. The woman-centered community at Hull House repressed open discussion of sex or sexuality.[65] Yet, Addams was both of and ahead of her time, in that she addressed prostitution in her writing despite her discomfort.

A New Conscience and an Ancient Evil employs slavery as the fundamental metaphor for prostitution in at least two ways. First, Addams views the battle to end prostitution as analogous to the battle to end slavery. She conceives of slavery as an evil that this nation recognized as immoral and, with great social effort, overcame. Similarly, she believes that the evil of prostitution can be mitigated if we are willing to make the collective effort. Drawing on the slavery analogy, Addams suggests that sympathetic knowledge is a crucial early step to the eradication of prostitution. First, the general public must understand the plight of the prostitute in a manner that elicits empathy: "The knowledge of the youth of [prostitution's] victims doubtless in a measure accounts for the new sense of compunction which fills the community."[66] As with the above description of young women like Marie, the epistemological/emotional connection is crucial. Knowledge creates possibilities for care and the sympathetic feelings that are the catalyst for social change. Addams wants her audience to know and understand the plight of prostitutes in a concrete way, which is why she uses many examples that she has gleaned from her Hull House experiences. Care and empathy are more likely to be evoked by the use of concrete examples from which personal connections are created rather than abstract statistical representations of prostitutes. Like the slave, as long as the prostitute remains a distant or abstract "other"—a category or stereotype for the populace—an emotive response, a caring desire for change, is unlikely.

The second way that prostitution resembles slavery in Addams's analysis is in its involuntary nature. Addams suggests that prostitutes are coerced through the use of economics, liquor, and/or deception. She devotes an entire chapter of the book to economics. The failure to allow women full participation in the economy gives them few substantial career choices. Addams reviews the traditional work possibilities for women of her day, including jobs as department store clerks, waitresses, and factory workers. She concludes that low wages, long hours, and tedious, sometimes dangerous, work make prostitution a more attractive career choice for women. She calls for a full-scale economic analysis of prostitution, including the impact of paying all forms of employment a "living wage"—a concept that gained attention in the first half of the twentieth century, but has long since been forgotten in favor of the meager minimum wage. "In addition to the monotony of work and the long hours, the small wages these girls receive have no relation to the standard of living which they are endeavoring to maintain. Discouraged and over-fatigued, they are often brought into sharp juxtaposition with the women who are obtaining much larger returns from their illicit trade."[67] Addams provides a subtle critique of capitalism: if the members of the economy are rational decision makers, as capitalists claim they are, then, for women, prostitution is a reasonable choice, given available alternatives. This approach places the onus on society to make economic policy that renders prostitution less economically attractive. Addams's economic analysis resembles, and was likely influenced by, Charlotte Perkins Gillman.[68]

Addams also views alcohol use as contributing to the coercion and slavelike grip of prostitution. Her Victorian upbringing led her to believe that drinking was a dangerous vice, and her experience at Hull House did not dissuade her: "Whoever has tried to help a girl making an effort to leave an irregular life she has been leading, must have been discouraged by the victim's attempts to overcome the habit of using alcohol and drugs."[69] Her caution that "consumption of liquor enormously increases the danger to young people," remains relevant.[70] Substance abuse continues to be a factor in many sex workers' lives.[71] Addams viewed social problems as interconnected. Just as economic justice would reduce prostitution, so too would a reduction in alcohol use.

In her view, male deception also contributes to prostitution and sexual slavery. A New Conscience is replete with stories like that of Marie, where innocent women are lured into elaborate schemes of prostitution. Addams describes a gendered division of morality. She suggests that when not socially restrained, men take sexual advantage of women. For example, when men come from small towns to visit Chicago, away from home their moral fortitude wanes: "They are supposedly moral at home, where they are well known and subject to the constant control of public opinion."[72] Once in the city, they give in to the ancient evil. She believes that men trick women into prostitution and then pander to a lack of restraint in other males. Addams's analysis retains validity today, as men continue to dominate the control of sex industries and traveling men are more likely to engage the sex industry.

A New Conscience has received much criticism. Addams's contemporary, Walter Lippmann, called the book "hysterical" and regarded it as unreflective moralism.[73] Sixty years later, Allen Davis's assessment is similar, describing the work as hysterical, sentimental, and naive.[74] Given the public's craving for depictions of sexual depravity and the rise of muckraking journalism, there is much to support these critiques of Addams's analysis. Nevertheless, aspects of her conclusions remain viable. For example, her economic response holds up well in the new millennium. Women continue to find barriers to economic success, such as the gendered division of labor, glass ceiling, wage gap, and the feminization of poverty, which make prostitution an attractive financial alternative. If society guaranteed a living wage, provided a safety net of social services, and allowed women equal participation in the economy, prostitution would be a less reasonable choice. Sociologist Julia O'Connell Davidson describes prostitution as based on "economic and political conditions that compel people to act in ways in which they would not choose to act."[75] Addams and Davidson agree that a change in economic conditions would alter much of the allure of prostitution. Addams's emphasis on education also remains relevant. The prevalence of modern myths about prostitution, such as the illusion that most prostitutes have freely chosen their work, indicates that a great deal of public education needs to take place.

A Reluctant Socialist

Addams studied Marx's work prior to starting Hull House.[76] In "A Modern Lear," *Democracy and Social Ethics,* and elsewhere, her economic analysis resonates with that of Karl Marx and Friedrich Engels, but it contains sharp distinctions, particularly in regard to the process of economic transformation. Addams acknowledged her sympathy with socialism: "I should have been most grateful at the time to accept the tenets of socialism."[77] Nevertheless, she could not agree that materialism creates social relations that are "merely historical and transitory products."[78] Addams was dissatisfied with the means/ends distinction put forth in socialism and preferred to understand social relationships as an experienced, organic whole. Accordingly, she was not interested in overthrowing all existing social relationships and starting anew. She sought to transform relationships so that human sympathies could become the driving force. In this respect, Addams's approach to economics has much in common with feminist economist Julie Nelson's concept of economics as *provisioning.*

For Nelson, feminist theory has an important critique to offer modern economic analysis. She finds contemporary economics overly concerned with decision science. Steeped in an individualistic concept of human nature, traditional economics tends to focus on a quantitative understanding of isolated choices by consumers within the free market system. Nelson finds that feminist theorists, who employ a more inclusive, imaginative rationality, infuse economics with a social, normative dimension that reframes the central concern of economic theory as "provisioning" or "the commodities and processes necessary to human survival."[79] In other words, economists have lost sight of the subject of economics. This in part explains why Addams's work on economics does not resemble most economic texts: it is grounded in experience, with particular human conditions at the forefront. Nelson's "provisioning economics" and Addams's lateral progress strike a common chord because of their commitments to human welfare over descriptive analysis.

Because, for Addams, continuity and connection were paramount, she envisioned social change brought about through inclusive deliberation and reflection. Marx's communist revolution represented a fundamental disruption of the social fabric in order to realign power relations. Marx would not have accepted Addams's approach of progressive ends-in-view. He claimed that communist ends "can be obtained only by the forcible overthrow of all existing social conditions. Let the ruling classes tremble at a Communist revolution."[80] Marx was willing to bring about social change by force and violence, justified by the historic force and violence levied by the bourgeoisie on the proletariat. Addams was unwilling to support violent revolution. Living at Hull House, she had daily exposure to the violence of industrial labor and its consequences. She was frustrated with capitalism as she witnessed the destructive impact of corporate free enterprise and the exploitation of workers. Nevertheless, violent revolution results in widespread suffering with no guarantees of a long-term peaceable equilibrium. The revolution Addams advocated is a participatory one that achieves the assent of the hearts and minds of society's constituencies without physical coercion.

It is somewhat ironic that traditional interpretations of Marx deem him the "radical" and Addams the "ameliorist." In many ways, the use of violent coercion or the blind adherence to ideology is unoriginal. Having faith that humans will act rationally to care for all members of society appears to be a much more radical idea, given widespread disillusionment over human nature. Historian Staughton Lynd describes Addams's approach as "vintage radicalism," which "saw itself not as a persecuted minority but as the voice of the people: in the minority, they thought, were the self-seeking men of power who resisted the changes for which the state of the nation cried aloud. Social revolution in their view was the fulfillment of the destiny of the American nation."[81]

As we have seen in her discussion of the division of labor, Addams and Marx shared a concern for the alienation of factory labor, but she integrated that concern into a critique of materialism. After contending that workers must master their machines, Addams suggests that at some point the public "will become inexpressibly bored by manufactured objects which reflect absolutely nothing of the minds of the men who made them."[82] She hints that America has become enthralled with industrial production for its own sake, leading to a cult of consumerism: "We are surrounded by stupid articles which give us no pleasure."[83] Addams's arguments imply that greater workplace democracy, participation, and education might lead to fewer, but more valuable, consumer goods. Her reflections on philanthropy demonstrate her class-consciousness. In the end, Addams, like many of the intellectuals of her day, was a socialist. Despite her complaints about ideology, she agreed with socialist analysis but disagreed about how to remedy the situation.

In proportion as the playtime of the child is lengthened, we have a new opportunity for adult culture. . . . Culture is not mere learning, pegging away and getting a lot of things in one's head, but it means the power of enjoyment as one goes along, the power to play with a fact and get pleasure out of it, and if we have not that, although we may be learned we are still uncultivated people.

—JANE ADDAMS

CHAPTER 8

Democracy, Education, and Play

Addams wrote about education early and often. A number of factors contributed to her interest in the subject. One was her personal positive experience. Addams had been a bright child who was intellectually encouraged at home and subsequently blossomed in college. The intellectual environment at Hull House recreated much of what she enjoyed at Rockford Seminary, and valuing education was reflected in her social philosophy. Education was also a sector of the public sphere where women's involvement was acceptable, although not in terms of leadership or administration. In addition, the time was ripe for engaging in educational discourse, because new ideas about pedagogical methods were circulating, especially among her intellectual colleagues such as Mead and Dewey, who specialized in educational theory. Finally, education fit squarely with her social philosophy. An essential element of sympathetic knowledge is learning about one another. Addams's work on education relates to her ideas about democracy, peace, diversity, and lateral progress because each requires empathetic understanding fostered by interpersonal transactions. Education is either implicitly or explicitly integrated into every issue Addams addressed.

Hull House was educative to its core. Historian Ellen Condliffe Lagemann describes Hull House as an "open university where a constant flow of talk about politics, ideas, public events, art, philosophy, and the immediate problems of a destitute family or a gang of neighborhood boys provided constantly evolving and lived meaning to such abstract concepts as citizenship, culture, assimilation, and education."[1] For Addams, part of what constituted this "open university" was the reciprocal character of Hull House. Settlement workers intended to learn from their poverty-stricken immigrant neighbors. Simultaneously, the neighborhood received educational opportunities through the variety of clubs, lectures, and classes sponsored by Hull House. There was, however, an interlocutor in this educational process: Addams's middle-class audience. Addams and her cohort acted as a conduit for social information, across class and culture, which few people had access to. Victoria Brown refers to Addams as playing the function of a "cross-class interpreter" who built a "bridge of human connection across the class divide."[2] Addams's prodigious corpus of articles, books, and lectures gave the public insight into the plight of Chicago's immigrant poor. For example, *Hull-House Maps and Papers* is a landmark exploration of the conditions of an immigrant neighborhood—social information not previously available to the public. The raw demographic data is the necessary condition, although not the sufficient condition, to inspire widespread sympathetic understanding. No one can care for those they have no knowledge of. In her other writings, Addams added the story of individual lives to the data, creating narratives that do foster care.

In this chapter, I discuss Addams's philosophy of education according to the age of the student—child, adolescent, or adult. Manifestations of her educational theory through Hull House projects, in particular the Labor Museum, occupy the latter part of the chapter. I conclude with a discussion of Addams's ongoing relevance in the philosophy of education.

Childhood Education: Play as the Basis for Democracy

Addams's work on childhood education endeavored to create opportunities for participation and institute reforms. She wanted all children to have an education, but she found external forces, such as child labor laws that would ensure children's availability for school, as well as the internal attractiveness and efficacy of that education, problematic. The former could be addressed with legislation, the latter required school reforms.

Universal childhood education has not always been secure, particularly at the end of the nineteenth century in the United States. In 1900, only 10 percent of students in the United States attended school after age fourteen. Although 70 percent of children claimed some education, the quality and quantity of school experience varied tremendously.[3] Not surprisingly, class and race played pivotal roles in the amount of education a child received. Uneven or nonexistent child labor laws exacerbated these inconsistent educational experiences. As early as 1897, Addams lectured to the National Education Association on how immigrant children missed opportunities for education: "If a boy is twelve or thirteen upon his arrival in America, his parents see him in a wage-earning factor, and the girl of the same age is already looking toward her marriage."[4] She emphasized family financial need as driving child labor. Later, her concerns extended to industry failures and government neglect. In 1907, she complained about the inconsistency "that the federal government should be willing to spend time and money to establish and maintain departments relating to the breeding, to the raising, to the distribution and to the exportation of cattle, sheep and hogs, and that as yet the federal government has nothing to see to it that the children are properly protected."[5] Not content with pointing the finger at government, Addams criticized business and industry for being "so ruthless and so self-centered that it has never given [children] a thought."[6] In 1904, Addams helped form the National Child Labor Committee to lobby for compulsory childhood education, and the requisite child labor laws, so that children could attend school. Despite her efforts, federal legislation banning child labor did not pass in her lifetime (the Fair Labor Standards Act was enacted in 1938).

Not surprisingly, Addams's methodological reforms emphasized matching educational efforts to the experiential needs of the learner: "Study the child and give him the things he so earnestly desires."[7] One of the desires of youth is play. Addams took play seriously. On May 5, 1895, the front page of the *Chicago Tribune* reported that the opening of the first public playground in Chicago, at Hull House, was "a wild scene of delight."[8] Today, joyous celebrations of public places of play are few, and rarer yet do playgrounds make front-page news. For Addams, a playground was not trivial. The playground is where the essence of her philosophy of play unfolds: "It is the little children who play in the streets. They are doing the work which cultivated people ought to be undertaking consciously and doing better. The children are the only ones that are coming together and showing how much stronger human nature is than any other tie."[9] Addams was a leading figure in the fledgling Playground Association of America, which in 1907 held its first national convention in Chicago.[10] Her analysis of playgrounds might be dismissed as domestic housekeeping—fit for "women's work," but she found more to child's play than mere diversion: she saw democratic skill building.

Addams's philosophy of childhood education emphasizes play, cooperative intelligence, contextual relevance, connected learning, and imaginative exploration. Drawing on the work of Friedrich Froebel, Dewey, Mead, Wayland Parker, and Ella Flagg Young, Addams advocates reshaping traditional institutional pedagogies. For example, she expresses concern that schools are overly focused on behavior control, so that "perhaps we have thought too much of order and quiet and too little of self-expression."[11] She insists on the alignment of educational philosophy with social philosophy in holistic development of the individual. Thus, her emphasis on sympathetic knowledge that provides the scaffolding for democracy extends to education. Furthermore, for Addams, education should engage the entire being—intellectually, imaginatively, and physically. Her approach is holistic and resourceful, utilizing and advocating various pedagogical tools, including play, literature, current events, and recreation, to develop the entire person and his or her connections to society. Because she claims social ethics is the necessity of the day, Addams values interactive education as preparing good citizens with sufficient resources to sympathetically understand others. A robust education, then, becomes an imperative of democracy.

The most intriguing aspect of Addams's educational philosophy is her emphasis on children playing with others and how she links play to democracy. She claims that a child "should have his full period of childhood and youth for this play expression, that he may cultivate within himself the root of that culture which can alone give his later activity a meaning."[12] Addams's accent on play is an outgrowth of the work of Friedrich Froebel (1782–1852) who founded the kindergarten movement. Hull House started a kindergarten prior to opening a playground. Kindergarten was already compulsory in parts of Europe when it was introduced in the United States in the 1840s. More than anyone, Froebel advanced the idea that children were not little adults, as was commonly held in the nineteenth century. His theory of education rests on the notions of self-directed activity, creativity, social participation, and physical activity. According to Froebel, play implies "an inner life and vigor" that can "arouse, feed, and elevate life."[13] He viewed play as the linchpin of education. Although many philosophers made mention of play's benefits, Froebel was the first to see it as crucial to human development. Play is an expression of a child's freedom. Froebel respected children's individuality and trusted them with their freedom. Such respect ran counter to prevailing ideas about childhood depravity and the need for discipline.[14] Addams adopted Froebel's cult of childhood.

Addams's good friend, George Herbert Mead, also makes play an important part of his theory of human development. Because Mead viewed the self as essentially social, the interactions involved in play are crucial for developing an empathetic imagination and constructing the self. When children play, they imaginatively "try out" roles such as mother, teacher, and police officer, and in doing so they experience social responses to these parts. Sometimes roles are simple and explicitly worked out in a relatively short period of play, and other times they evolve over extended experiences of play. These responses are used "in building a self," which children cumulatively "organize into a certain whole."[15] For Mead, without play, social lessons about roles must be learned elsewhere or else the child's sense of self may not fully develop its social connection. Play is therefore valued as a significant aspect of human social growth. Given their close personal relationship, it is likely that Mead and Addams discussed these ideas.

Although Dewey was not always meticulous when it came to citing his sources, he dedicated a chapter of *The School and Society* to the educational principles of Froebel. Dewey endorses Froebel's ideas with the caveat that more has been learned about child development since Froebel wrote his educational theory and we should always reevaluate teaching approaches, given new information. Dewey also views play as central to identity development, engaging "the free interplay of all the child's powers, thoughts, and physical movements, in embodying, in a satisfied form, his own images and interests."[16] Addams does not disagree with Dewey, Froebel, and Mead that play is central to identity and imagination formation, but she goes further to claim that social interactions found in children's play are the basis for a democratic citizenry that can sympathetically understand diverse community members: "Play is the great social stimulus, and it is the prime motive which unites children and draws them into comradeship. A true democratic relation and ease of acquaintance is found only among the children in a typical factory community because they readily overcome differences of language, tradition and religion, which form insuperable barriers to adults. 'It is in play that nature reveals her anxious care to discover men to each other' and this happy and important task children unconsciously carry forward day by day with all the excitement and joy of co-ordinate activity. They accomplish that which elders could not possibly do, and they render a most important service to the community."[17] When Addams refers to play stimulating a "true democratic relation," she is offering high praise. In her eyes, democracy is a political system and the highest ethical way of being.

For Addams, play involves a cooperative intelligence not always appreciated by adults. When children play with one another, they work out systems of engagement often through trial and error. The individual grows, but there is group development as well. Children learn to navigate their social group to achieve individual goals while learning about collective goals.[18] Addams emphasizes cooperation over competition as the primary goal of play: "What is it a child does when he plays? He anticipates the life about him and anticipates his life to follow. We cannot get culture merely by making an individual effort; we must also combine this with social relations."[19] She realizes that the emphasis on cooperative play is a difficult demand for public schools: "Sometimes the public school crushes out that very play spirit which this age needs as no other age has needed it."[20] Nevertheless, the development of cooperative faculties is too important in a diverse society for the public school to ignore the power of play.

One avenue of play Addams emphasizes is imaginative expression through the arts.[21] Children at Hull House were exposed to a variety of artistic media because, as she says, "we have found at Hull House that our educational efforts tend constantly toward a training for artistic expression; in a music school, a school of dramatics, classes in rhythm and dancing and the school of plastic and graphic arts."[22] Fostering aesthetic sensibilities in children becomes valuable when they participate in society as adults. The arts also serve to counteract the imagination-stifling, overcrowded, and impoverished city: "Each child lives not only in an actual environment visible to all, but in enchanted surroundings which may be reproduced by the child himself."[23] Hull House offered an "enchanted surrounding," creating expressive outlets for children in drama, dance, song, art, and crafts.

In addition to the imaginative properties of play and the development of cooperative intelligence, Addams emphasizes the importance of the contextual relevance of education. According to this approach, education should begin from the experience of the child and leverage relevant examples and situations to further his or her education. Addams had witnessed Italian immigrant children enter public school only to be frustrated by pedagogical methods with no relevance to their life experience: "We are impatient with the schools which lay all stress on reading and writing, suspecting them to rest upon the assumption that the ordinary experience of life is worth little, and knowledge and interest must be brought to the children through the medium of books. Such an assumption fails to give the child any clew [sic] to the life about him, or any power to usefully or intelligently connect himself with it."[24] This statement reveals how much Addams had matured through her Hull House experience: she loved books, was extremely well read, and was an accomplished writer, yet she recognized the limitation of education through a single medium. Her approach validates children's experiences and refocuses education on their particular situation and needs rather than the needs of the discipline. Such an approach resonates with Nel Noddings's dictum that the student is always more important than the subject.[25]

Adolescence and Sex Education

Although a concern for childhood developed in the eighteenth and nineteenth centuries, the notion of adolescence as a separate category of human development from that of children was still new in the early part of the twentieth century.[26] Unfortunately, the term *adolescence* connoted trouble. Whether real or perceived, juvenile delinquency in adolescence was a national concern. In 1909, Addams entered the fray with an upbeat account of young adults, *The Spirit of*

Youth and the City Streets. She views young people as essentially good, with an untapped desire to make a social contribution. She is disturbed that society shuns adolescents by limiting their opportunities for civic participation and not providing outlets for their youthful energies. The exasperations of young people are magnified in the city. Addams believes that cities were arranged around adult work opportunities but overlooked the needs of adolescents, particularly the need to play: "This stupid experiment of organizing work and failing to organize around play has, of course, brought about a fine revenge. The love of pleasure will not be denied, and when it has turned into all sorts of malignant and vicious appetites, then we, the middle aged, grow quite distracted and resort to all sorts of restrictive measures."[27]

Hull House provided opportunities for adolescents to engage in social play in the midst of the harsh city. In her autobiography, Hilda Satt Polacheck, who started frequenting Hull House as a teenager, gives us a glimpse of Addams facilitating social play among adolescents: "I remember Miss Addams stopping one day and asking me if I had joined the dancing class. She thought I worked too hard and needed some fun. So I joined the dancing class and learned the waltz, two-step, and schottische."[28] Her assistance to Polacheck exemplifies how Addams regarded socializing and play as an important part of education, and not exclusively the purview of young children.

Addams views the sex drive as part of the energy or "emotional force" of youth. She describes this erotic energy as unrefined, and capable of being channeled into many different ventures—some positive, some negative: "The spontaneous joy, the clamor for pleasure, the desire of the young people to appear finer and better and altogether more lovely than they are, the idealization not only of each other but of the whole earth which they regard but as a theater for their noble exploits, the unworldly ambitions, the romantic hopes, the make-believe world in which they live, if properly utilized, what might they not do to make our sordid cities more beautiful, more comfortable?"[29]

This approach to sexual energy prefigures Audre Lorde's notion of the erotic as power. Lorde describes the erotic as "providing the power which comes from sharing deeply any pursuit with another person. The sharing of joy, whether physical, emotional, psychic, or intellectual, forms a bridge between the sharers which can be the basis for understanding much of what is not shared between them, and lessens the threat of their difference."[30] She equates the erotic with the impulse toward communal consummations of all forms. Lorde is dissatisfied with narrow patriarchal definitions of *erotic* as sexy or titillating. Similarly, although she was not intending an explicit feminist critique, Addams combats labeling adolescent explorations, including sexual ones, as immorality. Furthermore, Lorde's description of the erotic maps onto Addams's experience of starting Hull House. Although Addams was not an adolescent in 1892, she brought a youthful zeal to the project—forming a community with a passionate energy, albeit tempered by decorum. In this sense, Hull House was an erotic endeavor. Thus, Addams understood that young people could funnel their abundant energy into social actions if given the means to do so.

The realities of women's lives in the immigrant community of Hull House certainly must have had an impact on Addams's thinking about sexuality. For example, two Hull House residents, Alice Hamilton and Rachelle Yarros, became national leaders in the birth control movement. Hamilton conducted studies on neighborhood families and discovered a link between large families, infant mortality, and poverty.[31] Hamilton and Yarros helped make Hull House a center for sex education and the distribution of contraceptives.[32] Although Addams never became as visible a force in the birth control movement as she was for other social causes, she helped foster the climate at Hull House that made groundbreaking efforts in sex education and contraception possible. Given her managerial involvement, Addams likely endorsed the efforts of Yarros and Hamilton. Sex education is another example of the interplay between the learning and educating of Hull House residents.

In *A New Conscience and an Ancient Evil,* Addams devotes an entire chapter to the moral education and protection of children. She applauds efforts by public schools to teach "sex hygiene" but is concerned that parents often respond negatively to such instruction.[33] Addams, like Charlotte Perkins Gilman, suggests that social progress requires shifting some of the responsibilities historically undertaken within families to the community, given an increasingly complex and specialized world. Sex education is one of those responsibilities. Addams also notes resistance to public sex education among educators, claiming that many act as if they "had never known that at fifteen or sixteen years of age, the will power being still weak, the bodily desires are keen and insistent."[34]

Not wishing to saddle the schools with all the work, in a 1912 article, Addams boldly challenges religious organizations to engage in sex education: "If it is clear that youth is ensnared because of its ignorance of the most fundamental facts of life, then it is the duty of the Church to promote public instruction for girls and lads which shall dignify sex knowledge and free it from all indecency."[35] This statement is striking, given that some religious institutions are reluctant to engage in sex education one hundred years later. Note the positive tone that Addams desires for sex education. Although her own upbringing made discussion of sexuality uncomfortable, and her same-sex identification was repressed by society, Addams advocates widespread and positive sex education for young adults.

Addams left an important legacy in the field of adult education. Prior to her efforts at Hull House, literature on adult education was largely nonexistent. In *Twenty Years at Hull-House,* Addams describes an early project: "Hull House in the very beginning opened what we called College Extension classes."[36] She characterized these classes as popular and predating extension courses offered by the University of Chicago. Addams, conscious of the distinction between childhood and adult education, recognized that all students could not be treated the same way. In a 1908 encyclopedia entry, she indicated that the residents of Hull House hoped to develop a technique of teaching "especially adapted to Adults."[37]

Addams's philosophy of adult education does not radically differ from her philosophy of childhood education, but she acknowledges a difference in social relations when adults teach adults: "The relation of students and faculty to each other and to the residents was that of guest and hostess, and at the close of each term the residents gave a reception to students and faculty which was one of the chief social events of the season. Upon this comfortable social basis some very good work was done."[38] Her approach to adult education, which might be called "socializing education," includes a relative sense of equality between teachers and students, as well as a sense of social ease to make the education process more readily acceptable to those who might be reluctant to participate.

For Addams, contextual relevance is essential for adult education. She uses the phrase "education by the current event" to describe a pedagogical approach to adult education that turned widespread interest in a news story into socially connected learning. This approach foreshadowed modern problem-based learning. In *The Second Twenty Years at Hull-House,* Addams mentions the controversial Scopes trial, the coming to power of the Labour Party in Britain, and racial tensions as news items that spurred wider discussions of historical and theoretical import.[39] She uses the metaphor of fire to describe the attention a significant news item can garner: "The newly moralized issue, almost as if by accident, suddenly takes fire and sets whole communities in a blaze, lighting up human relationships and public duty with new meaning. The event suddenly transforms abstract social idealism into violent political demands, entangling itself with the widest human aspiration. . . . At such a moment, it seemed possible to educate the entire community."[40] This form of education requires flexibility that is not tied to strict curricular boundaries. Such flexibility is necessary to take advantage of opportunities to engage the intellectual imaginations of adult learners.

Addams's approach to adult education is expansive and inclusive: "It was the business of the colleges, broadly speaking, to hand down the knowledge that had thus been accumulated and if they kindled an ardor for truth, each succeeding generation would add to the building of civilization. It was the business of the settlements to do something unlike either of these things. It was the function of the settlements to bring into the circle of knowledge and fuller life, men and women who might otherwise be left outside."[41] For Addams, education is a lifelong responsibility for citizens of a democracy, but it does not have to be limited to a school classroom. Hull House sponsored clubs and public lectures in addition to the college extension courses that also contributed to communal learning.

Educational theorists Ira Harkavy and John L. Puckett argue that universities can learn a great deal from Addams and Hull House in regard to the role of higher education in our society. They criticize contemporary universities because too often "esotericism has triumphed over public philosophy, narrow scholasticism over humane scholarship."[42] Harkavy and Puckett contend that it is in the best interest of universities to engage more actively in the concerns of their communities and society at large. The pursuit of "pure" scholarship, unencumbered by the realities and vicissitudes of contemporary life, has led to a missed educational opportunity: "The separation of universities from society, their aloofness from real-world problems, has deprived universities of contact with a necessary source of genuine creativity and academic vitality."[43] They also suggest that such social engagement models good citizenship, thus creating further opportunities for connection and better relations with those antagonistic toward higher education. The authors cite Hull House's break with the University of Chicago, because of the latter's pursuit of academic professionalism over social progress and activism, as a significant ideological decision. This break was a turning point in educational history, marking an epistemological shift: "The changing relationship of Addams and her Hull House colleagues with the Chicago sociologists from the 1890s to the late 1910s mirrored the American university's transition from an outwardly directed, service-centered institution to an inwardly directed, discipline-centered institution. It was also a marker of the separation of knowledge production from knowledge use, indeed, of social science from social reform, by the end of the Progressive Era."[44] Harkavy and Puckett challenge universities to function more like Addams's Hull House and to reconnect their academic work with the advancement of society.

Addams did not intend her philosophy of education to manifest itself only in social settlements. Addams, Dewey, and Ella Flagg Young (1845–1918), the first female superintendent of the Chicago school system, shared a vision of using public school facilities as social centers engaged in lifelong learning programs for the community when the schools were not occupied with their primary duties.[45] In 1904, Addams described her fantasy of public schools evolving into social centers that mimic the function of social settlements: "A glimpse of Hull House shops on a busy evening incites the imagination as to what the ideal public school might offer during long winter nights, if it becomes really a 'center' for its neighborhood."[46] She mused about a business professional teaching an immigrant English and math skills in exchange for craft skills. Addams applied pragmatist values by envisioning tapping into the collective resources of society for mutual benefit through educative reciprocity. It was also a practical dream, because it foresaw maximizing the use of existing infrastructure to achieve lateral progress.

Addams's philosophy of adult education shifted somewhat over the first decade of Hull House's existence. At first, she replicated her positive experiences of higher education by offering the aforementioned college extension courses. As her criticisms grew about the increasingly abstract direction in which scholarship at the University of Chicago was headed, she realized that Hull House needed to change its offerings as well: "The educational efforts of a settlement should not be directed primarily to reproduce the college-type culture but to work out a method and an ideal adapted to adults."[47] Addams then turned her attention to more creative forms of adult education.

The Hull House Labor Museum

A unique Hull House educational project was the Labor Museum: a historical exhibit of industrial practices that included live demonstrations by elder members of the community. By integrating cultural history with contemporary relevance and active participation, the Labor Museum manifested Addams's philosophy of education. Not surprisingly, the idea for the museum grew out of Addams's experience of the community and her reflection on how to promote social progress. Reporting on the Labor Museum's first year of operation, she outlines three goals: educating visitors about industrial processes in a manner more "picturesque" and with more "charm" than is usually offered; giving young people a greater appreciation of the "social connection of their work"; and allowing older members of the neighborhood an opportunity to "assert a position in the community" of respect, particularly for those immigrant elders who had become alienated from younger generations consumed with enculturation.[48] Addams subsequently describes how the success of the museum was grounded in providing concrete and connected knowledge: "When the materials of daily life and contact remind the student of his lesson and its connections, it would hold his interest and feed his thought as abstract and unconnected study utterly fails to do. . . . People were attracted to the museum who had never cared to attend the other educational advantages offered by Hull House."[49]

Although intended to demonstrate industrial arts in a number of functional areas, the textile exhibit, particularly spinning wheels from a variety of cultures, proved the most popular and intellectually fruitful. With the physical demonstration of spinning on Saturday evenings as the centerpiece of the exhibit, the Hull House residents arranged lectures and informative displays on the history and implication of textile labor. Many Hull House projects and clubs participated in Labor Museum activities. The students of the music school even sang labor songs at various events. Addams describes the museum as "connected directly with the basket weaving, sewing, millinery, embroidery and dressmaking constantly being taught at Hull House, and so far as possible with the classes in design and drawing."[50] Thus, the textile exhibition was a springboard for cross-disciplinary learning that made education come alive for the neighborhood. She characterizes two educational principles that emerged from the museum experience: "first, that it concentrates and dramatizes the inherited resources of a man's occupation, and, secondly, that it conceives of education as 'a continuing reconstruction of experience.'"[51] Addams redistributed the learning process to promote lateral progress, but in the process she transformed education. She recognized that education reconstructs experience, and she wanted that reconstruction to be concrete and personal.

Although Addams viewed the Labor Museum as successful, it has had its critics. T. J. Lears accuses Addams of being complicit with oppressive forms of capitalism by making arduous industrial labor palatable. He thinks that she promoted a "therapeutic approach" to industrial work and that "the key to this process was the Hull House Labor Museum."[52] Lears contends that progressive reformers were misguided in not advocating the overturn of oppressive systems. He accuses Addams and other like-minded social activists of "unwittingly accommodat[ing] themselves to the corporate system of organized capitalism. Assuming that education alone could overcome alienated labor, Addams ended in an intellectual position scarcely different from the unctuous paternalism of the 'job enrichment' programs now run by giant corporations."[53]

Lears's critique would be appropriate if the Labor Museum were removed from its multifaceted theoretical context. In addition to historical, geographical, cultural, and industrial education, the museum included programs on "trade unionism" and histories of collective worker activities. Addams did not conceive of "industrial education" as the term is commonly used today. In her opinion, industrial education could and should participate in a liberal arts education. The factory laborer should know the place of his or her work in the world historically, politically, aesthetically, philosophically, and economically. The goal of such education is not just greater productivity, as is the explicit goal of job enrichment programs. Her brand of industrial education would provide workers with the tools to understand and question the nature of their labor. An educated labor force can use its collective intelligence to improve society. Addams could not support the idea "that industrial education is one thing, and cultural education is of necessity quite another,"[54] given, for example, that one of the impetuses for the Labor Museum was to reconnect alienated generations.

Addams was not the kind of radical that Lears wants her to have been. She sought "internal" revolutions of social relations between rich and poor, employer and employee, and parents and children, but she did not endeavor to violently overturn external structures of American society. Kelley, Kinney, and Addams were important labor advocates at a time when unions were not limited in scope, as they are today. Contemporary collective bargaining is statically locked into antagonistic relations but offers little vision of fundamentally transforming workers' relation to corporate ownership. Unlike the present, widespread belief at the beginning of the twentieth century was that collective bargaining would eventually transform corporations into more participatory organizations. The Labor Museum was conceived as an empowering educative endeavor that fit with a dynamic labor movement.

Education, Democracy, and Sympathetic Knowledge

Addams viewed democracy and education as inexorably entangled. Just as she employs an expansive definition of democracy, including a normative component of mutual care through sympathetic knowledge, she also interjects an educative mandate. She ties education to democracy by claiming that collective intelligence is necessary for an effective democracy; that education is a lifelong proposition, essential in allowing democracy to change and adapt; and that education connects or binds democratic citizens by creating important links of understanding between individuals.

Addams's notion of the collective intelligence of society required for lateral progress is egalitarian, emphasizing the dignity of each person in assuming that all should educate themselves not just for individual gain but for mutual advantage. She describes the educative requirement of democracy: "As democracy modifies our conception of life, it constantly raises the value and function of each member of the community, however humble he may be. We have come to believe that the most 'brutish man' has a value in our common life, a function to perform which can be fulfilled by no one else. We are gradually requiring of the educator that he shall free the powers of each man and connect him with the rest of life."[55] Addams advocates education as the prerogative of all, not just an elite few. She prefers consequentialist to rights-based arguments: "We have become convinced that the social order cannot afford to get along without [individual citizens'] special contribution."[56] Developing collective intelligence is an imperative of lateral progress. If all members of society are to move forward and make common cause, then its constituency must have the tools found in widespread educational opportunities for that advancement.

Addams combines her inclusive approach to education mentioned above with her emphasis on play to advocate recreation, broadly defined, for men and women, as well as for all age groups: "We are told that the imaginative powers, are realized more easily in the sphere of joy and release, which we have come to call recreation."[57] She views sport as a means for crossing social divisions through common concern as player and spectator: "The opportunity which the athletic field provides for discussion of actual events and for comradeship founded upon the establishment of just relationships is the basis for a new citizenship."[58] The physicality and practices of sport appeal to a common denominator of humanity: the body. At Hull House, organized corporeal activity brought together people of different nationalities and classes, thus providing another social opportunity for interpersonal transactions resulting in sympathetic understanding.

Addams's feminism is apparent in her approach to physical activity, as Hull House sponsored numerous women's athletic courses, dance programs, and a successful women's basketball team.[59] The opportunities for women to use their bodies in an expression of physicality were groundbreaking, because the cult of domesticity had severely limited women's physical activity. Recreation programs were available to working women and not just youths. Linda Tomko finds an empowering connection between the social opportunities offered adult women and their physical performances: "Working women's dancing bodies were important resources for experimenting with the measure of social and sexual autonomy that derived from their wage labor."[60] Thus physicality was another expression of women's independence and a form of education as women learned about their bodies and their ability to move in public space previously reserved for men. Addams provided an opportunity for women to grow in confidence about their place and power in society.

Ultimately, Addams advocates lifelong learning. Hull House offered various forms of formal education intended to increase knowledge for all who would have it—children, adolescents, and adults. Public lectures, the Labor Museum, playgrounds, and theater performances were all potential learning opportunities. Addams viewed society and its structures as growing, changing, and adapting. To keep up with this growth, change, and adaptation, citizens of a democracy require continuing education, broadly defined. Sympathetic understanding of others is not a goal to be achieved but rather an ongoing process to be worked at. Sympathetic knowledge relies on a commitment to comprehensive, constant learning.

Addams values both the content of an education and its social function. Social epistemology is the bedrock of sympathetic understanding. In her view, a pluralistic democracy relies on an informed citizenry—informed not only in propositional knowledge (this or that fact), but informed about the entanglements of one another's lives. In this respect, Addams thinks that children who grow up in the city have an advantage that educational programs should capitalize on. City children "learn a method of knowing each other, of revealing themselves one to another, of consciously living in a city, which those of us who were born in the country and brought into cities when we were quite grown up, will never be able to attain."[61] Although she does not deny the value of basic education, she considers all education in the context of its social situations: "The isolation of the school from life—its failure to make life of more interest, and show its larger aspects—the mere equipping of the children with the tools of reading and writing, without giving them an absorbing interest concerning which they wish to read and write, certainly tends to defeat the very purpose of education."[62] Addams views democracy as a form of morality grounded in education.

Progressive Reforms, a Century Later

Given the vast expanse of public education in the United States, it is difficult to generalize about the quality of learning. Nevertheless, there are some indications that instruction has become stuck in a long-term pedagogical rut. In a historical review of educational methods, Arthur N. Applebee notes that texts chosen for literature courses demonstrate "remarkable stability since the 1890s."[63] More important, Applebee is concerned that traditions of education in the United States have too frequently placed an emphasis on "knowledge-out-of-context rather than knowledge-in-action."[64] In his opinion, the bulk of education today consists of the rote memorization and articulation of propositional knowledge learned as discrete facts—knowledge-out-of-context. Accordingly, he argues for knowledge that is living because it is tied to present-day conversations about subjects that matter. Applebee favors learning methodologies that are active and emphasize participation as well as connection to wider social discourses. To be fair, there are many obstacles to pedagogical innovation in the United States, including insufficient funding, bureaucratic inertia, and mandated emphasis on quantitative forms of accountability that mimic the free market—all of which collectively favor knowledge-out-of-context. Addams's ideas about education reform continue to appear relevant a century after their formulation. As Lagemann describes, "It is because Addams's writings on education invite fundamental reconsideration of the way we organize and think about education that they are worth reading still."[65]

Two modern educational reforms harmonize with Addams's educational philosophy: service-learning and learning communities. Service-learning is achieving increasing national popularity among high schools and universities. As the name implies, "service" and "learning" can exist in a symbiotic relationship that provides benefits for each. Students typically engage in structured community service endeavors while simultaneously thematizing the experience through complementary reading and writing assignments.[66] The educational experience weaves together physical activity, ethical purpose, social transactions, and critical thinking to create a dynamic learning opportunity. Service-learning projects can include volunteering at women's shelters, crisis help lines, low-income housing projects, hospice care, or environmental clean-up campaigns. In this manner, confronting issues and people in the community makes education more compelling for many students. To the extent that service-learning is reciprocal, benefiting and changing both the recipient and the student, it resembles the work of Hull House.

Traditionally, the discipline of philosophy has little to do with service-learning. Professional philosophers stereotypically keep social projects at arm's length, preferring to address intellectual problems over practical ones. This was not the case for Progressive Era philosophers, and there are signs that increasing numbers of philosophers are endeavoring to return to making social relevance a priority. A reconceptualization of epistemology can participate in such a shift. Goodwin Liu suggests that philosophy should elevate alternative epistemologies that integrate contextualized, politicized, moral, and relational knowledge, which underwrites service-learning. For Liu, service-learning is a clarion call to reassess dominant discourses on the philosophy of knowledge. He describes the voices necessary to develop an operative service-learning epistemology: "Whatever more can be said about the relation between epistemology and service-learning should be said, I believe, not by an armchair philosopher, but by reflective practitioners who witness the actual ways in which teaching, learning, and knowing occur."[67] Jane Addams was a philosopher and a practitioner.

Some of the theorists of today's service-learning movement claim Addams in their genealogy not because she assigned service-learning projects in her classes but because her philosophy and service were so intimately enmeshed. Nicholas V. Longo awards Addams founder status: "Addams allows us a glimpse into the origins of service-learning as a practice, as opposed to a theory. A history of service-learning that takes account of Addams also locates the origins of service-learning not in the schools, but in the community. And it places the origins of service-learning squarely in the movement for the expansion of the role of women in public life. Jane Addams's work is also a valuable reminder that service-learning may be understood not only as an educational technique, but also as a craft, whose greatest value is the unpredictable creativity that it brings to our public life. Each of these lessons for service-learning—practice, community, gender, and craft—is also vital to our contemporary efforts to link community learning with civic education."[68] For Longo and Gary Danes, Addams is more than an important forebearer of service-learning. Her century-old work at Hull House continues to inspire and provide insight into an alternative approach to education not dependent on traditional concerns about programs and disciplines that mark the politics of academia: "Her emphasis on narrative and relationship over statistics and programs, and her ability to make good on the promise of collaboration among diverse people should impel others to greater agility and wisdom in service-learning work."[69]

Another contemporary endeavor in education that resonates with Addams's philosophy of education is the learning community. Although learning communities have various manifestations on college campuses, they have in common a commitment to a shared process of learning in which every member of the community contributes to the intellectual journey. The collective approach of learning communities stands in contrast to the single instructor–driven model of traditional educational experiences. In learning communities, the teacher/learner distinctions are blurred as the educational responsibilities are shared. Learning communities are most often interdisciplinary affairs guided by a theme or project rather than the absorption of a static body of knowledge. Hull House was a quintessential learning community. Residents brought varied skills and education together, not to achieve an educational objective, but to participate in a dynamic learning experience. Hull House lacked a financial incentive for its residents, but it did provide an intellectual one. Theory and practice, seminar and laboratory, Hull House was an unparalleled learning community with rich intellectual energy. Addams defined the settlement as "an institution attempting to learn from life itself."[70]

The concluding chapter of Nel Noddings's influential book *Caring* is dedicated to moral education. Noddings describes a reformulation of education that places caring at the heart of learning. She finds the growth and blossoming of individuals and society tied to fostering the ability to meet one another morally. To this end, she advocates comprehensive and lifelong learning grounded in affective relation: "Moral education is, then, a community-wide enterprise and not a task exclusively reserved for home, church, or school."[71] For Noddings, all education is moral education. Accordingly, the relationship of the teacher to the learner is not ancillary to what is learned, but an integral element in knowledge creation. Noddings does not dismiss the significance of propositional knowledge, but she finds the affective knowledge of caring just as important, not only for individual development but for the benefit of society as well. Addams did not have the language of care ethics available to her, but the social democracy she envisioned entailed interpersonal understanding through rich and varied caring transactions such as those found in play, the arts, and education, thereby providing the continual creation of sympathetic knowledge.

Christian proponents of the social gospel thought it benefited their cause to claim [Addams] as one of their own. But wishing could not make it so. Jane did not simply refuse to impose Christian beliefs on her neighbors, she declined to identify with organized Christianity herself.

—VICTORIA BROWN

CHAPTER 9

Civic Religion and Utopia

Many feminists are wary of sexist elements in the teachings, interpretations, and leadership of mainstream religious organizations. The domination of men over women is reified through sacredly ordained phenomena, making the task of deconstructing asymmetrical power relations in society all the more difficult. The messages and actions of mainstream Christian denominations in the United States have resisted women's empowerment through notions that wives should be subservient to husbands, that a woman's place is in the home, and that same-sex identification as well as reproductive control is sinful. In the nineteenth and twentieth centuries, feminists such as Elizabeth Cady Stanton and Charlotte Perkins Gilman risked public ridicule by daring to challenge the sexism found in religious institutions.

In the last decades of her life, Elizabeth Cady Stanton (1815–1902) was preoccupied with the gender oppression generated by religious institutions. In 1885, she wrote, "What power is it that makes the Hindu woman burn herself on the funeral pyre of her husband? Her religion. What holds the Turkish woman in the harem? Her religion. By what power do the Mormons perpetuate their system of polygamy? By their religion. Man, of himself, could not do this: but when he declares, 'Thus said the Lord,' of course he can do it. So long as ministers stand up and tell us that as Christ is the head of the church, so is man the head of the woman, who are we to break the chains which have held women down through the ages?"[1] By 1895, Stanton felt so strongly about the negative impact of religion that she wrote an alternative commentary on the Bible with the subversive title *The Woman's Bible*. In it, she disavows women's responsibility for bringing evil into the world, denies the divinity of Jesus, and does not accept the doctrine of the virginity of Jesus's mother, Mary.

In a similar critique, Addams's contemporary and friend, Charlotte Perkins Gilman, declares that "all the old religions made by men" are "forced on women whether they liked it or not."[2] In 1923, Gilman wrote *His Religion and Hers*, where, like Stanton, she feels compelled to challenge Christian tenets of social morality because of their promotion of gender oppression. Gilman describes male religion as "death-based" because of its preoccupation with individualism and the resulting bellicosity. "His" religion needs the corrective of "her" religion, which stresses social harmony and progress. Stanton and Gilman exemplify a significant branch of feminism that challenges the divine status of sexist theology and biblical hermeneutics. No such straightforward condemnation of religion came from Jane Addams.

Religion is not a topic that she addressed directly in any sustained manner, and with good reason: Addams was ambivalent about religion, personally and publicly. As a pragmatist, she found it difficult to accept significant tenets and dogmas of mainstream Christianity. Philosopher Richard Bernstein describes the pragmatist approach to religion: "Pragmatism is not indifferent or hostile to the religious life. It is not a form of 'aggressive atheism.' On the contrary, all the classical pragmatists argued that a pragmatic orientation can help us to clarify the concrete meaning of religious life. A major contribution of pragmatism has been its insistence on ongoing, open, fallibilistic public criticism. Pragmatism opposes all forms of dogmatism, fanaticism, and fundamentalism."[3] Accordingly, Addams resisted ideological alignment. Nevertheless, she recognized religion's social influence and knew it could be a motivating force for social progress. This was particularly apparent given the achievements of the contemporaneous social gospel movement, the religious version of the social settlement movement. Personally, Addams's identification with Christianity waxed and waned, but largely her identification was of a small "c" variety that had more in common with humanism than any specific denomination.[4] Addams admired the moral teachings of Jesus but never accepted the divinity of Christ.

The claim that Addams embraced a form of Christian humanism is vexing to some Addams scholars who wish to read into her work a level of religiosity that she simply never held. Given the imprint of Christianity on U.S. culture, there is a widespread belief that to be influential in a moral movement, an individual must be a devoted Christian. Addams was indeed very knowledgeable about Christianity because of her upbringing and her education at Rockford Seminary. Furthermore, from time to time she expressed a desire to reconcile herself to religious belief. Nevertheless, to characterize her as deeply religious is to ignore her writings and actions. Part of the confusion may derive from the character of Addams's feminist projects as compared with those of Stanton and Gilman. Addams was primarily interested in advancing social democracy through sympathetic understanding. Deconstructing existing power structures was useful to her as long as it assisted in the task of social progress. Stanton and Gilman sought to undermine oppressive religious institutions and were less concerned about building coalitions among social organizations. As a public philosopher who had to negotiate many institutions and forces, Addams found it useful to use her knowledge of Christianity to cajole the churches toward social progress. She chided religious institutions when necessary, but she never intentionally alienated them. Ultimately, Addams's religion was social progress, and her faith was in humanity.

What follows in this chapter suggests that Addams's philosophy is that of Christian humanism and that her frustrations over finding a moral vocation, combined with her religious uncertainty, lead her to reconstruct Hull House as a civic church and a feminist utopia.

Addams's Ambiguous Relationship with Christianity

From childhood, Addams was tenuous concerning her religious beliefs. There is every indication that she earnestly sought to share the Christian faith of her friends, but she was thwarted by her own rational reflection. In *Twenty Years at Hull-House,* Addams recounts a significant childhood conversation she had with her father. She confronted her father about her inability to understand the Christian concept of predestination (the idea that God, prior to human existence, determines who will achieve eternal salvation and who is destined for eternal damnation). As Addams explains it, her father was unconcerned by her lack of understanding: "He then proceeded to say other things of which the final impression left upon my mind was, that it did not matter much whether one understood [predestination] or not, but that it was very important not to pretend to understand what you didn't understand and that you must always be honest with yourself inside, whatever happened."[5] Whether her account is apocryphal or not, it does portend the approach to religion that she would hold, regardless of how sincere her desire to understand Christian spirituality was.

She gravitated toward the spirit of Christian concern for the well-being of fellow human beings while eschewing dogma, ritual, and theology.

Although John Addams did not send his daughter to Rockford Female Seminary to obtain a proper Christian education, evangelism and missionary work were the hallmarks of the school under the leadership of its founder and headmistress, Anna P. Sill. Of Sill, Addams writes, "She does everything for people merely from love of God alone and that I do not like."[6] The time that Addams spent at Rockford was a period of intense soul searching and spiritual questioning. In the close-knit women's community at the school, she was under considerable pressure to make an overt and active commitment to Christianity. Addams resisted "every sort of evangelical appeal," and she was "singularly unresponsive to these forms of emotional appeal."[7] Despite the evangelization, regular chapel, church-related activities, the Christian content of the curriculum, the prodding of her dearest friend, Ellen Gates Starr, and her fondness for translating the gospels from the Greek in private sessions with her favorite instructor, Sarah Blaisdell, Addams never accepted, nor denounced, Christianity.[8] Her resistance likely made evangelical efforts toward her more intense, because she was the visible social and intellectual leader on campus. Many found it irksome that she was not "more" of a Christian.

In an 1880 letter to Starr, Addams continued their ongoing discussion regarding Addams's lack of traditional Christian convictions: "Whatever else I am I mean to be honest in the subject of religion, I have tried to-day and made a failure."[9] Despite Addams's humility, the failure is not hers, but that of religion, and specifically Christian theology, to rationally persuade her of its veracity. She was neither comforted nor convinced by the central tenets of Christianity. Addams wrote to Starr, "you long for a beautiful faith and experience of this kind—I only feel that I need religion in a practical sense."[10] She described experimenting with prolonged periods of not praying only to find that she felt no worse off for the hiatus.[11]

Even in her mid-twenties, when she was baptized into a small Cedarville Presbyterian congregation in 1886, Addams equivocated about her Christianity.[12] In the one paragraph devoted to her baptism in *Twenty Years at Hull-House*, she interprets her baptism in social and political terms: "There was also growing within me an almost passionate devotion to the ideals of democracy, and when in all history had these ideals been so thrillingly expressed as when the faith of the fisherman and the slave had been boldly opposed to the accepted moral belief that the well-being of a privileged few might justly be built upon the ignorance and sacrifice of the many?"[13] Christianity is part of her personal identification only as an inspiration for social democracy. Religious dogma, even when central to Christian beliefs, did not sit well with Addams, as exemplified in her statement to Starr, "I don't think God embodied himself in Christ."[14] Neither her religious education nor the decade of illness and angst prior to starting Hull House brought Addams into any more harmony with Christianity, and yet, she did not disclaim it.

Addams, ever introspective, desired to resolve her spiritual quest and believed that such a resolution was necessary for her to be successful in her life's work. She decided to build her religion from "the Bible and observation, from books and people, and in no small degree from Carlyle."[15] She most identified with the early Christian movement before it had achieved institutional status. For Addams, the early underground church represented a purer form of Christianity focused on Jesus's teaching of love and committed to building a caring community rather than venerating a deified Christ figure. In the 1890s, Addams frequently wore a "Chi-Rho" cross, which Victoria Brown describes as "symbolic of the pre-Constantinian era, as well as a pre-crucifix era, when Jesus was a guide to peaceful love in this life, not disembodied salvation in the next."[16] Although Addams did not have the benefit of the historical scholarship of the twentieth century, she was correct to see the connection between early Christian communities and social settlements. Progressive Era social settlements and first-century Christian communities shared small-group autonomy, convictions about communal care, a lack of grand plans, and they enlisted prominent women leaders.[17] Hull House was founded as such a Christian community, employing Addams's definition of Christianity as a humanistic endeavor committed to social progress.

The Civic Church of Hull House

In *Twenty Years at Hull-House,* Addams reminisces about how early in the project she smugly used idealistic religious imagery to describe the settlement project as a "cathedral of humanity." She had hoped the settlement would "house a fellowship of common purpose" that could be "beautiful enough to persuade men to hold fast to the vision of human solidarity."[18] She saw that Christianity had the potential to contribute to lateral progress by motivating social activism as exhibited by Starr, the most religious of the Hull House residents. Ultimately, for Addams, Christianity was not an absolute or intrinsic good. As with feminism and socialism, she supported Christianity to the extent that it contributed to social cohesion and advancement. Addams's Christian convictions ran as deep as the religion's social utility. Her religious convictions lay with the care and advancement of humanity.

Addams's secular Hull House community poses a contrast in religious orientation to the social gospel movement as well as to many other social settlements. Historian Kathryn Kish Sklar acknowledges the unique position of Hull House: "Although Hull House residents have generally been interpreted as reformers with a religious motivation, it now seems clear that they were instead motivated by political goals. . . . In, but not of, the Social Gospel movement, the women of Hull House were a political boat on a religious stream advancing political solutions to social problems."[19] The settlement movement and the social gospel movement each shared a passion for social improvement, but social gospelers were explicitly working from a religious framework. Furthermore, many settlements exhibited a greater Christian character than did Hull House. Nevertheless, Hull House was not an atheistic endeavor, if atheism implies antagonism to religion and spirituality. Addams refused to align Hull House with any Christian church, but the residents were not adverse to cooperative efforts with religious organizations, nor did Addams shy away from having religious leaders speak at Hull House.

The religious status of Hull House was controversial when Addams was alive and remains a point of contention today. In Graham Taylor's autobiography, he indicates that the settlement movement embodied the spirit of the Pilgrims. In a letter to Taylor, Addams retorts, "the settlement was rather a revolt *against* Puritan conceptions than a continuation of them—a substitute of 'works' for dogma."[20] Although socialists claimed that Hull House was not radical enough, church officials frequently claimed that Hull House lacked sufficient religiosity. In 1903, the *Chicago Chronicle* dispelled the popular belief that Hull House was a Christian endeavor: "The fact that Hull house conducts its great work for the uplifting of humanity without religious teaching of any kind will be news to many people."[21] In *Twenty Years at Hull-House*, Addams recounts how she engaged in three years of lecturing for the Home and Foreign Missionaries in Chicago only to be rebuked when nominated for a trustee position because Hull House lacked religious instruction.[22]

Today, the dispute over Addams's religiosity continues. In an audacious critique of her work, R. A. R. Edwards decries her relationship to religion: "Addams used, in a fairly unreflective way, religious words to describe essentially secular concerns."[23] Edwards describes Addams as "naive" in her optimism about human nature, and as a result of this naïveté, her work is co-opted by capitalism. Edwards ultimately advocates that religious institutions keep their critical distance from society "abandoning a belief in progress."[24] Edwards is not the first commentator to accuse Addams (or progressives) of being naive, although he might be unique in claiming that Addams was unreflective. In *The Tragedy of American Compassion*, Marvin Olasky claims that Addams's philosophy and her work at Hull House helped set in motion a liberal system of dependency that would dominate social thinking for decades. Olasky mixes economic and religious commentary in his assessment of Addams: "Deletion of the idea of a sinful nature and delight in utopian hopes worked hand-in-hand, for if handouts no longer were corrupting, mass transformation down a broad highway of material distribution became not only possible but preferable. The settlement house movement's emphasis on volunteer residency was excellent, but its stress on societal transformation rather than personal change turned some of the settlement clients into means to an end."[25] Olasky implicates the lack of religiosity at Hull House in fostering a mistaken shift from the salvation of the individual to the salvation of society: "The settlement house movement, through its emphasis on the material over the spiritual and the political over the personal, became the inspiration of governmental social work programs of the 1930's and community action programs of the 1960's."[26]

Olasky's and Edwards's positions contrast with Eleanor Stebner's claim that Hull House was fundamentally a Christian community. Stebner contends that Addams "embodied a liberal Christian tradition that emerged within a growing pluralistic society."[27] This statement can only be true if "liberal" can be stretched to include denying the divinity of Jesus. Stebner overstates Addams's spirituality in a manner that longs to find a fundamental religious conviction that was not present. Her statements are not as exaggerated as those of theologian Georgia Harkness, who in 1960 claimed that what Addams "drew from the Gospels motivated her both to a faith in God and to works of love."[28] Addams is perceived as religious by some, and not religious enough by others, but such perceptions were incidental to Addams herself, who was more concerned with advocating social democracy.

Addams frequently wrote articles for religious periodicals such as the *Christian Century* and *Religious Education* and spoke at religious gatherings. She skillfully managed to be respectful while simultaneously offering sharp criticism of church organizations. She often used her familiarity with Christian discourse without revealing her own lack of religious conviction. Addams transcended simple dichotomous categories such as that of religious/not religious by offering an understanding of Christianity grounded in social action and devoid of theological dogma. In this manner, Hull House was a civic church and Addams was the pastor.

Only a few years after founding Hull House, and just prior to the publication of William T. Stead's social commentary, *If Christ Came to Chicago*, Addams wrote "A New Impulse to an Old Gospel." Here she outlines three motivations for social settlements. The first is to expand the notion of democracy beyond mere political forms, thus foreshadowing her book *Democracy and Social Ethics*. The second motivation arises out of realization that everyone shares in the social life, but there are many who are not allowed to participate fully. The third is what she refers to as a renaissance in Christianity grounded in humanitarianism. Addams engages in an exegesis of the gospels that reveals more about her religious philosophy than it does Christian history: "The impulse to share the lives of the poor, the desire to make social service, irrespective of propaganda, express the spirit of Christ, is as old as Christianity itself. We have no proof from the records themselves that the early Roman Christians . . . considered this 'good news' a religion. Jesus had imposed no cult nor rites. He had no truths labeled 'religious.' . . . His teaching had no dogma."[29] Addams's interpretation of Christianity reflects her own convictions: nondogmatic, unconcerned with religious institutions or theology, yet attracted to the religious potential for social activism. If Addams could mold Christianity according to these convictions—a pragmatist feminist Christianity—then she would be willing to be a Christian.

In a 1901 article, "The College Woman and Christianity," Addams crafts a critique and new vision of Christianity while skirting issues of theology. Addams claims that college-educated women can devote themselves to the work of Christianity, but she defines Christianity strictly in terms of social work. She begins by stating that Christianity must adapt to social circumstances. If it fails to do so, "it will suffer, rightly or wrongly, an eclipse in favor of a theory, doctrine, or a social life which shall exhibit sufficient energy to deal adequately with the social situation."[30] Similar criticism of religion underwrites concerns regarding religion from many feminists, including Addams's contemporaries, and modern scholars such as Mary Daly, Rosemary Radford Ruether, and Elisabeth Schussler Fiorenza. These intellectuals observe that most institutional religions hold to historical positions, such as limiting the roles of women, against countervailing contemporary evidence. Addams's commitment to progress, which leads her to believe that morality and democracy must adapt to present circumstances, also extends to religion.

Ever careful to walk the fine line between confrontation and antagonism, Addams defends Christianity while continuing to prod: "We are not willing to admit that Christianity showed a loss of power of adaptation, which is the unfailing symptom of decadence."[31] She suggests that Christian humanism grounded in social activism has much to offer college women. According to Addams, academic life can become fixated on preparation rather than action; it can promote alienation between the college-educated and those who are not; and it can produce graduates who are too concerned with reflection and not "ready to act." She concludes the article by praising Jesus, who "alone of all great teachers made a masterly combination of method, aim and source of motive power."[32] Addams's praise does not contain any attribution of divinity but notably couches Jesus as a social activist.

Addams's critique of religion, although never dismissive, became more severe over the course of her career. In 1909, and again in 1911, Addams demonstrated her ability to identify with Christianity while simultaneously undermining it. She wrote "The Reaction of Modern Life upon Religious Education" and "Religious Education and Contemporary Social Conditions" for *Religious Education*. In these articles, Addams is not afraid to label the Christian church as a "failure" in regard to inspiring young people and adjusting to face modern social problems.[33] She reiterates the moral mandate of the Christian churches to address social problems if they are to remain viable social institutions. She claims, "There are several reasons why life at this moment should have seemed more real outside of that which we call the religious world, than it did within it."[34] Addams chides the churches for failing to combat poverty and oppressive working conditions: "The church apparently felt no lure in the hideously uncouth factories in which men sometimes worked twelve hours a day for seven days in the week until they were utterly brutalized by fatigue; nor in the unsanitary tenements so crowded that the mere decencies of life were often impossible; nor in the raw towns of newly arrived immigrants where the standard of life was pushed below that of their European poverty unmitigated either by natural beauty or social resources."[35]

With autobiographical resonance, Addams accuses religious educators of alienating "ardent young people" who are smitten with a social impulse but find no satisfactory outlet in Christian theology and practices. She views the Christian churches as overly concerned with individual salvation at the expense of social progress, and she makes it clear that she is not beholden to any denominational doctrine: "The particular faith from which we preach is not important" as long as the message includes social morality. She continues, "Conduct is the supreme and efficient test of religious validity."[36] Addams repeats the assertion that religious institutions must evolve: "To convince thousands of young people of the validity of religion, the church must go out to meet them both willing to take their point of view, and to understand social methods."[37] She demands of religion what she demands of democratic citizenship: sympathetic understanding and the flexibility to adjust to social conditions. For Addams, a rigid dogmatism of individual salvation is not merely wrongheaded, it indicates a moral failure to respond to contemporary needs. Although leaving the door open to the empowering potential of humanistic religion, she makes no concession to Christian theology. In these articles, Addams fails to mention God or the divinity of Jesus while addressing Christianity. She enlists her hero, Abraham Lincoln, as a role model for her view that religious conviction should be grounded in social morality. She claims that Lincoln was no "religious individualist," but, like herself, "he saw the promise of religion, not for one man, but in the broad reaches of national affairs and in the establishment of social justice."[38] Because Lincoln is the quintessential American, Addams is hinting that a socially grounded religiosity is part of the American tradition.

In 1927, Addams contributed an article to the *Christian Century* titled "A Book That Changed My Life." Although making no personal religious commitments, she carefully constructs an essay that again challenges Christianity and praises humanism. Discussing Tolstoy's *What Then Must We Do?*, Addams acclaims Tolstoy's "religious impulse to share in the sacrament of work" as a powerful and influential religious impulse.[39] She finds Tolstoy's morality more authentic than that of the leaders of the Christian churches who think that "they were emphasizing the social message of Christianity."[40] She appreciates Tolstoy's radical solidarity with laborers. For Addams, Tolstoy is a Christian who does not merely write in behalf of the poor but follows up his words with direct action. Her reflections on Tolstoy are complex. As previously mentioned, Addams views Tolstoy as setting an impractical standard for social service, although she admires his dedication to principles. Despite her differences with his methodology, she still praises his social convictions. Addams uses Tolstoy's work to imply a lack of ecclesiological integrity when it comes to Christian concern for the oppressed.

If the purpose of Christianity, as Addams's writing indicates, is to bring about social progress through communal understanding and action, or sympathetic knowledge, then Hull House was a form of civic church. The work done there gave its secular ministers, the residents, a meaningful vocation and a sense that they were participating in a transcendent endeavor: creating a dynamic social organism. This work represented a "realized eschatology"—trying to make heaven on earth. The neighborhood around Hull House never achieved anyone's image of heaven, but a sense of hope was restored to many. To make this possible, Addams not only worked to bring about positive change in the here and now, but as manifested in her writing, she imagined a better future.

A Feminist Pragmatist Utopia?

Whether we trace utopian theory to Thomas More's *Utopia* or Plato's *Republic*, philosophy has a long-standing relationship to an idealized state of communal being. Among feminists, utopian literature is particularly rich, partly out of a motivation that "there must be something better than this," and partly because of the fundamental feminist belief that oppressive social relations are constructed, and therefore changeable. Hull House is rarely considered in the utopian literature, and it is seldom conceived as a feminist utopia. This is understandable because Hull House included male residents, albeit in a separate apartment; had few if any founding principles, utopian or otherwise; and was situated in the middle of one of the most overpopulated and destitute parts of the city. Halsted Street in Chicago hardly elicits traditional utopian imagery of harmonious communities operating in bucolic settings. Nevertheless, Hull House was a utopia of a certain sort: a feminist pragmatist utopia.

Hull House was created by women, for women, was often funded by women, and addressed issues that were important to women—sex education, contraception information, child care, labor organizing, and athletic expression, among others. As a woman-centered utopia, Hull House was an exception to the rule. According to Patricia Huckle, of the five hundred utopian communities created in the nineteenth century, there was only one in the extant records that was developed by and for women—and she does not include Hull House.[41] Much of the analysis on feminist utopias of that era centers on fictional accounts rather than physical communities. In the twentieth century, the rising tide of feminism led to experiments in communal living, as well as further literary explorations. Huckle claims that feminist utopias of the twentieth century were particularly concerned with eliminating social oppression.[42] Hull House straddled the two centuries and pointed the way for later feminist communities.

How are feminist utopias differentiated from other utopias? Elaine Hoffman Baruch, who coedited an anthology of feminist utopias, offers a few distinctions: "If male utopias, whether in literary or social thought, seek to turn the world upside down, then feminism is the arch utopia with its negation not only of a particular social order, but of the entire principle of patriarchy."[43] According to Baruch, although male utopias often exchange freedoms for uniform rules and regulations, women's utopias tend to seek the freedoms that society does not offer. Many male utopias imagine an ideal state; feminist utopias tend to be stateless. Another significant difference is played out over the human body. Some male utopias have sought escape from the "tyranny" of sexuality by imposing restrictions beyond the then-current social norms. Feminist utopias tend to emphasize sexual liberty, some by including the acceptance of lesbian relationships.[44] In the utopian novel *Herland,* Addams's contemporary, Charlotte Perkins Gilman, envisions a world without men in a society perpetuated through parthenogenesis. Heterosexuality is not necessary and not missed.

Hull House can be viewed as a feminist utopia, given Baruch's parameters. It imposed few regulations and provided women with freedoms they could not experience elsewhere. Robyn Muncy describes the empowering nature of the Hull House community: "Settlements promised women independence from their families, unique possibilities for employment, and the sort of communal living arrangement they had cherished in college."[45] For most women of this era who wished to avoid social stigmatization, the choice was often between marriage, which entailed surrendering career plans for devotion to husband and children, or religious life, which entailed living under the constraints of patriarchal religious institutions. Hull House was such a unique opportunity for women that Eleanor Stebner suggests theorists lack a "conceptual language to talk about women living and working together, tying together spiritual, vocational, and friendship ideals" outside of a religious understanding.[46] Hull House residency required a commitment to social interaction and improvement, plus labor to maintain the household, in return for cooperative support and opportunities to pursue one's chosen profession. Not everyone was comfortable with this commitment. For example, Gilman, a lifelong admirer of Addams, could manage only a brief residency at Hull House because she was uncomfortable with the group's difficult social endeavors given the blighted conditions of the neighborhood. Nevertheless, those who aligned with the mission of the group flourished, and they often moved on to other projects of their own. Hull House was clearly not a controlling, totalizing utopia, as its residents rejoiced when their colleagues took on endeavors outside the community.

Sexuality was a largely unspoken component of Hull House's utopian existence. Addams set the tone for a women's space that was accepting and supportive of lesbian relationships—without using overt sexual language. Most, but not all, of the women who led Hull House, including Addams, did not enter into romantic relationships with men, and many had long-term, committed relationships with other women activists. Addams began Hull House in a close relationship with Ellen Gates Starr, but that faded when Mary Rozet Smith became Addams's constant companion and life partner. Hull House was a living utopia for women who wished to resist compulsory heterosexuality. Feminist historian Gerda Lerner refers to Addams as a *deviant* from male-defined norms.[47] Shannon Jackson describes Hull House as exhibiting a form of queer bonding in the creation of alternative family arrangements.[48] Intimate relations among residents, exhibited by pet names and effusive statements of affection, served to provide a structure of support for women residents who confronted the challenges of a patriarchal society not entirely certain of whether to embrace or rebuke these reformers. A community of middle-class, neo-Victorian women using polite euphemisms to confront social issues of the day might not be a common image of a feminist utopia, but in the late nineteenth and early twentieth centuries, Hull House was an important feminist enclave.

Although feminist utopias are intelligible, the term *pragmatist utopia* seems to be an oxymoron. If pragmatist philosophy is based on the centrality of human experience, how can it muster language to characterize utopias that are by definition beyond that which is currently experienced? Pragmatists keep utopias at arm's length. John Stuhr argues that "pragmatism, a faith in intelligence, carries no overarching or advance guarantees . . . supports neither utopian thinking nor even optimism in the abstract."[49] The challenge lies in the definition of utopia. If utopia is defined as an abstract state of perfection, then indeed pragmatists have cause to be wary. Such utopias tend to have an unattainable, static *telos*, with a totalitarian vision of policies and behavior. A single image of perfection that locks in values universally accepted by its constituents makes up the "end-state utopia" that has become a pariah to philosophers. Such static visions of utopia defy critical thinking and reflection in lieu of an overarching ideology. In *The Task of Utopia*, Erin McKenna describes four forms of utopia: end-state, anarchist, process, and feminist models. McKenna identifies an end-state utopia as preoccupied with ends over means; as having a static imagination, whereby followers work toward a goal, but subsequently return to a passive, spectator position; as pursuing conformity among its members; and as having a dualistic notion of perfection. Pragmatists like Addams do not seek such a utopia.

Hull House was a pragmatist utopia because it valued direct experience, experimental inquiry, and action while recognizing its own fallibility. By locating "among the common throng,"[50] those in the settlement movement accumulated knowledge that was leveraged into action. Given the surrounding squalor, Hull House residents did not have the luxury to seek absolute certainty but instead attempted to attain sufficient understanding so as to inform expedient action. As Addams describes, "It was the function of the settlements to bring into the circle of knowledge and fuller life men and women who might otherwise be left outside."[51] When, in "The Function of a Social Settlement," Addams sets out to delineate its purpose, she turns to John Dewey and William James on the relationship between knowledge and action. She cites Dewey: "When a theory of knowledge forgets that its value rests in solving the problem out of which it has arisen, that of securing a method of action, knowledge begins to cumber the ground. It is a luxury, and becomes a social nuisance and disturber."[52] Similarly, Addams quotes William James's famous speech introducing pragmatism: "Beliefs, in short, are really rules of action, and the whole function of thinking is but one step in the production of habits of action."[53] Addams later chided academic endeavors for relinquishing their social commitment and moving to an even more abstract, distant, and professional stance.

American pragmatists, particularly those of the Chicago school, have made social ethics and social improvement a significant part of their philosophy. Such a moral agenda requires a vision beyond current experience, a sense of how things might be better. If a utopia has a more tenuous vision—one that is amendable, fallible, and pluralistic, as well as responsive to new experience—then it can be understood as pragmatist. Erin McKenna reads Dewey as providing five criteria for a "great community": (1) Provide free and open participation to help develop critical habits of the mind. (2) View both limits and possibilities so as to find realistic choices of action. (3) Avoid dogmatism. (4) Avoid narrowly focusing on single or specific ends. (5) Facilitate new possibilities through an awareness of interconnectedness and diversity.[54] Rather than an unattainable vision, Dewey's utopia is just past the horizon, an ends-in-view, with the difference between the goal state, or ends, and the journey, or means, not nearly as clear as in the more rigid end-state utopia.[55] Therefore, pragmatist utopias can exist in the present as ongoing works in progress.

According to McKenna, a process utopia is marked by a cycle of achievable visions, referred to as ends-in-view, which once achieved become the means to the next goal.[56] The utopia described is tenuous and dynamic rather than fixed and perfect. Means and ends are collapsed into one another such that the path is almost as important as the goal, and perhaps unfolds into the goal. Hull House clearly met this standard of fluidity as it moved from one campaign to another—sometimes successful and sometimes not so successful, but always looking to fill the next need dictated by the neighborhood. McKenna describes the characteristics of the process/ends-in-view model as participatory, realistic (in terms of considering the past and present circumstances), flexible (and thus able to adjust to unforeseen variables), integrative of means and ends such that the goal does not overshadow the skills necessary to achieve it, and open to new possibilities for further ends-in-view. The boarding cooperative, Jane Club, was just one of many projects that demonstrate how Hull House exemplified this process model of utopia.

McKenna views process utopias and feminist utopias as sharing a great deal in terms of rejecting dualisms and hierarchy, but feminist utopias emphasize pluralism and recognition of the multiple communities that everyone is a part of.[57] Of course, not only was Hull House a woman-centered operation and a woman-centered community, it existed at the nexus of multiple communities. In addition to interacting with the eighteen immigrant groups that lived in its immediate neighborhood,[58] it was also the crossroad for those from all points on the educational and class continuum to meet. Charlene Haddock Seigfried describes Addams's approach: "By seeking to include in the process all those who are affected, Addams rejects the top-down imposition of solutions by political, professional, religious, or other elites. Instead, she provides a means to empower participants as they collectively work to establish and carry out common ends."[59] Addams's Hull House was an amalgamation of activities in support of multiple communities, thus meeting McKenna's criteria for a feminist utopia.

Hull House residents were not end-state utopians. Some have criticized them as naive in the belief that they could end poverty and antagonism on the streets of Chicago, but this was never their claim.

Utopia without Ideology

The claim that Hull House was a feminist pragmatist utopia is important for at least three reasons. First, the notion of feminist pragmatism is relatively new and unexplored. Seigfried coined the term in 1996, and although she offers a cogent argument for efficacious connection, the idea has not exactly taken philosophy by storm. A handful of scholars have adopted the moniker of feminist pragmatist, but mainstream American philosophers and mainstream feminist philosophers have not embraced the integration. Hull House provides a concrete historical example of one version of how feminist pragmatism in action might look, and Addams demonstrates how to integrate the two in philosophy. Hull House and the writings of Addams can provide a fruitful experiment in how feminism and pragmatism can work with one another.

Second, recognizing Hull House as a feminist pragmatist utopia can give philosophers permission to dream. Despite Stuhr's claim that pragmatist philosophers avoid utopias, perhaps, like Richard Rorty, they can dream: "My sense of the holy, insofar as I have one, is bound up with the hope that someday, any millennium now, my remote descendants will live in a global civilization in which love is pretty much the only law. In such a society, communication would be domination-free, class and caste would be unknown, hierarchy would be a matter of temporary pragmatic convenience, and power would be entirely at the disposal of the free agreement of a literate and well-educated electorate."[60] The dreams do not have to be of a universalized notion of perfection, but why can't philosophy take the risk of offering tenuous, fallible, and amendable visions of a better life? The example of Hull House models a way of being and working together that does not require perfect replication but instead provides a glimpse of human potential worthy of striving for. Hull House represents not a utopia of ends, but a utopia of means. It is the shared journey and struggle that is utopian.

Finally, philosophy desperately needs social engagement of the sort Hull House offered. Addams created a working balance between action and reflection. Evenings at Hull House were often filled with lively debates while the days were busy with working for social improvement. The residents were neither knee-jerk reactionaries nor were they disengaged theorists. They were college-educated, intelligent women working out their ideas while striving to help the community. Today, the bulk of society considers philosophers to be quirky academics whose jobs might be eliminated as frivolous if a liberal arts education ever fell out of favor. Addams was a levelheaded social organizer and philosopher who defies the stereotype. William James once said, "What *you* want is a philosophy that will not only exercise your power of intellectual abstraction, but that will make some positive connexion with this actual world of finite human lives."[61] Jane Addams's work exemplified just such a philosophy.

Hope is an indispensable seasoning in our human,
historical experience. Without it, instead of history
we would have pure determinism. — PAULO FREIRE

Certainly in America we have a chance to employ
something more active and virile, more inventive,
more in line with our temperament and tradition,
than the mere desire to increase commercial
relations by armed occupation. — JANE ADDAMS

Afterword

COSMOPOLITAN HOPE

The social philosophy of Jane Addams supports hope rooted in cosmopolitanism. She is hopeful that war can be mitigated, racism curtailed, and
that labor can be made fulfilling. Addams is also hopeful that democracy, her
term for a rich social morality, will flourish in an educative atmosphere of
inquiry and meaningful exchanges. She is confident that society can "extend
democracy beyond its political expression" if America can live up to its ideals and
update its expression to match the needs of the time.[1] Addams did not hold an
unfounded hope. She translated her social philosophy into action on a regular
basis, accomplishing intermediary advancements toward her vision of social
democracy. This social democracy welcomes and is empowered by pluralism
rather than flees from it. In the words of her contemporary, Graham Taylor,
Addams not only had a "sense of being identified with others, but also gives
others the sense of being identified with her. This constitutes her democracy
and makes her its most prophetic interpreter."[2] Because of this sense of shared
identification, Addams was able to coalesce the activities of others around her
hopes for democracy to motivate action.

Jane Addams in a contemplative mood, ca. 1890s.

Hope is not a term one finds in *The Oxford Dictionary of Philosophy,* but it has received attention from theorists who wish to give social philosophy a sense of purpose. For example, philosopher Patrick Shade develops a pragmatist notion of hope as "conditioned transcendence," which balances grounding hope in present conditions with producing new and better conditions.[3] His pragmatist theory of hope is eminently practical because it maintains an ability to motivate and sustain those working for social change without relying on the cosmological justice of a supernatural being. As such, we are ultimately responsible for hope's creation and re-creation. Shade draws on the work of Peirce, James, and Dewey, and in particular the pragmatist understanding of ends-in-view as descriptive of hope as an activity. An end-in-view collapses means and ends such that the end is continuous with the means, and can lead to further as well as multiple other ends-in-view. For Shade, it is habits of hope, particularly persistence, resourcefulness, and courage, that help sustain us and bring us closer to the ends of hope.[4] He concludes his uplifting account of hope's practicality with a chapter on celebrating hope in stories both fictional and historical. The chapter praises volunteerism and briefly mentions the work of the founder of the Catholic Worker movement, Dorothy Day, as indicative of "active involvement in ends whose realization does not solely or immediately affect ourselves. It thus represents the growth of agency and the expansion of horizons of meaning in light of new and diverse ends and means."[5] Shade makes no mention of Addams, although her social philosophy fits his description of pragmatist hope so well.

Addams did not posit a supernatural basis for hope. The work of Hull House was relatively unique among settlements for its lack of religious foundation.[6] Her hope rested with the proven ability of human beings to overcome barriers and sympathetically understand one another. For example, when Addams set out to combat prostitution, or more accurately, sexual slavery, she drew hope from the country's ability to overcome slavery.[7] She made no reference to divine intervention, but instead hailed the resilience of the country and its leaders to progress beyond the blight of racial domination. Similarly, Addams held out hope for lateral economic progress led by labor organizing. To help achieve this end, she assisted the local labor organizations in multivariate and unique ways. She exhibited the characteristics that Shade describes as sustaining hope: persistence, resourcefulness, and courage. Addams's work moves beyond the common definition of volunteerism in that her efforts cannot be compartmentalized: Addams lived her dream of social democracy at Hull House. All of her work, reflection, and writing are aligned behind a hope for a better future.

Two contemporary theorists who engage in extended discussions of hope are bell hooks and Paulo Freire. What is intriguing about their engagement with hope is that, like Addams, they juxtapose education, social justice, and hope. In *Pedagogy of the Oppressed,* Freire offers a theory of education to subvert systems of domination: "The central problem is this: How can the oppressed, as divided, unauthentic beings, participate in developing the pedagogy of their liberation? Only as they discover themselves to be 'hosts' of the oppressor can they contribute to the midwifery of their liberating pedagogy."[8] Freire views the "banking approach" to education as fostering a disconnection and gulf between the teacher and student that transforms students into passive entities susceptible to domination. For education to be libratory, it must reconnect student, teacher, and inquiry, and in doing so help reconnect a world torn apart. "The teacher is no longer merely the one-who-teaches, but one who is himself taught in dialogue with the students, who in turn while being taught also teach. They become jointly responsible for a process in which all grow."[9] He describes education as the crucial means of knitting humanity back together to embrace a common journey. No matter how bleak circumstances may be, education provides the hope for action and change. For Freire, social justice begins with "the preeminence of education experience and . . . its eminently ethical character, which in its turn leads us to the radical nature of 'hope.' In other words, though I know that things can get worse, I also know that I am able to intervene to improve them."[10]

bell hooks also valorizes hope but contributes a feminist character to Freire's libratory theory. She agrees with Freire's integration of justice, education, and hope in insisting that "progressive educators, democratic educators, must be consistently vigilant about voicing hope and promise as well as opposition to those dominating forces that close off free speech and diminish the power of dialogue."[11] However, hooks goes further in her notion of inclusion by embracing "radical openness" and distinguishing diversity from pluralism. Quoting from Judith Simmer-Brown, hooks understands diversity as "a fact of modern life—especially in America," whereas pluralism is the response to the phenomenon of diversity.[12] Accordingly, education should not strive for assimilation but rather create community out of diversity, and in turn that community becomes a wellspring for hope.[13]

The resonance between the social philosophies of Addams, hooks, and Freire is striking. Each views hope as an action verb, not as a passive state of wishing. As Addams states, "We continually forget that the sphere of morals is the sphere of action."[14] Addams also sees the libratory implications of education and sought to make Hull House a thoroughgoing educational institution with illuminating implications for class, race, and gender. For Hull House residents, the distinction between teacher and student was blurred, as all shared in journeys of inquiry. Like hooks, Addams finds great hope for the world in the local experiences of pluralistic community building. She embraces the potential of cosmopolitan community—a community not built on homogeneity nor merely an amalgamation of autonomous agents, but a community actively valuing points of continuity and discontinuity among its members.

A Cosmopolitan Future

In a world made ever smaller and interdependent, philosopher Kwame Anthony Appiah finds the term *cosmopolitanism* a hopeful approach to the border crossings necessary to address modern ethical dilemmas. The notion of "citizens of the cosmos" reframes moral concerns around that which is shared across diverse peoples rather than absolute claims of right and wrong. Appiah explains, "Cosmopolitans suppose that all cultures have enough overlap in their vocabulary of values to begin a conversation. But they don't suppose, like some universalists, that we could all come to agreement if only we had the same vocabulary."[15] Rather than principles of adjudication, Appiah esteems the experience of diversity as invigorating the requisite empathy and imagination for individuals to understand the standpoint of others and thus work toward solutions to social problems, even if the requisite agreement on values is not yet present. For Appiah, discussions across boundaries of identity start with "imaginative engagement," and such conversations foster an affective process of familiarity that is perhaps more important than a rational attempt to gain widespread assent to a moral argument.[16]

Addams's commitment to cosmopolitan ideals goes beyond many of her fellow progressives. For Addams, cosmopolitanism is a phenomenon grounded in the multicultural experience of the big city: "Because of their differences in all external matters, in all of the non-essentials of life, the people in a cosmopolitan city are forced to found their community of interests upon the basic and essential likenesses of their common human nature; for, after all, the things that make men alike are stronger and more primitive than the things that separate them."[17] Addams comes to a cosmopolitan outlook as an extension of her interactions in Chicago. She daily witnessed the conflict of cultures and subsequent resolutions that occurred in the city and felt that much was to be gained from getting to know the rich diversity of people in her neighborhood. She foreshadows the conclusions of Iris Marion Young, who opposes attempts to formulate "ideal communities" and who suggests that city life provides a non-utopian ideal of the "being together of strangers in openness to group difference."[18] Addams and Young are comfortable with the plurality of "unassimilated otherness" found in the city.[19] Social justice in such an environment does not derive from homogenization of the community, but rather through a group process respectful of all the voices within the community: in a word, cosmopolitanism. Addams claims, "I believe that when we once apprehend the international goodwill which is gathering in the depths of the cosmopolitanism peoples, that we will there discover a reservoir of that moral devotion which has fostered 'the cause of the people,' so similar in every nation, throughout all the crises in the world's history."[20] She proposes that cosmopolitanism fosters sympathetic understanding, which in turn makes violent conflict less possible.

Cosmopolitanism operates within the tension between the one and the many: between diversity and commonality. Although pluralism is celebrated, cosmopolitanism also seeks common ground among the diversity. Addams's social democracy revels in that tension: "As the acceptance of democracy brings a certain life-giving power, so it has its own sanctions and comforts. Perhaps the most obvious one is the curious sense which comes to us from time to time, that we belong to the whole, that a certain basic well being can never be taken away from us whatever the turn of fortune."[21] Note that Addams is not comforted by a higher power. Her demanding social democracy that calls for sympathetic understanding constitutes a connected community that emerges out of the diversity. That connected community brings hope grounded in a faith in humanity. Addams experienced and wrote about the local workings of cosmopolitan ethics and extended the idea globally.

A Jane Addams Moment

At the outset of the twenty-first century, hope is a precious commodity. War, political scandal, and corporate disasters have created a warranted cynicism over collective efforts, while the celebrated material success of an elite class reinforces the pursuit of egoistic endeavors. It appears that the only sense of progress prevalent today is one rooted in individual material success. Simultaneously, philosophers suffer from a perception of disengagement that has left few publicly recognized intellectual leaders. This perceived disengagement gives the appearance that philosophy is ill-equipped to offer suggestions for reinvigorating the notion of social advancement. Seigfried notes the significance of philosophical disengagement: "I think that for the good of the world in which we live and for our own self-respect as philosophers, it is vitally important for us to relate rational arguments and intellectual rigor to the state of the world today and the pressing cultural, social, economic, and political issues which face all of us."[22] Seigfried is not merely arguing to repair the academic discipline of philosophy, but because philosophy represents a crucial component of the reflective life of humanity, repairing philosophy means helping the world understand its potential. Similarly, bell hooks laments the cynicism surrounding feminism:

In recent years mass media have told the public that the feminist movement did not work, that affirmative action was a mistake, that combined with cultural studies all alternative programs and departments are failing to educate students. To counter these public narratives it is vital that we challenge all this misinformation. That challenge cannot be simply to call attention to the fact that it is false; we also must give an honest and thorough account of the constructive interventions that have occurred as a consequence of all our efforts to create justice in education. We must highlight all the positive, life-transforming rewards that have been the outcome of collective efforts to change our society, especially education, so that it is not a site for the enactment of domination in any form.[23]

A rediscovery of the social philosophy of Jane Addams can help reconnect philosophy to the world and interject hope in the power of reflection and action to build a better society.

Addams is a monumental figure of the early twentieth century, but she is also the most significant feminist pragmatist intellectual who captures and reinforces a progressive social philosophy. Her social philosophy of sympathetic knowledge need not be lost. Historian Howard Zinn describes the potential for historical continuity: "Surely history does not start anew with each decade. The roots of one era branch and flower in subsequent eras. Human beings, writings, invisible transmitters of all kinds, carry messages across the generations."[24] The social philosophy of Jane Addams reminds us of an idea that was so viable a century ago: a rich social democracy that values lateral progress can advance through processes of sympathetic knowledge.

NOTES

INTRODUCTION. A REMARKABLE LIFE, A REMARKABLE MIND

1 For those unfamiliar with Addams, I recommend beginning your exploration by reading her autobiographical work, *Twenty Years at Hull-House*. Here, Addams describes the first half of her life and the beginning of her great odyssey as part of the social settlement movement. Alternatively, I suggest reading one of the modern biographies (see the bibliography of this book), particularly because much has been discovered about her life that early biographies did not address. In addition, early biographies tended toward romantic hagiography.

2 Tarbell, *The Business of Being a Woman*, 104.

3 Historian Rosalind Rosenberg observes the tremendous impact Hull House had on the field of social work, noting that in 1889, "less than 3 percent of all social workers were women. By 1910 women were a majority, due largely to Addams's efforts." Rosenberg, *Divided Lives*, 29.

4 Addams, "A Function of the Social Settlement," 187.

5 Curti, "Jane Addams on Human Nature," 240.

6 Romano, "Mulling (Not Hulling) Jane Addams," B11.

7 Addams, "The Subjective Necessity for Social Settlements." Addams, "The Objective Value of a Social Settlement." Addams, "A Function of the Social Settlement."

8 Addams, "A Function of the Social Settlement," 186.

9 Ibid.

10 Ibid.

11 Brown, *The Education of Jane Addams*, 295.

12 James quoted in Lasch, *The Social Thought of Jane Addams*, 62.

13 Jessie A. Charters, a student of John Dewey in his last years at the University of Chicago, wrote, "One of my pleasant recollections [of a 1901 philosophy course] is of Dr. Dewey inviting Jane Addams to his class, his tributes to her, and his having us students buy Jane Addams *Democracy and Social Ethics*" (quoted in Seigfried, "Socializing Democracy," 219).

14 Seigfried, "Where Are All the Pragmatist Feminists?" 10–14.

15 For example, leading American philosopher John J. Stuhr's *Genealogical Pragmatism: Philosophy, Experience, and Community*, despite addressing topics germane to Addams's writings, makes no mention of Addams whatsoever.

16 Dewey, "Philosophy and Democracy," 45.

17 Seigfried, *Pragmatism and Feminism*, 27.

18 Lerner, "Why Have There Been So Few Women Philosophers?" 13.

19 Deegan, *Jane Addams and the Men of the Chicago School, 1892–1918*, 49.

20 Fischer, *On Addams*, i.

21 Deegan, *Jane Addams and the Men of the Chicago School, 1892–1918*.

22 Baggini and Stangroom, *What Philosophers Think*, 5.

23 Seigfried, *Pragmatism and Feminism*, 11.

24 Mahowald, "What Classical American Philosophers Missed: Jane Addams, Critical Pragmatism, and Cultural Feminism," 45.

25 Curti, "Jane Addams on Human Nature," 240.

26 The Metaphysical Club consisted of a small group of intellectuals, including Oliver Wendell Holmes Jr., John Dewey, William James, and Charles Sanders Peirce, who started meeting in Cambridge, Massachusetts, in 1872 to discuss philosophy and in particular the turn away from metaphysics. The impact of these figures is romanticized in the Pulitzer Prize-winning work, *The Metaphysical Club* by Louis Menand.

CHAPTER I. INTELLECTUAL INFLUENCES

Portions of this and subsequent chapters first appeared in my article, "Jane Addams," *Stanford Encyclopedia of Philosophy* (Fall 2007): http://plato.stanford.edu/archives/fall2007/entries/addams-jane. Reprinted with permission from the *Stanford Encyclopedia of Philosophy*.

1 Addams, *Twenty Years at Hull-House*, 33.

2 A possible exception to the disjointed Progressive movement was the short-lived Progressive Party. Largely because of the skill and popularity of Addams, the Progressive Party influenced the 1912 presidential election, although its candidate, Theodore Roosevelt, did not win.

3 Davis, *Spearheads for Reform*, xiii.

4 Kleinberg, *Women in the United States, 1830–1945*, 188.

5 Addams, "A Function of the Social Settlement," 21.

6 Addams, *Democracy and Social Ethics*, 41. Other reasons for the strong participation of women in the social settlement movement include the following: (1) The lingering association of women with morality made this an appropriate activity for women. (2) Similarly, because women were engaging in a form of "social housekeeping," settlements were viewed as an extension of "women's work." (3) The settlement movement followed on the heels of the temperance movement, which began in the 1870s and was another woman-identified reform campaign that thus paved the way for greater women's involvement in society. (4) Women's social clubs had become a well-developed network of associations that gave women social and political opportunities as well as a means for garnering clout to support women's activism—such as social settlements.

7 Davis, *Spearheads for Reform*, 12.

8 Articles such as "The Objective Value of a Social Settlement," "The Subjective Necessity for Social Settlements," and "A Function of the Social Settlement," as well as her famous biographical account, *Twenty Years at Hull-House*, provide some of the defining philosophical underpinnings of the movement.

9 Noddings, *Starting at Home*, ix.

10 Muncy, *Creating a Female Dominion in American Reform, 1890–1935*, xii.

11 Addams, *Twenty Years at Hull-House*, 38.
12 Ibid., 45.
13 Addams made the celebration of Lincoln's birthday an annual event at Hull House. Bryan, Bair, and de Angury, *The Selected Papers of Jane Addams*, 4.
14 Addams, *Twenty Years at Hull-House*, 25.
15 Ibid., 27.
16 Many other women who achieved prominence in the face of gender oppression, such as Florence Kelley, had strong connections to their fathers. Sherrick, "Their Father's Daughters."
17 Brown, *The Education of Jane Addams*, 47.
18 Linn, *Jane Addams*, 19.
19 G. J. Barker-Benfield argues that Addams's bouts with illness in her early life were responses to her father's dominance, and that not coincidently upon his death, she recovered and founded Hull House. Barker-Benfield, "Mother Emancipator: The Meaning of Jane Addams' Sickness and Cure," 395–97. Victoria Brown's research does not support this conclusion. Brown, *The Education of Jane Addams*, 60.
20 Addams, *Twenty Years at Hull-House*, 32.
21 Delzell, *The Unification of Italy, 1859–1861*, 25–35.
22 Mazzini, *The Duties of Man and Other Essays*, 86–89, 122.
23 Ibid., 90.
24 Jane Addams to Eva Campbell in Bryan, Bair, and de Angury, *The Selected Papers of Jane Addams*, 273.
25 Thomas Carlyle, quoted in Brown, *The Education of Jane Addams*, 84.
26 Carlyle, *On Heroes and Hero Worship and the Heroic in History*, 99.
27 Ruskin, *The Works of John Ruskin*, 19:197.
28 Ibid., 19:266.
29 Ruskin, "The Crown of Wild Olive," *The Works of John Ruskin*, 18:435.
30 Addams, *Twenty Years at Hull-House*, 191–95.
31 Ibid., 192.
32 Ibid.
33 Ibid., 197.
34 Addams, "Tolstoy and Gandhi," 437.
35 Addams, *Twenty Years at Hull-House*, 195.
36 H. Barnett, "The Beginning of Toynbee Hall," 239–54.
37 S. Barnett, "A Retrospective of Toynbee Hall," 257.
38 Addams, "A Function of the Social Settlement," 344–45.
39 Ibid., 323–24.
40 Sklar, *Florence Kelley and the Nation's Work*, 204.
41 Kadish, *Apostle Arnold*.
42 Arnold quoted in Kadish, *Apostle Arnold*, 210.
43 Addams, *Twenty Years at Hull-House*, 25.
44 Webb, "A Fabian Visits Hull House," 66.
45 Muncy, *Creating a Female Dominion in American Reform, 1890–1935*, 10.
46 When Kelley's abusive husband sought custody of their children, Addams found a safe home for them. The Hull House community acted as a modern domestic violence center in protecting Kelley and her children. Sklar, *Florence Kelly and the Nation's Work*, 178–80.
47 Alice Hamilton quoted in Schierman, *Alice Hamilton*, 113.
48 Kelley allegedly ridiculed evening prayer and Bible readings into extinction at Hull House. Sklar, *Florence Kelley and the Nation's Work*, 195.

49 Davis, *American Heroine,* 77–78.

50 Sklar, *Florence Kelley and the Nation's Work,* 185.

51 Kelley, "I Go to Work," 271.

52 Jackson, *Lines of Activity,* 64.

53 Polikoff, *With One Bold Act,* 216.

54 Sadovnik and Semel, *Founding Mothers and Others,* 113.

55 Ross, "Gendered Social Knowledge," 237.

56 Sawaya, "The Authority of Experience," 49.

CHAPTER 2. RADICAL PRAGMATISM

1 Recent anthologies of American philosophers such as Marsoobian and Ryder, *The Blackwell Guide to American Philosophy,* mention Addams more frequently than do older anthologies, but she is still saddled with secondary status.

2 James, *Pragmatism and Other Essays,* 25.

3 Ibid., 23.

4 Ibid.

5 Ibid., 26.

6 Ibid.

7 James, "The Experience of Activity," 84.

8 James, *Pragmatism and Other Essays,* 58.

9 William James, quoted in Lasch, *The Social Thought of Jane Addams,* 84.

10 Addams, "A Function of the Social Settlement," 187.

11 Ibid., 188.

12 Ibid., 197.

13 Addams, "The Revolt against War," 86.

14 Addams, "A Toast to John Dewey," 27.

15 Dewey, *Logic,* 4.

16 Dewey, *The Quest for Certainty,* 16.

17 Ibid., 28.

18 Ibid., 82.

19 Ibid., 90.

20 Addams, "The Objective Value of a Social Settlement," 44.

21 Dewey quoted in Pratt, *Native Pragmatism,* 282–83.

22 Deegan notes the frequency of contact with many members of the Chicago school. Deegan, *Jane Addams and the Men of the Chicago School, 1892–1918,* 164.

23 John Dewey quoted in Menand, *The Metaphysical Club,* 313.

24 Ibid., 314.

25 Pratt, *Native Pragmatism,* 284.

26 Seigfried, "Socializing Democracy," 213.

27 Lasch, *The Social Thought of Jane Addams,* 176.

28 Deegan, "Play from the Perspective of George Herbert Mead," xliii–xliv.

29 Deegan, *Jane Addams and the Men of the Chicago School, 1892–1918,* 118.

30 Ibid., 5–6.

31 Ibid., 121.

32 Mead quoted in ibid., 119.

33 Deegan, "Play from the Perspective of George Herbert Mead," lxxxiii.

34 Deegan, *Jane Addams and the Men of the Chicago School, 1892–1918,* 118–21; Jackson, "Civic Play-Housekeeping: Gender, Theatre, and American Reform," 343; and Aboulafia, "Was George Herbert Mead a Feminist?" 11.

35 Jackson, "Civic Play-Housekeeping," 343.
36 West, *The American Evasion of Philosophy*, 5.
37 Ibid., 6.
38 Ibid., 69.
39 Bernstein quoted in Anderson, "The Public Intellectual," 40.
40 West, *The American Evasion of Philosophy*, 83.
41 Ibid., 106.
42 Ibid., 107–10.
43 Ibid., 78–79.
44 Ibid., 84.
45 Seigfried, *Pragmatism and Feminism*, 6.
46 Ibid.
47 Ibid., 45.
48 Ibid., 7.
49 Ibid., 10.
50 Addams, "A Modern Lear," 175.
51 Ibid.
52 Addams, "The Subjective Necessity for Social Settlements," 127.
53 William James, quoted in Lasch, *The Social Thought of Jane Addams*, 62.
54 Addams, "Trade Unions and Public Duty," 456.
55 Ibid., 461.
56 Addams, *Democracy and Social Ethics*, 11–12.
57 Addams, "The Objective Value of a Social Settlement," 45.
58 Ibid., 34.
59 Deegan, *Jane Addams and the Men of the Chicago School, 1892–1918*, 248.
60 Ibid.
61 Sociologists Joe R. Feagin and Hernán Vera view Addams as radically reconstructing social theory. They describe "liberation theory" as marked by societal betterment, questioning of social hierarchy, increasing humanization, facing challenges in the community, listening to the people, and taking a moral stand. Furthermore, they name Addams and W. E. B. DuBois as exemplary of liberation sociology despite being overlooked in traditional accounts of the discipline. Feagin and Vera, *Liberation Sociology*, 17–27.
62 Historian Christopher Lasch offers another way of understanding Addams's social criticism. He distinguishes "new radicals" from progressives, although he sees them emerging at the same period of time. For Lasch, new radicals were motivated more by pervasive reform than by the more narrow political reforms sought by progressives: ". . . new radicals were more interested in the reform of education, culture, and sexual relations than they were in political issues." Lasch, *The Social Thought of Jane Addams*, xiv. Lasch suggests that new radicalism was an intellectual-led movement that translated into reformist activities. He views Addams as a bridge figure who did not embrace radical labels such as "socialist" or "anarchist," but because she envisioned widespread social change, as her work on lateral progress indicates, and was not afraid to embrace aspects of radical ideals, she had more in common with new radicals than her reputation reveals. Addams was certainly influenced by radical discourse. Not only did she read widely, but Hull House was also a forum for a variety of speakers, including socialists, anarchists, and feminists. Addams was a thoughtful listener who was not afraid to acknowledge a good idea no matter what its sources.
63 Seigfried, *Pragmatism and Feminism*, 44–45.

1 For example, Dale Spender's *Feminist Theories: Three Centuries of Women's Intellectual Traditions* includes twenty-two women such as Charlotte Perkins Gilman; however, Addams receives no mention. Two possible explanations for Addams's exclusion from the listing of founding feminist theorists are the problem of intellectual appreciation between waves of feminism and Addams's rhetorical style. Part of the difficulty in assessing her feminism stems from the challenge of reading a "first-wave" feminist from the perspective of "second-" or "third-wave" feminism. In her analysis of the various waves, Cathryn Bailey finds that distinctions between waves are made to solidify identity by "stressing what are perceived as discontinuities with earlier feminist thoughts and activities" and that more continuity and value exists among historical waves than is professed. Bailey, "Making Waves and Drawing Lines," 181. Stylistically, Addams's philosophy lacks the sharp edge in criticizing patriarchy that is often employed by second- and third-wave feminists. She detests unwarranted antagonism, preferring to employ indirect and euphemistic language in her critiques in order to keep all parties engaged in the conversation. Anne Marie Pois says that Addams's political style, "grounded in Victorian notions of service and ladylike responsibility[,] contrasts sharply with contemporary feminist resistance." Addams employs a rhetorical style that balances argumentation with humility. Pois, "Foreshadowings," 439.

2 Jane Addams never claimed to be a feminist, and neither did most women of her era. However, in a 1913 book titled *Women as World Builders: Studies in Modern Feminism,* Floyd Dell devotes a chapter to Addams and Emmeline Pankhurst, in which he describes Addams as feminist. Unfortunately, Dell employs exceptionalism: "Miss Addams has by her magnificent anomalies shown us what women are not like. Can anyone doubt this? Can anyone, seeing the long eminence of Miss Addams, assert that imaginative sympathy, patience, and the spirit of conciliation are the ordinary traits of women?" Dell's adulation denigrates other women in order to elevate Addams, a common formulation of prejudice (exceptional members of an oppressed group are praised for being more like the dominant group). Dell, *Women as World Builders,* 38.

3 See Tong, *Feminist Thought,* chap. 1.

4 Addams, "Aspects of the Woman's Movement," 280.

5 Addams, "What War Is Destroying," 64.

6 Ibid.

7 Ibid., 65.

8 Addams, *Twenty Years at Hull-House,* 139.

9 Addams, *Democracy and Social Ethics,* 52.

10 Ibid., 53–62.

11 Addams, "Why Women Are Concerned with the Larger Citizenship," 9:2,135–36.

12 Ibid., 9:2,130.

13 Deegan, *Jane Addams and the Men of the Chicago School, 1892–1918,* 225–26.

14 Ibid., 227.

15 Addams, *Newer Ideals of Peace,* 183.

16 Bonnie Mann describes how accusations of "essentialism" have become a means of disciplining scholarship in contemporary feminism. Because assumptions about women's nature so often serve to oppress women, many feminist theorists treat any hint of essentialism as a cause for alarm. This trend may contribute to devaluing Addams's work. Mann, *Women's Liberation and the Sublime,* 13.

17 Frye, *The Politics of Reality,* 96.

18 Mead quoted in Crunden, *Ministers of Reform,* 32.

19 Craig, "The Woman's Peace Party and Questions of Gender Separatism," 373.

20 Addams to Carrie Chapman Catt, quoted in Craig, "The Woman's Peace Party and Questions of Gender Separatism," 373.

21 Harding, *The Feminist Standpoint Theory Reader*, 6.

22 Robin May Schott, "Introduction," in *Feminist Interpretations of Immanuel Kant*, 5.

23 Some feminist philosophers read Kant differently, contending that the content of the moral agent's decision to be tested by the categorical imperative for universalizability provides the necessary flexibility to consider experience. See, for example, Sedgewick, "Can Kant's Ethics Survive Feminist Critique?"

24 Harding, *Feminism and Methodology*, 185.

25 Code, "Epistemology," 180.

26 Lugones and Spelman, "Have We Got a Theory for You!" 498–99.

27 Addams, *Democracy and Social Ethics*, 9.

28 Lugones and Spelman, "Have We Got a Theory for You!" 501.

29 Addams, *Twenty Years at Hull-House*, 80.

30 Weeks, *Constituting Feminist Subjects*, 7.

31 Addams, "A Belated Industry," 538.

32 Ibid., 540.

33 Ibid., 536.

34 Seigfried, *Pragmatism and Feminism*, x.

35 Addams, *The Long Road of Woman's Memory*, 7–8.

36 Ibid., 8.

37 Ibid., 9.

38 Ibid., 11.

39 Ibid.

40 Ibid., 28.

41 Ibid., 29.

42 Baier, *Postures of the Mind*, 84; and Code, *What Can She Know?* 82.

43 I am being intentionally brief in providing background on care ethics. In the twenty-five years since this term was coined, care ethicists have developed a rich and varied corpus of literature. For a more thorough literature review, see Hamington, *Embodied Care*.

44 Addams, *The Spirit of Youth and the City Streets*, 56–57.

45 Ibid., 71.

46 Addams, *Democracy and Social Ethics*, 8.

47 Addams, "The Objective Value of a Social Settlement," 39.

48 Addams, "A Function of the Social Settlement," 187.

49 Hoagland, "Why Lesbian Ethics?" 197.

50 Deegan, "'Dear Love, Dear Love,'" 599.

51 Ibid., 592–93.

52 Faderman, *Odd Girls and Twilight Lovers*, 25.

53 Ibid., 25.

54 Rupp, "Sexuality and Politics in the Early Twentieth Century," 7.

55 Addams, *The Second Twenty Years at Hull-House*, 192–93.

56 Davis, *American Heroine*, 13. Emphasis on standpoint and experience, as well as the burgeoning field of lesbian ethics, makes exploring the significance of Addams's sexuality to her philosophy seem appropriate. Nevertheless, the significance of heterosexual philosophers' sexuality is rarely explored.

57 Another term applied to romantic phenomena similar to spooning is *smashing*, in which college women of this era "developed crushes, fell madly in love, courted, wrote love notes, and exchanged presents" with one another. D'Emilio and Freedman, *Intimate Matters*, 191.

58 Bryan, Bair, and de Angury, *The Selected Papers of Jane Addams*, 196.

59 Ibid., 198.

60 Addams, *Twenty Years at Hull-House*, 49.

61 Bryan, Bair, and de Angury, *The Selected Papers of Jane Addams*, 548–49.

62 Faderman, *Odd Girls and Twilight Lovers*, 24–25.

63 Linn, *Jane Addams*, 147.

64 Faderman, *Odd Girls and Twilight Lovers*, 26–27.

65 Rupp, "Sexuality and Politics in the Early Twentieth Century," 20.

66 Davis, *American Heroine*, 88.

67 Ibid., 85.

68 Faderman, *Odd Girls and Twilight Lovers*, 28.

69 Sklar, *Florence Kelley and the Nation's Work*, 373n48.

70 Diliberto, *A Useful Woman*, 186–87.

71 Martindale and Saunders, "Realizing Love and Justice."

72 Hoagland, *Lesbian Ethics*, 22.

73 Ibid., 25.

74 Ibid., 285.

75 Penelope, "The Lesbian Perspective," 92.

76 Addams, "Widening the Circle of Enlightenment," 276.

77 Addams, *Democracy and Social Ethics*, 37.

78 Rosenberg, *Divided Lives*, 33.

79 Addams, "Votes for Women and Other Votes," 367.

80 Ibid.

81 Ibid., 368.

82 Hypothetical cases of gender reversal are a technique employed by numerous feminists to foreground asymmetrical gender beliefs. See, for example, Gilman, "If I Were a Man," and Steinem, "What if Freud Were Phyllis?"

83 Addams, "If Men Were Seeking the Elective Franchise," 229–30.

84 Ibid.

85 Addams, "My Experiences as a Progressive Delegate," 12.

86 Addams, "As I See Women," 11.

87 Ibid.

88 Addams, "Why Women Should Vote," 1. For a thorough discussion of the impact of this article and pamphlet, see Brown, "Jane Addams, Progressivism, and Woman Suffrage."

89 Ibid., 13.

CHAPTER 4. SYMPATHETIC KNOWLEDGE

1 For a discussion of the imaginative dimension of care ethics, see Hamington, *Embodied Care*, chap. 3, "Caring Imagination."

2 Addams, *The Spirit of Youth and the City Streets*, 13.

3 Ibid., 14.

4 Addams, *Democracy and Social Ethics*, 99.

5 Addams, *A New Conscience and an Ancient Evil*, 15.

6 Seigfried, "Introduction to the Illinois Edition," xxv–xxvi.

7 Ibid., xxx.

8 Addams, *Democracy and Social Ethics*, 119.

9 Walker, "Moral Epistemology," 366.

10 Addams, *Democracy and Social Ethics*, 118–19.

11 UNICEF, "Nutrition."

12 Addams, *Newer Ideals of Peace,* 9.

13 Ibid., 10.

14 Ibid.

15 Ibid.

16 On several occasions in this chapter, I pose Addams's social philosophy in opposition to the Western tradition of philosophy and/or liberalism. This is not intended as a wholesale dismissal of either, but recognition of lacunae within these traditions that Addams's philosophy is poised to fill.

17 Addams, *Democracy and Social Ethics,* 119.

18 Ibid., 35.

19 Addams, "A Function of the Social Settlement," 187.

20 Seigfried, "Introduction to the Illinois Edition," xiii.

21 Addams, *Democracy and Social Ethics,* 5.

22 Ibid., 6.

23 Ibid.

24 Ibid., 7.

25 Ibid.

26 Ibid.

27 Ibid., 8.

28 Ibid., 12.

29 Ibid., 17.

30 Lasch, *The Social Thought of Jane Addams,* 63.

31 Addams, *Democracy and Social Ethics,* 11.

32 Ibid., 98.

33 Addams, *The Spirit of Youth and the City Streets,* 146. I published an earlier version of this section as "Addams's Radical Democracy: Moving beyond Rights."

34 Addams, *Newer Ideals of Peace,* 20–21.

35 Addams, *Democracy and Social Ethics,* 117.

36 Ibid.

37 Ibid.

38 Addams, *A New Conscience and an Ancient Evil,* 29–30.

39 Ibid., 98.

40 Addams, *Newer Ideals of Peace,* 21.

41 Addams, *A New Conscience and an Ancient Evil,* 6.

42 Ibid., 7.

43 Royce quoted in Addams, *Newer Ideals of Peace,* 21.

44 Addams, "Widening the Circle of Enlightenment," 279.

45 Leffers, "Pragmatists Jane Addams and John Dewey Inform the Ethics of Care."

46 As of this writing, my *Embodied Care* is the only extended treatment of feminist pragmatism and care ethics.

47 Hekman, *Moral Voices, Moral Selves,* 2.

CHAPTER 5. ULTIMATE SOCIAL PROGRESS: PEACE

1 Zinn, *A People's History of the United States: 1492–Present,* 351.

2 Addams, "The Revolt against War," 78–79.

3 Lasch, *The Social Thought of Jane Addams,* xxiv.

4 Addams, "What War Is Destroying, 65.

5 Addams, "Presidential Address."

6 Addams, *The Second Twenty Years at Hull-House,* 167.

7 Ibid., 168.

8   Julia Gulliver quoted in Walhout, "Recovering Our Predecessors," 74.

9   Addams, "Patriotism and Pacifists in Wartime," 69.

10 *New York Herald* quoted in Degen, *The History of the Woman's Peace Party*, 200.

11 Sklar, "Jane Addams's Peace Activism, 1914–1922," 35.

12 The reference to "virgins" is an intriguing slur, but overall this statement is meant as a compliment to women, as Addams and Rankin are presented as exceptions to the nature of womanhood. *Cleveland News,* June 12, 1917, quoted in Degen, *The History of the Woman's Peace Party*, 201.

13 Addams, "Woman's Special Training for Peacemaking," 253–54.

14 Addams, "What War Is Destroying," 63.

15 Addams, "Women and War," 440.

16 Addams, "What War Is Destroying," 62.

17 Addams places these words in quotes and yet acknowledges that they are a composite drawn from conversations with two women. Although these are ostensibly not Addams's words, we may infer that she had a hand in editing them to support her contentions. "War Times Challenging Woman's Traditions," 135.

18 Segal, *Is the Future Female?* 203.

19 Addams, Balch, and Hamilton, *Woman at The Hague,* 60.

20 Addams, "What Peace Means," 11.

21 Ibid.

22 Ibid., 12.

23 Ibid., 14.

24 Addams, "Democracy or Militarism," 2.

25 Ibid., 3.

26 Addams, *Newer Ideals of Peace,* 5.

27 Levine, *Jane Addams and the Liberal Tradition,* 95.

28 James, *Pragmatism and Other Essays,* 290.

29 Ibid., 295.

30 William James quoted in Joslin, *Jane Addams,* 80.

31 Joslin, *Jane Addams,* 7.

32 Ibid., 83.

33 For further analysis of the differences between the two approaches, see Linda Schott, "Jane Addams and William James on Alternatives to War."

34 James, *Pragmatism and Other Essays,* 297.

35 Ibid., 293.

36 Ibid., 299.

37 Addams, *Newer Ideals of Peace,* 183.

38 Addams, "The New Ideals of Peace," 53.

39 Addams, "Democracy or Militarism."

40 Addams, "The New Ideals of Peace," 53.

41 Addams, *Newer Ideals of Peace,* 17.

42 Addams, "Statement of Miss Jane Addams," 115.

43 Addams, *Newer Ideals of Peace,* 13.

44 Ibid., 17.

45 Dewey, "Democratic versus Coercive International Organization," xvi.

46 Addams, *Newer Ideals of Peace,* 23.

47 Alonso, *Peace as a Woman's Issue,* 102.

48 Addams, *The Second Twenty Years at Hull-House,* 184

49 Bok, *A Strategy for Peace,* 6.

50 Addams, "Factors in Continuing the War," 41.

51 Addams, "Exaggerated Nationalism and International Comity," 168.
52 Farrell, *Beloved Lady*, 215.
53 Addams, *The Second Twenty Years at Hull-House*, 170.
54 Addams, *Newer Ideals of Peace*, 13.
55 Ibid., 237.
56 Addams, "Our National Self-Righteousness," 442.
57 Addams, "Hearing before the Committee on Military Affairs," 113.
58 Dewey, "Democratic versus Coercive International Organization," xviii.
59 Dawley, *Changing the World*, 299.
60 See, for example, Tuana, *Woman and the History of Philosophy*, 58–69.
61 See, for example, Miller, "A Kantian Ethic of Care."
62 Addams makes a fleeting reference to Kant's article in her 1915 "Presidential Address," 70.
63 Armstrong, "Kant's Philosophy of Peace and War," 197–98.
64 "Appendix 3: Resolutions Adopted by the International Congress of Women at The Hague, May 1, 1915," *Women at The Hague*, 72–77.
65 Addams, "Women and Internationalism," 66.
66 Addams, "How to Build a Peace Program?" 220.
67 Kant, "Perpetual Peace," 107.
68 Ibid., 108.
69 Ibid.
70 Degen, *The History of the Woman's Peace Party*, 153.
71 Kant, "Perpetual Peace," 108.
72 Addams, "How to Build a Peace Program?" 219–20.
73 Kant, "Perpetual Peace," 115.
74 Ibid., 123.
75 Addams, *Peace and Bread in Time of War*, 83.
76 Addams, "Is a United Peace Front Desirable?" 60.
77 Kant, "Perpetual Peace," 111, 115.
78 Ibid., 118.
79 Ibid., 113.
80 Ibid., 114.
81 Audoin-Rouzeau and Becker, *14–18: Understanding the Great War*, 34.
82 Mosse, *Fallen Soldiers*, 244.
83 Cuomo, *The Philosopher Queen*, 20.

CHAPTER 6. WIDENING THE CIRCLE

Portions of this chapter first appeared in my article, "Jane Addams and Ida B. Wells on Lynching," *Journal of Speculative Philosophy* 19, no. 2 (2005): 167–74. Reprinted with permission from the *Journal of Speculative Philosophy*.

1 West, *Race Matters*, 6.
2 Addams, "Widening the Circle of Enlightenment," 279.
3 Knight, *Citizen*, 179.
4 Holbrook, "Map, Notes, and Comments," 60.
5 Green, "Building a Cosmopolitan World Community through Mutual Hospitality," 213.
6 Gilman, *The Home*, 311.
7 Voris, *Carrie Chapman Catt*, 15–16.
8 Acker, *Class Questions*, 6.

9   See, for example, Addams, "Social Control," 22.
10 Although some claim that Rice faced discrimination at Hull House, it appears that she was frustrated more by wider racist practices that forced her to engage in social work for which she had little interest. Knight, *Citizen*, 387–88.
11 African American leaders were more than acquaintances to Addams. Deegan contends that the women of Hull House, and particularly Addams, were extremely influential in DuBois's developing "applied sociology." Deegan notes that there were twenty documented professional contacts between Addams and DuBois. "W. E. B. DuBois and the Women of Hull House, 1895–1899," 308. In her autobiography, Mary Church Terrell recounts her collaborations with Addams. In 1919, Terrell was a delegate to the Women's International League for Peace and Freedom at the International Peace Congress in Zurich, Switzerland, with Addams. On one evening, Addams asked Terrell to present resolutions before the congress on behalf of the American delegation, thus representing the American contingent. On another occasion, bogus accusations of impropriety by French African troops in Germany resulted in a petition being circulated among the WILPF executive committee to have these troops removed. Terrell refused to sign the petition and with trepidation wrote a letter to Addams indicating her decision. Addams wrote back that she concurred with Terrell about the fallacious nature of the accusations. *A Colored Woman in a White World*, 329–35, 359–64. Hull House also supported the causes of Native American women activists such as Susan LaFlesche and Gertrude Bonin. Pratt, *Native Pragmatism*, 282.
12 Brown, *The Education of Jane Addams*, 389–90.
13 Addams, *Twenty Years at Hull-House*, 77.
14 Clarke, *Ellen Swallow*, 128.
15 Jackson, *Lines of Activity*, 129.
16 Addams, *Twenty Years at Hull-House*, 103.
17 Addams, "Has the Emancipation Act Been Nullified by National Indifference?" 566.
18 Tuskegee Institute Archives, Tuskegee, Alabama. http://www.law.umkc.edu/faculty/projects/ftrials/shipp/lynchingyear.html.
19 Addams, "Social Control," 22.
20 Ibid.
21 Addams, *Twenty Years at Hull-House*, 78.
22 Ibid., 83.
23 Addams quoted in Davis, *American Heroine*, 71; and Jackson, *Lines of Activity*, 155.
24 Seigfried, "Introduction to the Illinois Edition," xii.
25 Jackson, *Lines of Activity*, 216.
26 Addams, "Social Control," 22.
27 Ibid., 23.
28 Addams, *The Second Twenty Years at Hull-House*, 367.
29 Ibid., 14.
30 Addams, "Americanization," 246.
31 Addams, "Immigration," 9.
32 Ibid.
33 Ibid., 10.
34 Ibid.
35 Ibid.
36 Ibid., 18.
37 Ibid.
38 Addams, "The Progressive Party and the Negro," 170.
39 Ibid., 173–74.

40 Joslin, *Jane Addams*, 133–34.

41 Perhaps the most negative assessment of Addams's work on race and culture can be found in Lissak, *Pluralism and Progressives*. Lissak claims that Addams was primarily concerned with the assimilation of immigrants (40–41). For a response to Lissak, see Sullivan, "Reciprocal Relations between Races," 43–60; and Seigfried, "Introduction to the Illinois Edition," xxxv n. 8.

42 Sullivan, "Reciprocal Relations between Races," 48.

43 Ibid., 49.

44 Ibid., 53.

45 Deegan, *Race, Hull-House, and the University of Chicago*, 72.

46 Ibid., 70.

47 Wells, *Crusade for Justice*, 257–60.

48 Ibid., 274–78.

49 Ibid., 259.

50 Addams, "Respect for Law," 23.

51 Ibid.

52 Ibid.

53 Ibid., 25–27.

54 Ibid., 27.

55 West, *Race Matters*, 13.

56 Outlaw, *On Race and Philosophy*, 187.

57 Ibid., 204.

CHAPTER 7. THE RELUCTANT SOCIALIST

1 Working conditions in 1900 included new and untested federal antitrust laws, no federal minimum wage or maximum hours laws, no federal safety guidelines, few child labor laws, no hiring or firing practices controls, and few labor organizing protection laws.

2 Zinn, *The Twentieth Century*, 31–32.

3 For example, in 1890, 18 percent of children between the ages of ten and fourteen were employed in nonagricultural work. Greenwood, *The Gilded Age*, 62.

4 Quandt, *From the Small Town to the Great Community*, 90.

5 Addams, *Twenty Years at Hull-House*, 82.

6 Addams, "One Menace to the Century's Progress," 11.

7 Addams, *Twenty Years at Hull-House*, 137.

8 Smith, *An Inquiry into the Nature and Causes of the Wealth of Nations*.

9 Addams, *Democracy and Social Ethics*, 93.

10 Ibid., 94.

11 Ibid., 93.

12 Ibid.

13 Addams quoted in Farrell, *Beloved Lady*, 99.

14 Addams quoted in ibid., 100. Addams's contextualization of labor parallels modern "stakeholder theory," although Addams targets employees, whereas stakeholder theory focuses on corporations. According to stakeholder theory, corporations maintain connection to various social constituencies by identifying who holds a stake in their decisions—employees, customers, the local community, and suppliers, as well as shareholders. Addams desires that workers understand how their labor connects to society, and stakeholder theorists desire that corporations understand how their decisions impact society. Mitchell, Agle, and Wood, "Toward a Theory of Stakeholder Identification and Salience," 853–86.

15 Addams, *Newer Ideals of Peace*, 127.

16 Addams quoted in Brown, *The Education of Jane Addams*, 246.

17 Addams, *Twenty Years at Hull-House*, 156–57.

18 Addams, "Trade Unions and Public Duty," 450.

19 Addams, "The Settlement as a Factor in the Labor Movement," 202.

20 Addams, "Trade Unions and Public Duty," 459–60.

21 Addams finds some of the workers in the Pullman strike taking an overly self-interested position. She prefers that worker emancipation be directed toward "human affection and social justice" and encompass "those who think they lose, as well as those who think they gain." Only thus can it become the doctrine of a universal movement. Addams, "A Modern Lear," 174–75.

22 Addams, "Trade Unions and Public Duty," 461.

23 Addams, *Newer Ideals of Peace*, 148.

24 Ibid.

25 Lindsey, "Paternalism and the Pullman Strike," 272.

26 Ibid., 273.

27 Ibid., 282.

28 Ibid., 285.

29 Winston, "The Significance of the Pullman Strike," 541.

30 Hirsch, "The Search for Unity among Railroad Workers," 44.

31 Brown, "Advocate for Democracy," 134.

32 Ibid., 132.

33 Addams, "A Modern Lear," 164.

34 Ibid., 167.

35 Ibid.

36 Ibid., 163.

37 Ibid., 164.

38 Ibid., 165.

39 Ibid., 167.

40 There is a gendered dimension to "A Modern Lear." Addams, like Cordelia, was the honest daughter. Both confronted a complacent society, and told its citizens what they did not always want to hear. Addams adored her father, yet she fought many patriarchs in society. The Pullman strike was another opportunity for Addams to transgress traditional gender boundaries and confront the King Lears of the community.

41 Addams, "A Modern Lear," 170.

42 Ibid., 171.

43 Addams, *Twenty Years at Hull-House*, 86.

44 Ibid., 148.

45 Addams, "Child Labor Legislation—A Requisite for Industrial Efficiency," 133–34.

46 Addams, *Newer Ideals of Peace*, 169.

47 Ibid., 158.

48 Addams, *Twenty Years at Hull-House*, 153.

49 Addams, "National Protection for Children," 60.

50 Knight, "Jane Addams's Views on the Responsibilities of Wealth," 120.

51 Flanagan, "Introduction," xv.

52 Bowen, *Growing Up with a City*, 85.

53 Stebner, *The Women of Hull House*, 174–75.

54 Bowen, *Growing Up with a City*, 93–95.

55 Addams quoted in Brown, *The Education of Jane Addams*, 262.

56 Addams, *Twenty Years at Hull-House*, 79.

57 Addams, *Democracy and Social Ethics*, 52.

58 Ibid., 54.
59 Ibid., 57.
60 Ibid., 60–61.
61 Addams, *A New Conscience and an Ancient Evil*, 9.
62 Ibid., 11.
63 Ibid., 6.
64 Ibid.
65 Diliberto, *A Useful Woman*, 186.
66 Addams, *A New Conscience and an Ancient Evil*, 25.
67 Ibid., 27.
68 Joslin, "Introduction to the Illinois Edition," xxiii.
69 Addams, *A New Conscience and an Ancient Evil*, 185.
70 Ibid., 151.
71 Davidson, *Prostitution, Power, and Freedom*, 47, 70, 81.
72 Addams, *A New Conscience and an Ancient Evil*, 90.
73 Lippmann, *A Preface to Politics*, 79.
74 Davis, *American Heroine*, 183.
75 Davidson, *Prostitution, Power, and Freedom*, 4.
76 Linn, *Jane Addams*, 195.
77 Addams, *Twenty Years at Hull-House*, 139.
78 Ibid.
79 Nelson, "The Study of Choice or the Study of Provisioning?" 32.
80 Marx, "Manifesto of the Communist Party," 500.
81 Lynd, "Jane Addams and the Radical Impulse," 59.
82 Addams, *The Spirit of Youth and the City Streets*, 128.
83 Ibid.

CHAPTER 8. DEMOCRACY, EDUCATION, AND PLAY

 1 Lagemann, *Jane Addams: On Education*, x.
 2 Knight, *Citizen*, 273.
 3 Thattai, "A History of Public Education in the United States."
 4 Addams, "Foreign-Born Children in the Primary Grades," 104.
 5 Addams, "National Protection for Children," 57.
 6 Ibid., 60.
 7 Addams, "Child Labor and Education," 367.
 8 *Chicago Daily Tribune*, "Opens in Jolly Romp," 1.
 9 Addams, "Work and Play as Factors in Education," 253.
10 Tomko, *Dancing Class*, 140.
11 Addams, "The Child at the Point of Greatest Pressure," 26–30.
12 Addams, "Child Labor Legislation—A Requisite for Industrial Efficiency," 131.
13 Froebel and Hailmann, *The Education of Man*, 303.
14 Downs, *Friedrich Froebel*, 61.
15 Mead, "Self," 215.
16 Dewey, *The School and Society*, 118–19.
17 Addams, "Child Labor Legislation," 132.
18 Ibid., 135.
19 Addams, "Work and Play as Factors in Education," 253.
20 Ibid.
21 For an excellent discussion of the significance of art at Hull House, see Ganz and Strobel, *Pots of Promise*.

22 Addams, *The Second Twenty Years at Hull-House,* 345.
23 Ibid., 344.
24 Addams, *Democracy and Social Ethics,* 81.
25 Noddings, *Caring,* 174.
26 Davis, "Introduction," ix–x.
27 Addams, *The Spirit of Youth and the City Streets,* 6.
28 Polacheck, *I Came a Stranger,* 76–77.
29 Addams, *The Second Twenty Years at Hull-House,* 16.
30 Lorde, *Sister Outsider,* 53–59.
31 Stebner, *The Women of Hull House,* 137.
32 Haslet, "Hull House and the Birth Control Movement," 261–78.
33 Addams, *A New Conscience and an Ancient Evil,* 45.
34 Ibid., 47.
35 Addams, "A Challenge to the Contemporary Church," 198.
36 Addams, *Twenty Years at Hull-House,* 295.
37 Addams, "Hull House (Chicago)," 587.
38 Addams, *Twenty Years at Hull-House,* 295.
39 Addams, *The Second Twenty Years at Hull-House,* 380–404.
40 Ibid., 381.
41 Ibid., 404.
42 Harkavy and Puckett, "Lessons from Hull House for the Contemporary Urban University," 300.
43 Ibid.
44 Ibid., 303.
45 Taylor, "Ella Flagg Young," 620. Addams describes Young as having "more general intelligence and character than any woman I know." Addams quoted in Sadovnik and Semel, *Founding Mothers and Others,* 164.
46 Addams, "The Humanizing Tendency of Industrial Education," 120.
47 Addams, *Hull-House Annual Report 1906/1907,* 8.
48 Addams, "First Report of the Labor Museum at Hull-House, Chicago 1901–1902," 1–2.
49 Ibid., 3.
50 Addams, *Hull-House Annual Report 1906/1907,* 12.
51 Ibid., 16.
52 Lears, *No Place of Grace,* 80.
53 Ibid.
54 Addams, "Discussion," 94.
55 Addams, *Democracy and Social Ethics,* 80.
56 Ibid.
57 Addams, *The Second Twenty Years at Hull-House,* 367.
58 Addams, "Recreation as a Public Function in Urban Communities," 190.
59 Jackson, *Lines of Activity,* 117.
60 Tomko, *Dancing Class,* 147.
61 Addams, "The Child at the Point of Greatest Pressure," 26–30.
62 Addams, "Foreign-Born Children in the Primary Grades," 112.
63 Applebee, *Curriculum as Conversation,* 27.
64 Ibid., 21.
65 Lagemann, *Jane Addams: On Education,* xiii.
66 Davis, *Tools for Teaching,* 166–67.
67 Liu, "Knowledge, Foundations, and Discourse," 28.

68 Longo, "Recognizing the Role of Community in Civic Education," 6.

69 Daynes and Longo, "Jane Addams and the Origins of Service-Learning Practice in the United States," 11.

70 Addams, *The Second Twenty Years at Hull-House*, 408.

71 Noddings, *Caring*, 171.

CHAPTER 9. CIVIC RELIGION AND UTOPIA

1 Elizabeth Cady Stanton, quoted in Banner, *Elizabeth Cady Stanton*, 157.

2 Gilman, *The Man-Made World*, 115.

3 Bernstein, "Pragmatism's Common Faith," 140.

4 Much of the early press coverage surrounding Hull House superimposed a Christian character on Addams that she did not warrant. Victoria Brown reports, for example, that after the Pullman strike, one newspaper described Hull House as a "non-Catholic convent," ascribing spiritual leadership to Addams. "Advocate for Democracy," 149 n. 2.

5 Addams, *Twenty Years at Hull-House*, 9–10.

6 Brown, *The Education of Jane Addams*, 59.

7 Addams, *Twenty Years at Hull-House*, 49.

8 See Bryan, Bair, and de Angury, introduction to part 2 in *The Selected Papers of Jane Addams*, 1:159–87.

9 Addams to Ellen Gates Starr, January 29, 1880, quoted in Bryan, Bair, and de Angury, *The Selected Papers of Jane Addams*, 333.

10 Ibid., 334.

11 Farrell, *Beloved Lady*, 35.

12 Louise Knight identifies a number of reasons for the twenty-five-year-old Addams's decision to be baptized into the Cedarville Presbyterian Church, none of which include an acceptance of the doctrines of the denomination. Knight, *Citizen*, 146. James Weber Linn more pointedly describes Addams's conversion: "she may be said not so much to have accepted it as to have undergone it." Linn, *Jane Addams*, 81.

13 Addams, *Twenty Years at Hull-House*, 48.

14 Addams to Ellen Gates Starr, January 29, 1880, quoted in Bryan, Bair, and de Angury, *The Selected Papers of Jane Addams*, 335.

15 Addams quoted in Farrell, *Beloved Lady*, 35.

16 Brown, *The Education of Jane Addams*, 264.

17 For more on the prominent role of women in early Christianity, see Torjesen, *When Women Were Priests*.

18 Addams, *Twenty Years at Hull-House*, 50.

19 Sklar, "Hull House in the 1890s," 663.

20 Addams quoted in Lasch, *The New Radicalism in America, 1889–1963*, 11.

21 *Chicago Chronicle*, "Hull-House, Irreligious and Socialistic," 120.

22 Addams, *Twenty Years at Hull-House*, 51.

23 Edwards, "Jane Addams, Walter Rauschenbusch, and Dorothy Day," 154.

24 Ibid., 162.

25 Olasky, *The Tragedy of American Compassion*, 124.

26 Ibid., 125.

27 Stebner, *The Women of Hull House*, 69.

28 Harkness, "Jane Addams in Retrospect," 39.

29 Addams, "A New Impulse to an Old Gospel," 353.

30 Addams, "The College Woman and Christianity," 1,852.

31 Ibid.

32 Ibid., 1,855.

33 Addams, "The Reaction of Modern Life upon Religious Education," 23.

34 Addams, "Religious Education and Contemporary Social Conditions," 197.

35 Ibid., 198.

36 Addams, "The Reaction of Modern Life upon Religious Education," 26.

37 Addams, "Religious Education and Contemporary Social Conditions," 203.

38 Addams, "The Reaction of Modern Life upon Religious Education," 29.

39. Addams, "A Book That Changed My Life," 1,198.

40 Ibid., 1,197.

41 Huckle, "Women in Utopias," 120.

42 Ibid., 128.

43 Baruch and Rohrlich, *Women in Search of Utopia*, xii.

44 Ibid., xi–xv.

45 Muncy, *Creating a Female Dominion in American Reform, 1890–1935*, 9.

46 Stebner, *The Women of Hull House*, 5.

47 Lerner, *The Majority Finds Its Past*, 147.

48 Jackson, *Lines of Activity*, 170.

49 Stuhr, *Genealogical Pragmatism*, 246.

50 William James quoted in Addams, "A Function of the Social Settlement," 186.

51 Addams, "Widening the Circle of Enlightenment," 276.

52 John Dewey quoted in Addams, "A Function of the Social Settlement," 186.

53 William James quoted in Addams, "A Function of the Social Settlement," 186.

54 McKenna, *The Task of Utopia*, 108.

55 See, for example, Dewey, *The Public and Its Problems*.

56 McKenna, *The Task of Utopia*, 86.

57 Ibid., 129.

58 Holbrook, "Map, Notes, and Comments."

59 Seigfried, "Introduction to the Illinois Edition," xxxiv.

60 Rorty, "Anticlericalism and Atheism," 40.

61 James, "Pragmatism," 12.

AFTERWORD. COSMOPOLITAN HOPE

 1 Addams, "The Subjective Necessity for Social Settlements," 15.

 2 Taylor, "Jane Addams—Interpreter, an Appreciation," 680.

 3 Shade, *Habits of Hope*, 6–7.

 4 Ibid., 77.

 5 Ibid., 211–12.

 6 Mink, *Settlement Folk*, 219 n. 38.

 7 Addams, *A New Conscience and an Ancient Evil*, 3.

 8 Freire, *Pedagogy of the Oppressed*, 33.

 9 Ibid., 67.

10 Freire, *Pedagogy of Freedom*, 53.

11 hooks, *Teaching Community*, 111.

12 Judith Simmer-Brown quoted in hooks, *Teaching Community*, 47.

13 hooks, *Teaching Community*, xv.

14 Addams, *Democracy and Social Ethics*, 119.

15 Appiah, *Cosmopolitanism*, 57.

16 Ibid., 85.

17 Addams, *Newer Ideals of Peace*, 17.

18 Young, *Justice and the Politics of Difference*, 256.

19 Ibid., 227.
20 Addams, "The New Internationalism," 19.
21 Addams, *Democracy and Social Ethics,* 120.
22 Seigfried, "Has Passion a Place in Philosophy?" 42.
23 hooks, *Teaching Community,* xii–xiii.
24 Zinn, *The Zinn Reader,* 661.

BIBLIOGRAPHY

BOOKS BY JANE ADDAMS

Democracy and Social Ethics. 1902. Urbana: University of Illinois Press, 2002.
The Excellent Becomes the Permanent. New York: Macmillan, 1932.
Hull-House Annual Report 1906/1907. Chicago, 1907.
The Long Road of Woman's Memory. 1916. Urbana: University of Illinois Press, 2002.
My Friend, Julia Lathrop. 1935. Urbana: University of Illinois Press, 2004.
A New Conscience and an Ancient Evil. 1912. Urbana: University of Illinois Press, 2002.
Newer Ideals of Peace. 1906. Urbana: University of Illinois Press, 2007.
Peace and Bread in Time of War. 1922. Urbana: University of Illinois Press, 2002.
The Second Twenty Years at Hull-House. New York: Macmillan, 1930.
The Spirit of Youth and the City Streets. 1909. Urbana: University of Illinois Press, 1972.
Twenty Years at Hull-House. 1910. Urbana: University of Illinois Press, 1990.
With Emily G. Balch and Alice Hamilton. *Women at The Hague: The International Congress of Women and Its Results.* 1915. Urbana: University of Illinois Press, 2003.
With Residents of Hull-House. *Hull-House Maps and Papers.* 1895. Urbana: University of Illinois Press, 2007.

CITED ARTICLES BY JANE ADDAMS

"Americanization." 1919. In *The Jane Addams Reader,* edited by Jean Bethke Elshtain, 240–47. New York: Basic Books, 2002.
"As I See Women: In an Informal Talk with a Friend." *Ladies Home Journal* 32, no. 8 (August 1915): 11, 54.
"Aspects of the Woman's Movement." 1930. In *The Jane Addams Reader,* edited by Jean Bethke Elshtain, 275–93. New York: Basic Books, 2002.
"A Belated Industry." *American Journal of Sociology* 1, no. 5 (March 1896): 536–50.
"A Book That Changed My Life." *Christian Century* 44 (October 13, 1927): 1,196–98.
"A Challenge to the Contemporary Church." *Survey* 28 (May 4, 1912): 195–98.
"The Child at the Point of Greatest Pressure." *National Conference of Charities and Correction Proceedings* (1912): 26–30.

"Child Labor and Education." *National Conference of Charities and Correction Proceedings* (1908): 364–68.

"Child Labor Legislation—A Requisite for Industrial Efficiency." 1905. In Jane Addams, *On Education,* 124–35. New Brunswick, N.J.: Transaction Publishers, 1994.

"The College Woman and Christianity." *Independent* 53 (August 8, 1901): 1,852–55.

"Democracy or Militarism." 1899. In *Jane Addams' Essays and Speeches,* edited by Marilyn Fischer and Judy D. Whipps, 1–4. New York: Continuum International Publishing Group, 2005.

"Exaggerated Nationalism and International Comity." *Survey Graphic* 23 (April 1934): 168–70.

"Factors in Continuing the War." 1915. In Jane Addams, Emily G. Balch, and Alice Hamilton, *Women at The Hague: The International Congress of Women and Its Results,* 36–46. Urbana: University of Illinois Press, 2003.

"First Report of the Labor Museum at Hull-House, Chicago 1901–1902." Chicago, 1902.

"Foreign-Born Children in the Primary Grades." National Education Association's *Journal of Proceedings and Addresses* 36 (1897): 104–12.

"A Function of the Social Settlement." 1899. In *The Social Thought of Jane Addams,* edited by Christopher Lasch, 183–99. Indianapolis: Bobbs-Merrill, 1965.

"Has the Emancipation Act Been Nullified by National Indifference?" *Survey* 29, no. 18 (February 1, 1913): 565–66.

"Hearing before the Committee on Military Affairs, House of Representatives, Sixty-fourth Congress, First Session, Thursday, January 13, 1916." In *Jane Addams on Peace, War, and International Understanding, 1899–1932,* edited by Allen F. Davis, 113–26. New York: Garland Publishing, 1976.

"How to Build a Peace Program? William Hard Asks—Jane Addams Answers, an Interview over the Network of the National Broadcasting Company." 1932. In *Jane Addams on Peace, War, and International Understanding, 1899–1932,* edited by Allen F. Davis, 213–27. New York: Garland Publishing, 1976.

"Hull House (Chicago)." In *Encyclopedia of Social Reform,* edited by William D. P. Bliss, 587–90. New York: Funk and Wagnalls, 1908.

"The Humanizing Tendency of Industrial Education." 1904. In *Jane Addams: On Education,* edited by Ellen Condliffe Lagemann, 120–23. New Brunswick, N.J.: Transaction Publishers, 1994.

"If Men Were Seeking the Elective Franchise." 1913. In *The Jane Addams Reader,* edited by Jean Bethke Elshtain, 229–34. New York: Basic Books, 2002.

"Immigration: A Field Neglected by the Scholar." *Commons* 10 (January 1905): 9–19.

"Is a United Peace Front Desirable?" *Survey Graphic* 23:2 (Feb. 1934): 60, 96.

"A Modern Lear." 1896 (written); first published in 1912. In *Jane Addams and the Dream of American Democracy,* edited by Jean Bethke Elshtain, 163–76. New York: Basic Books, 2002.

"My Experiences as a Progressive Delegate." *McClure's Magazine* 40 (November 12, 1912): 12–14.

"National Protection for Children." *Annals of the American Academy of Political and Social Science* 29 (January–June 1907): 327–30.

"The New Ideals of Peace." 1907. In *Jane Addams on Peace, War, and International Understanding, 1899–1932,* edited by Allen F. Davis, 51–55. New York: Garland Publishing, 1976.

"A New Impulse to an Old Gospel." *Forum* 14 (November 1892): 345–58.

"The New Internationalism." 1907. In *Jane Addams' Essays and Speeches,* edited by Marilyn Fischer and Judy D. Whipps, 43–45. New York: Continuum International Publishing Group, 2005.

"The Objective Value of a Social Settlement." 1893. In *Jane Addams and the Dream of American Democracy,* edited by Jean Bethke Elshtain, 29–45. New York: Basic Books, 2002.

"One Menace to the Century's Progress." 1901. In *Jane Addams' Essays and Speeches,* edited by Marilyn Fischer and Judy D. Whipps, 9–12. New York: Continuum International Publishing Group, 2005.

"Our National Self-Righteousness." 1933. In *The Jane Addams Reader,* edited by Jean Bethke Elshtain, 442–48. New York: Basic Books, 2002.

"Patriotism and Pacifists in Wartime." 1917. In *The Jane Addams Reader,* edited by Jean Bethke Elshtain, 352–64. New York: Basic Books, 2002.

"Presidential Address." 1915. In *Jane Addams on Peace, War, and International Understanding, 1899–1932,* edited by Allen F. Davis, 67–71. New York: Garland Publishing, 1976.

"The Progressive Party and the Negro." 1912. In *The Social Thought of Jane Addams,* Christopher Lasch, 169–74. Indianapolis: Bobbs-Merrill, 1965.

"The Reaction of Modern Life upon Religious Education." *Religious Education* 4 (April 1909): 23–33.

"Recreation as a Public Function in Urban Communities." *American Journal of Sociology* 17 (March 1912): 615–19.

"Religious Education and Contemporary Social Conditions." 1911. In *The Jane Addams Reader,* edited by Jean Bethke Elshtain, 196–204. New York: Basic Books, 2002.

"Respect for Law." 1899. In *Lynching and Rape: An Exchange of Views,* edited by Bettina Apthecker, 22–27. New York: American Institute for Marxist Studies, 1977.

"The Revolt against War." 1915. In *Jane Addams on Peace, War, and International Understanding, 1899–1932,* edited by Allen F. Davis, 72–90. New York: Garland Publishing, 1976.

"The Settlement as a Factor in the Labor Movement." 1895. In *The Jane Addams Reader,* edited by Jean Bethke Elshtain, 46–61. New York: Basic Books, 2002.

"The Sheltered Woman and the Magdalen." 1913. In *The Jane Addams Reader,* edited by Jean Bethke Elshtain. 264–69. New York: Basic Books, 2002.

"Social Control." *Crisis: A Record of the Darker Races* 1, no. 3 (January 1911): 22–23.

"Statement of Miss Jane Addams before the Committee on Military Affairs." 1916. In *Jane Addams on Peace, War, and International Understanding, 1899–1932,* edited by Allen F. Davis, 113–26. New York: Garland Publishing, 1976.

"The Subjective Necessity for Social Settlements." 1893. In *The Jane Addams Reader,* edited by Jean Bethke Elshtain, 14–28. New York: Basic Books, 2002.

"A Toast to John Dewey." 1929. In *Feminist Interpretations of John Dewey,* edited by Charlene Haddock Seigfried, 25–30. University Park: Penn State University Press, 2002.

"Tolstoy and Gandhi." 1931. In *The Jane Addams Reader,* edited by Jean Bethke Elshtain, 436–41. New York: Basic Books, 2002.

"Trade Unions and Public Duty." *American Journal of Sociology* 4, no. 4 (1899): 448–62.

"Votes for Women and Other Votes." *Survey* 28 (June 1, 1912): 367–68.

"War Times Challenging Woman's Traditions." 1916. In *Jane Addams on Peace, War, and International Understanding, 1899–1932,* edited by Allen F. Davis, 127–39. New York: Garland Publishing, 1976.

"What Peace Means." 1899. In *Jane Addams on Peace, War, and International Understanding, 1899–1932,* edited by Allen F. Davis, 11–14. New York: Garland Publishing, 1976.

"What War Is Destroying." 1915. In *Jane Addams on Peace, War, and International Understanding, 1899–1932,* edited by Allen F. Davis, 62–66. New York: Garland Publishing, 1976.

"Why Women Are Concerned with the Larger Citizenship." In *The Woman Citizen's Library,* edited by Shailer Mathews, 9:2,135–36. Chicago: Civics Society, 1913.

"Why Women Should Vote." *Ladies Home Journal* 27 (January 1910): 21–22.

"Widening the Circle of Enlightenment." *Journal of Adult Education* 2, no. 3 (June 1930): 276–79.

"Women and Internationalism." 1915. In *Women at The Hague: The International Congress of Women and Its Results,* edited by Jane Addams, Emily G. Balch, and Alice Hamilton, 59–66. Urbana: University of Illinois Press, 2003.

"Women and War." 1915. In *Famous Speeches by Eminent American Statesmen,* edited by Frederick C. Hicks, 440. St. Paul, Minn.: West Publishing, 1929.

"Women's Special Training for Peacemaking." 1909. In *Jane Addams' Essays and Speeches,* edited by Marilyn Fischer and Judy D. Whipps, 47–48. New York: Continuum International Publishing Group, 2005.

"Work and Play as Factors in Education." *Chautauqua* 42 (November 1905): 251–55.

COLLECTIONS OF JANE ADDAMS'S WRITINGS

Bryan, Mary Lynn McCree, Barbara Bair, and Maree de Angury, eds. *The Selected Papers of Jane Addams.* Vol. 1, *Preparing to Lead, 1860–81.* Urbana: University of Illinois Press, 2003.

Cooper Johnson, Emily, ed. *Jane Addams: A Centennial Reader.* New York: Macmillan, 1960.

Davis, Allen F., ed. *Jane Addams on Peace, War, and International Understanding, 1899–1932.* New York: Garland Publishing, 1976.

Elshtain, Jean Bethke, ed. *The Jane Addams Reader.* New York: Basic Books, 2002.

Fischer, Marilyn, and Judy D. Whipps, eds. *Jane Addams' Essays and Speeches.* New York: Continuum International Publishing Group, 2005.

Lagemann, Ellen Condliffe, ed. *Jane Addams: On Education.* New Brunswick, N.J.: Transaction Publishers, 1994.

Lasch, Christopher, ed. *The Social Thought of Jane Addams.* Indianapolis: Bobbs-Merrill, 1965.

SELECTED SECONDARY LITERATURE ON ADDAMS'S THEORETICAL WORK

Deegan, Mary Jo. *Jane Addams and the Men of the Chicago School, 1892–1918.* New Brunswick, N.J.: Transaction Books, 1988.

Elshtain, Jean Bethke. *Jane Addams and the Dream of American Democracy.* New York: Basic Books, 2002.

Farrell, John C. *Beloved Lady: A History of Jane Addams' Ideas on Reform and Peace.* Baltimore: Johns Hopkins University Press, 1967.

Fischer, Marilyn. *On Addams.* Belmont, Calif.: Wadsworth, 2004.

Fischer, Marilyn, Carol Nackenoff, and Wendy Chmielewski, eds. *Jane Addams and the Practice of Democracy.* Urbana: University of Illinois Press, 2009.

Hamington, Maurice. *Embodied Care: Jane Addams, Maurice Merleau-Ponty, and Feminist Ethics.* Urbana: University of Illinois Press, 2004.

———. "Jane Addams." *Stanford Encyclopedia of Philosophy* (Fall 2007): http://plato.stanford.edu/archives/fall2007/entries/addams-jane.

Levine, Daniel. *Jane Addams and the Liberal Tradition.* Madison: State Historical Society of Wisconsin, 1971.

Seigfried, Charlene Haddock. *Pragmatism and Feminism: Reweaving the Social Fabric.* Chicago: University of Chicago Press, 1996.

BIOGRAPHIES OF JANE ADDAMS

Brown, Victoria Bissell. *The Education of Jane Addams.* Philadelphia: University of Pennsylvania Press, 2004.

Davis, Allen F. *American Heroine: The Life and Legend of Jane Addams*. London: Oxford, 1973.

Diliberto, Gioia. *A Useful Woman: The Early Life of Jane Addams*. New York: Scribner, 1999.

Joslin, Katherine. *Jane Addams: A Writer's Life*. Urbana: University of Illinois Press, 2004.

Knight, Louise. *Citizen: Jane Addams and the Struggle for Democracy*. Chicago: University of Chicago Press, 2005.

Linn, James Weber. *Jane Addams: A Biography*. Urbana: University of Illinois Press, 2000.

Polikoff, Barbara Garland. *With One Bold Act: The Story of Jane Addams*. Chicago: Boswell Books, 1999.

OTHER WORKS CITED

Aboulafia, Mitchell. "Was George Herbert Mead a Feminist?" *Hypatia* 8, no. 2 (Spring 1993): 145–58.

Acker, Joan. *Class Questions: Feminist Answers*. Lanham, Md.: Rowman and Littlefield, 2006.

Ake, Claude. "The African Context for Human Rights." *Africa Today* 34, no. 142 (1987): 5–13.

Alonso, Harriet Hyman. *Peace as a Woman's Issue: A History of the U.S. Movement for World Peace and Women's Rights*. Syracuse, N.Y.: Syracuse University Press, 1993.

Andermahr, Sonya, Terry Lovell, and Carol Wolkowitz. *A Glossary of Feminist Theory*. New York: Hodder Arnold, 1997.

Anderson, Jervis. "The Public Intellectual." *New Yorker* 69, no. 46 (January 17, 1994): 39–46.

Appiah, Kwame Anthony. *Cosmopolitanism: Ethics in a World of Strangers*. New York: W. W. Norton, 2006.

Applebee, Arthur N. *Curriculum as Conversation: Transforming Traditions of Teaching and Learning*. Chicago: University of Chicago Press, 1996.

Armstrong, A. C. "Kant's Philosophy of Peace and War." *Journal of Philosophy* 28, no. 8 (April 1931): 197–204.

Audoin-Rouzeau, Stéphane, and Annette Becker. *14–18: Understanding the Great War*. New York: Hill and Wang, 2000.

Baggini, Julian, and Jeremy Stangroom. *What Philosophers Think*. New York: Barnes and Noble Books, 2003.

Baier, Annette. *Postures of the Mind: Essays on Mind and Morals*. Minneapolis: University of Minnesota Press, 1985.

Bailey, Cathryn. "Making Waves and Drawing Lines: The Politics of Defining the Vicissitudes of Feminism." *Hypatia* 12, no. 3 (Summer 1997): 17–29.

Banner, Lois. *Elizabeth Cady Stanton: A Radical for Woman's Rights*. Boston: Little, Brown, 1980.

Barker-Benfield, G. J. "Mother Emancipator: The Meaning of Jane Addams' Sickness and Cure." *Journal of Family History* 4, no. 4 (Winter 1979): 395–420.

Barnett, Henrietta. "The Beginning of Toynbee Hall." In *Towards Social Reform*, edited by Samuel Augustus Barnett, 239–54. New York: MacMillan, 1909.

Barnett, Samuel Augustus. "A Retrospect of Toynbee Hall." In *Towards Social Reform*, edited by Samuel Augustus Barnett, 255–70. New York: MacMillan, 1909.

Baruch, Elaine Hoffman, and Ruby Rohrlich. *Women in Search of Utopia: Mavericks and Mythmakers*. New York: Schocken, 1984.

Bernstein, Richard J. "Pragmatism's Common Faith." In *Pragmatism and Religion*, edited by Stuart Rosenbaum, 129–41. Urbana: University of Illinois Press, 2003.

Bok, Sissela. *A Strategy for Peace: Human Values and the Threat of War*. New York: Vintage Books, 1989.

Bowen, Louise de Koven. *Growing Up with a City*. Urbana: University of Illinois Press, 2002.

Brown, Victoria. "Advocate for Democracy: Jane Addams and the Pullman Strike." In *The Pullman Strike and the Crisis in the 1890s: Essays on Labor and Politics*, edited by Richard Schneirov, Shelton Stromquist, and Nick Salvatore, 130–58. Urbana: University of Illinois Press, 1999.

———. "Jane Addams, Progressivism, and Woman Suffrage: An Introduction to 'Why Women Should Vote.'" In *One Woman, One Vote: Rediscovering the Woman Suffrage Movement*, edited by Marjorie Spruill Wheeler, 179–202. Troutdale, Ore.: NewSage Press, 1995.

Bryan, Mary Lynn McCree, and Allen F. Davis, eds. *100 Years at Hull-House*. Bloomington: Indiana University Press, 1969.

Carlyle, Thomas. *On Heroes and Hero Worship and the Heroic in History*. New York: A. L. Burt, 1910.

Carr, Albert Z. "Is Business Bluffing Ethical?" In *Essentials of Business Ethics*, edited by Peter Madsen and Jay M. Shafritz, 62–78. New York: Meridian, 1990.

Chicago Chronicle. "Hull-House, Irreligious and Socialistic." September 16, 1903. In *100 Years at Hull-House*, edited by Mary Lynn McCree Bryan and Allen F. Davis. 120–21. Bloomington: Indiana University Press, 1969.

Chicago Daily Tribune. "Opens in Jolly Romp: Throngs of Children Besiege the Hull House Playground." May 5, 1895, 1.

Clarke, Robert. *Ellen Swallow: The Woman Who Founded Ecology*. Chicago: Follett Publishing, 1973.

Code, Lorraine. "Epistemology." In *A Companion to Feminist Philosophy*, edited by Alison Jaggar and Iris Young, 173–84. New York: Blackwell Publishers, 1999.

———. *What Can She Know?* Ithaca, N.Y.: Cornell University Press, 1991.

Craig, John. "The Woman's Peace Party and Questions of Gender Separatism." *Peace and Change* 19, no. 4 (October 1994): 373–98.

Crunden, Robert M. *Ministers of Reform: The Progressives' Achievement in American Civilization, 1889–1920*. Urbana: University of Illinois Press, 1984.

Cuomo, Chris. *The Philosopher Queen*. Lanham, Md.: Rowman and Littlefield, 1999.

Curti, Merle. "Jane Addams on Human Nature." *Journal of the History of Ideas* 22, no. 2 (April 1961): 240–53.

Davidson, Julia O'Connell. *Prostitution, Power, and Freedom*. Ann Arbor: University of Michigan Press, 1998.

Davis, Allen F. *American Heroine: The Life and Legend of Jane Addams*. New York: Oxford University Press, 1977.

———. "Introduction." In Jane Addams, *The Spirit of Youth and the City Streets*, vii–xxx. New York: Macmillan, 1930.

———. *Spearheads for Reform: The Social Settlements and the Progressive Movement, 1890–1914*. New York: Oxford University Press, 1967.

Davis, Barbara Gross. *Tools for Teaching*. San Francisco: Jossey-Boss, 1993.

Dawley, Alan. *Changing the World: American Progressives in War and Revolution*. Princeton, N.J.: Princeton University Press, 2003.

Daynes, Gary, and Nicholas V. Longo. "Jane Addams and the Origins of Service-Learning

Practice in the United States." *Michigan Journal of Community Service Learning* 11, no. 1 (Fall 2004): 5–13.

Deegan, Mary Jo. "'Dear Love, Dear Love': Feminist Pragmatism and the Chicago Female World of Love and Ritual." *Gender and Society* 10, no. 5 (October 1996): 590–607.

———. *Jane Addams and the Men of the Chicago School, 1892–1918.* New Brunswick, N.J.: Transaction Books, 1990.

———. "Play from the Perspective of George Herbert Mead." In George Herbert Mead, *Play, School, and Society,* edited by Mary Jo Deegan. New York: Peter Lang, 1999.

———. *Race, Hull-House, and the University of Chicago: A New Conscience against Ancient Evils.* Westport, Conn.: Praeger, 2002.

———. "W. E. B. DuBois and the Women of Hull House, 1895–1899." *American Sociologist* 19, no. 4 (Winter 1988): 301–11.

Degan, Mary Louise. *The History of the Woman's Peace Party.* New York: Burt Franklin Reprints, 1974.

Dell, Floyd. *Women as World Builders: Studies in Modern Feminism.* Chicago: Forbes, 1913.

Delzell, C. F. *The Unification of Italy, 1859–1861: Cavour, Mazzini, or Garibaldi?* New York: Holt Rinehart and Winston, 1965.

D'Emilio, John, and Estelle B. Freedman. *Intimate Matters: A History of Sexuality in America.* 2nd ed. Chicago: University of Chicago Press, 1997.

Dewey, John. *Democracy and Education.* 1916. In *John Dewey: The Middle Works, 1899–1924,* edited by Jo Ann Boydston, 9:1–370. Carbondale: Southern Illinois University Press, 1985.

———. "Democratic versus Coercive International Organization: The Realism of Jane Addams." 1945. In Jane Addams, *Peace and Bread in Time of War,* ix–xx. Boston: G. K. Hall, 1960.

———. *Logic: The Theory of Inquiry.* 1938. In *John Dewey: The Later Works, 1925–1953,* edited by Jo Ann Boydston, 12:1–527. Carbondale: Southern Illinois University Press, 1991.

———. "Philosophy and Democracy." 1919. In *John Dewey: The Middle Works, 1899–1924,* edited by Jo Ann Boydston, 11:42–54. Carbondale: Southern Illinois University Press, 1991.

———. *The Public and Its Problems.* 1927. In *John Dewey: The Later Works, 1925–1953,* edited by Jo Ann Boydston, 2:235–372. Carbondale: Southern Illinois University Press, 1984.

———. *The Quest for Certainty.* 1933. In *John Dewey: The Later Works, 1925–1953,* edited by Jo Ann Boydston, 4:1–250. Carbondale: Southern Illinois University Press, 1991.

———. *The School and Society.* 1915. Chicago: University of Chicago Press, 1990.

Downs, Robert Bingham. *Friedrich Froebel.* Boston: Twayne Publishers, 1978.

Edwards, R. A. R. "Jane Addams, Walter Rauschenbusch, and Dorothy Day: A Comparative Study of Settlement Theology." In *Gender and the Social Gospel,* edited by Wendy J. Deichmann Edwards and Carolyn De Swarte Gifford, 150–66. Urbana: University of Illinois Press, 2003.

Faderman, Lillian. *Odd Girls and Twilight Lovers: A History of Lesbian Life in Twentieth-Century America.* New York: Penguin, 1991.

Feagin, Joe R., and Hernán Vera. *Liberation Sociology.* Boulder, Colo.: Westview Press, 2001.

Flanagan, Maureen A. "Introduction." In Louise de Koven Bowen, *Growing Up with a City,* ix–xxiv. Urbana: University of Illinois Press, 2002.

Freire, Paulo. *Pedagogy of Freedom: Ethics, Democracy, and Civic Courage.* Translated by Patrick Clarke. Lanham, Md.: Rowman and Littlefield, 1998.

———. *Pedagogy of the Oppressed.* Translated by Myra Bergman Ramos. New York: Herder and Herder, 1972.

Froebel, Friedrich, and W. N. Hailmann. *The Education of Man.* New York: D. Appleton, 1895.

Frye, Marilyn. *The Politics of Reality.* Trumansburg, N.Y.: Crossing Press, 1983.

Ganz, Cheryl R., and Margaret Strobel, eds. *Pots of Promise: Mexicans and Pottery at Hull-House, 1920–40.* Urbana: University of Illinois Press, 2004.

Gilman, Charlotte Perkins. *The Home: Its Work and Influence.* 1903. New York: Source Book Press, 1970.

———. "If I Were a Man." 1914. In *The Yellow Wallpaper and Other Stories,* 57–62. Toronto: Dover Thrift Editions, 1997.

———. *The Living of Charlotte Perkins Gilman: An Autobiography.* Madison: University of Wisconsin Press, 1935.

———. *The Man-Made World.* 1911. Amherst, N.Y.: Humanity Books, 2001.

———. *Women and Economics: The Economic Factor between Men and Women as a Factor in Social Evolution.* 1898. New York: Harper and Row, 1966.

———. "The Yellow Wallpaper." 1892. In *Herland, The Yellow Wall-Paper, and Selected Writings,* 166–82. New York: Penguin Books, 1999.

Green, Judith. "Building a Cosmopolitan World Community through Mutual Hospitality." In *Pragmatism and the Problem of Race,* edited by Bill E. Lawson and Donald F. Koch, 203–24. Bloomington: Indiana University Press, 2004.

Greenwood, Janette Thomas. *The Gilded Age: A History in Documents.* New York: Oxford University Press, 2000.

Hamington, Maurice. "Addams's Radical Democracy: Moving beyond Rights." *Journal of Speculative Philosophy* 18, no. 3 (2004): 216–23.

———. "Jane Addams and Ida B. Wells on Lynching." *Journal of Speculative Philosophy* 19, no. 2 (2005): 167–74.

Harding, Sandra, ed. *Feminism and Methodology.* Bloomington: Indiana University Press, 1987.

———. *The Feminist Standpoint Theory Reader: Intellectual and Political Controversies.* New York: Routledge, 2004.

———. "Subjectivity, Experience, and Knowledge: An Epistemology from/for Rainbow Coalition Politics." In *Feminist Theory,* edited by Mary F. Rogers, 97–108. Boston: McGraw-Hill, 1998.

Harkavy, Ira, and John L. Puckett. "Lessons from Hull House for the Contemporary Urban University." *Social Science Review* (September 1994): 299–321.

Harkness, Georgia. "Jane Addams in Retrospect." *Christian Century* 77, no. 2 (January 13, 1960): 39–41.

Haslet, Diane C. "Hull House and the Birth Control Movement: An Untold Story." *Journal of Women and Social Work* 12, no. 3 (Fall 1997): 261–78.

Hekman, Susan. *Moral Voices, Moral Selves: Carol Gilligan and Feminist Moral Theory.* University Park, Pa: Pennsylvania State University Press.

Hirsch, Susan E. "The Search for Unity among Railroad Workers: The Pullman Strike." In *The Pullman Strike and the Crisis in the 1890s: Essays on Labor and Politics,* edited by Richard Schneirov, Shelton Stromquist, and Nick Salvatore, 43–64. Urbana: University of Illinois Press, 1999.

Hoagland, Sarah Lucia. *Lesbian Ethics.* Palo Alto, Calif.: Institute of Lesbian Studies, 1988.

———. "Why Lesbian Ethics?" *Hypatia* 7, no. 4 (Autumn 1992): 195–206.

Holbrook, Agnes Sinclair. "Map, Notes, and Comments." In *Hull House Maps and Papers: A Presentation of Nationalities and Wages in a Congested District of Chicago,* 53–62. New York: Thomas Y. Crowell, 1895.

hooks, bell. *Teaching Community: A Pedagogy of Hope*. New York: Routledge, 2003.

Huckle, Patricia. "Women in Utopias." In *The Utopian Vision: Seven Essays on the Quin-centennial of Sir Thomas More*, edited by E. D. S. Sullivan, 115–36. San Diego: San Diego State University Press, 1983.

Jackson, Shannon. "Civic Play-Housekeeping: Gender, Theatre, and American Reform." *Theatre Journal* 48, no. 3 (1996): 337–61.

———. *Lines of Activity: Performance, Historiography, Hull-House Domesticity*. Ann Arbor: University of Michigan Press, 2000.

James, William. "The Experience of Activity." In *Essays in Radical Empiricism and a Pluralistic Universe*, edited by Ralph Barton Perry, 81–99. New York: E. P. Dutton, 1971.

———. *Pragmatism and Other Essays*. 1907. New York: Washington Square Press, 1963.

Jenni, Kathie. "Vices of Inattention." *Journal of Applied Philosophy* 20, no. 3 (2003): 279–95.

Joslin, Katherine. "Introduction to the Illinois Edition." In Jane Addams, *A New Conscience and an Ancient Evil*, ix–xxxii. Urbana: University of Illinois Press, 2002.

Kadish, Alon. *Apostle Arnold: The Life of Death of Arnold Toynbee 1852–1883*. Durham, N.C.: Duke University Press, 1986.

Kant, Immanuel. "Perpetual Peace: A Philosophical Sketch." 1795. In *Perpetual Peace and Other Essays on Politics, History, and Morals*, translated by Ted Humphrey, 107–44. Indianapolis: Hackett, 1983.

Kelley, Florence. "I Go to Work." *Survey* 58, no. 5 (June 1, 1927): 271–77.

Kleinberg, S. J. *Women in the United States, 1830–1945*. New Brunswick, N.J.: Rutgers University Press, 1999.

Knight, Louise W. "Jane Addams's Views on the Responsibilities of Wealth." In *The Responsibilities of Wealth*, edited by Dwight F. Burlingame, 118–37. Bloomington: Indiana University Press, 1992.

Kuklick, Bruce. *A History of Philosophy in America, 1720–2000*. Oxford: Oxford University Press, 2001.

Lasch, Christopher, ed. *The New Radicalism in America, 1889–1963: The Intellectual as a Social Type*. New York: W. W. Norton, 1965.

Lears, T. J. Jackson. *No Place of Grace*. New York: Pantheon Books, 1981.

Leffers, M. Regina. "Pragmatists Jane Addams and John Dewey Inform the Ethics of Care." *Hypatia* 8, no. 2 (Spring 1993): 64–78.

Lerner, Gerda. *The Majority Finds Its Past: Placing Women in History*. New York: Oxford University Press, 1979.

———. "Why Have There Been So Few Women Philosophers?" In *Presenting Women Philosophers*, edited by Cecile T. Tougas and Sara Ebenreck, 5–14. Philadelphia: Temple University Press, 2000.

Liebschner, Joachim. *A Child's Work: Freedom and Play in Froebel's Educational Theory and Practice*. Cambridge: Lutterworth, 2001.

Lindsey, Almont. "Paternalism and the Pullman Strike." *American Historical Review* 44, no. 2 (January 1939): 272–89.

Lippmann, Walter. *A Preface to Politics*. New York: Mitchell Kennerley, 1914.

Lissak, Rivka Shpak. *Pluralism and Progressives: Hull House and the New Immigrants, 1889–1919*. Chicago: University of Chicago Press, 1989.

Liu, Goodwin. "Knowledge, Foundations, and Discourse: Philosophical Support for Service-Learning." In *Beyond the Tower: Concepts and Models for Service-Learning in Philosophy*, edited by C. David Lisman and Irene E. Harvey, 11–34. Washington D.C.: American Association for Higher Education, 2000.

Longo, Nicholas V. "Recognizing the Role of Community in Civic Education." *Circle Working Paper* 30 (April 2005): 1–17. Available at http://www.civicyouth.org.

Lorde, Audre. *Sister Outsider.* Freedom, Calif.: Crossing Press, 1984.

Lugones, Maria C., and Elizabeth V. Spelman. "Have We Got a Theory for You! Feminist Theory, Cultural Imperialism, and the Demand for 'the Woman's Voice.'" In *Feminism and Philosophy: Essential Readings in Theory, Reinterpretation and Application,* edited by Nancy Tuana and Rosemarie Tong, 494–507. Boulder, Colo.: Westview Press, 1995.

Lynd, Staughton. "Jane Addams and the Radical Impulse." *Commentary* 32 (July 1961): 54–59.

Mahowald, Mary B. "What Classical American Philosophers Missed: Jane Addams, Critical Pragmatism, and Cultural Feminism." *Journal of Value Inquiry* 31, no. 1 (March 1997): 39–54.

Mann, Bonnie. *Women's Liberation and the Sublime: Feminism, Postmodernism, Environment.* New York: Oxford University Press, 2006.

Marsoobian, Armen T., and John Ryder. *The Blackwell Guide to American Philosophy.* Malden, Mass: Blackwell Publishing, 2004.

Martindale, Kathleen, and Martha Saunders. "Realizing Love and Justice: Lesbian Ethics in the Upper and Lower Case." *Hypatia* 7, no. 4 (Fall 1992): 148–72.

Marx, Karl. "Manifesto of the Communist Party." In *The Marx-Engels Reader,* 2nd ed., edited by Robert C. Tucker, 469–500. New York: W. W. Norton, 1978.

Mazzini, Joseph. *The Duties of Man and Other Essays.* New York: J. M. Dent, 1907.

McKenna, Erin. *The Task of Utopia: A Pragmatist and Feminist Perspective.* Lanham, Md.: Rowman and Littlefield, 2001.

Mead, George Herbert. *Play, School, and Society,* edited by Mary Jo Deegan. New York: Peter Lang, 1999.

———. "Self." In *George Herbert Mead: On Social Psychology,* edited by Anselm Strauss, 196–246. Chicago: University of Chicago Press, 1956.

Menand, Louis. *The Metaphysical Club: A Story of Ideas in America.* New York: Farrar, Straus and Giroux, 2001.

Miller, Sarah Clark. "A Kantian Ethic of Care." In *Feminist Interventions in Ethics and Politics,* edited by Barbara S. Andrew, Jean Keller, and Lisa H. Schwartzman, 111–27. Lanham, Md.: Rowman and Littlefield, 2005.

Mink, Gwendolyn. *Settlement Folk: Social Thought and the American Settlement Movement, 1885–1930.* Chicago: University of Chicago Press, 1990.

Mitchell, Ronald K., Bradley R. Agle, and Donna J. Wood. "Toward a Theory of Stakeholder Identification and Salience: Defining the Principle of Who and What Really Counts." *Academy of Management Review* 22, no. 4 (1997): 853–86.

Mosse, George L. *Fallen Soldiers: Reshaping the Memory of the World Wars.* Oxford: Clarendon Press, 1990.

Muncy, Robyn. *Creating a Female Dominion in American Reform, 1890–1935.* New York: Oxford University Press, 1991.

Nelson, Julie A. "The Study of Choice or the Study of Provisioning? Gender and the Definition of Economics." In *Beyond Economic Man: Feminist Theory and Economics,* edited by Marianne A. Ferber and Julie A. Nelson, 23–36. Chicago: University of Chicago Press, 1993.

Noddings, Nel. *Caring: A Feminine Approach to Ethics and Moral Education.* Berkeley: University of California Press, 1984.

———. *Starting at Home: Caring and Social Policy.* Berkeley: University of California Press, 2002.

Olasky, Marvin. *The Tragedy of American Compassion.* Washington, D.C.: Regnery Publishing, 1992.

Outlaw, Lucious T. *On Race and Philosophy.* New York: Routledge, 1996.

Penelope, Julia. "The Lesbian Perspective." In *Lesbian Philosophies and Cultures,* edited by Jeffner Allen, 89–108. Albany, N.Y.: State University of New York Press, 1986.

Pois, Anne Marie. "Foreshadowings: Jane Addams, Emily Greene Balch, and the Ecofeminism/Pacifist Feminism of the 1980's." *Peace and Change* 20, no. 4 (October 1995): 439–66.

Polacheck, Hilda Satt. *I Came a Stranger: The Story of a Hull-House Girl.* Urbana: University of Illinois Press, 1991.

Pratt, Scott. *Native Pragmatism.* Bloomington: Indiana University Press, 2002.

Quandt, Jean B. *From the Small Town to the Great Community: The Social Thought of Progressive Intellectuals.* New Brunswick, N.J.: Rutgers University Press, 1970.

Romano, Carlin. "Mulling (Not Hulling) Jane Addams." *Chronicle of Higher Education* 48, no. 29 (March 29, 2002): B11.

Rorty, Richard. "Anticlericalism and Atheism." In *The Future of Religion,* edited by Santiago Zabala, 29–42. New York: Columbia University Press, 2005.

Rosenberg, Rosalind. *Divided Lives: American Women in the Twentieth Century.* New York: Hill and Wang, 1992.

Ross, Dorothy. "Gendered Social Knowledge: Domestic Discourse, Jane Addams, and the Possibilities of Social Science." In *Gender and American Social Science: The Formative Years,* edited by Helene Silverberg, 235–64. Princeton, N.J.: Princeton University Press, 1998.

Royce, Josiah. *Philosophy of Loyalty.* Nashville, Tenn.: Vanderbilt University Press, 1995.

Rupp, Leila J. "Sexuality and Politics in the Early Twentieth Century: The Case of the International Women's Movement." *Feminist Studies* 23, no. 3 (Fall 1997): 577–606.

Ruskin, John. *The Works of John Ruskin.* Vols. 18 and 19. Edited by E. T. Cook and Alexander Wedderburn. London: George Allen, 1903–12.

Sadovnik, Alan R., and Susan F. Semel. *Founding Mothers and Others: Women Educational Leaders during the Progressive Era.* New York: Palgrave, 2002.

Sawaya, Francesca. "The Authority of Experience: Jane Addams and Hull House." In *Women's Experience of Modernity, 1875–1945,* edited by Ann L. Ardis and Leslie W. Lewis, 47–62. Baltimore: Johns Hopkins University Press, 2003.

Schierman, Barbara. *Alice Hamilton: A Life in Letters.* Urbana: University of Illinois Press, 2003.

Schott, Linda. "Jane Addams and William James on Alternatives to War." *Journal of the History of Ideas* 54, no. 2 (April 1993): 241–54.

Schott, Robin May. "Introduction." In *Feminist Interpretations of Immanuel Kant,* edited by Robin May Schott, 1–18. University Park, Pa: Pennsylvania State University Press, 1997.

Sedgewick, Sally. "Can Kant's Ethics Survive Feminist Critique?" In *Feminist Interpretations of Immanuel Kant,* edited by Robin May Schott, 77–100. University Park, Pa: Pennsylvania State University Press, 1997.

Segal, Lynne. *Is the Future Female? Troubled Thoughts on Contemporary Feminism.* New York: Peter Bedrick Books, 1988.

Seigfried, Charlene Haddock. "Has Passion a Place in Philosophy?" In "Philosophy in America at the Turn of the Century." APA Centennial Supplement, *Journal of Philosophical Research* (Charlottesville, Va.: Philosophy Documentation Center) (2003): 35–54.

———. "Introduction to the Illinois Edition." In Jane Addams, *Democracy and Social Ethics,* ix–xxxviii. Urbana: University of Illinois Press, 2002.

———. *Pragmatism and Feminism.* Chicago: University of Chicago Press, 1996.

———. "Socializing Democracy: Jane Addams and John Dewey." *Philosophy of the Social Sciences* 29, no. 2 (1999): 207–30.

———. "Where Are All the Pragmatist Feminists?" *Hypatia* 6, no. 2 (Summer 1991): 1–20.

Shade, Patrick. *Habits of Hope: A Pragmatic Theory*. Nashville, Tenn.: Vanderbilt University Press, 2001.

Sherrick, Rebecca. "Their Father's Daughters: The Autobiographies of Jane Addams and Florence Kelley." *American Studies* 27, no. 1 (Spring 1986): 39–53.

Sklar, Kathryn Kish. *Florence Kelley and the Nation's Work: The Rise of Women's Political Culture, 1830–1900*. New Haven, Conn.: Yale University Press, 1995.

———. "Hull House in the 1890s: A Community of Women Reformers." *Signs* 10 (Summer 1985): 658–77.

———. "Jane Addams's Peace Activism, 1914–1922: A Model for Women Today?" *Women's Studies Quarterly* 23 (Fall–Winter 1995): 32–47.

Smith, Adam. *An Inquiry into the Nature and Causes of the Wealth of Nations*. 1776. London: Methuen, 1904. Available at http://www.econlib.org/LIBRARY/Smith/smWN1.html.

Spender, Dale. *Feminist Theories: Three Centuries of Women's Intellectual Traditions*. London: Women's Press, 1983.

Stebner, Eleanor J. *The Women of Hull House: A Study in Spirituality, Vocation, and Relationship*. Albany, N.Y.: State University of New York Press, 1997.

Steinem, Gloria. "What if Freud Were Phyllis?" In *Moving beyond Words: Age, Rage, Sex, Power, Money, Muscles; Breaking the Boundaries of Gender*, 32–92. New York: Simon and Schuster, 1995.

Stuhr, John J. *Genealogical Pragmatism: Philosophy, Experience, and Community*. Albany, N.Y.: State University of New York Press, 1997.

Sullivan, Shannon. "Reciprocal Relations between Races: Jane Addams's Ambiguous Legacy." *Transactions of the Charles S. Peirce Society* 39, no. 1 (Winter 2003): 43–60.

Tarbell, Ida M. *The Business of Being a Woman*. New York: Macmillan, 1912. Available at http://manybooks.net/titles/tarbelli1657716577-8.html#.

Taylor, Graham. "Ella Flagg Young: First Woman Superintendent of Chicago Schools and President of National Education Association." *Survey* 24, no. 17 (July 23, 1910): 619–21.

———. "Jane Addams—Interpreter, an Appreciation." *Review of Reviews* 40 (December 1909): 680.

Terrell, Mary Church. *A Colored Woman in a White World*. 1940. New York: G. K. Hall, 1996.

Thattai, Deeptha. "A History of Public Education in the United States." Available at http://www.servintfree.net/~aidmn-ejournal/publications/2001–11/PublicEducationInThe UnitedStates.html.

Tomko, Linda J. *Dancing Class: Gender, Ethnicity and Social Divides in American Dance, 1890–1920*. Bloomington: Indiana University Press, 1999.

Tong, Rosemarie. *Feminist Thought: A Comprehensive Introduction*. Boulder, Colo.: Westview Press, 1989.

Torjesen, Karen Jo. *When Women Were Priests: Women's Leadership in the Early Church and the Scandal of Their Subordination in the Rise of Christianity*. San Francisco: HarperSan Francisco, 1993.

Tuana, Nancy. *Woman and the History of Philosophy*. New York: Paragon, 1992.

UNICEF. "Nutrition." UNICEF Press Centre, http://www.unicef.org/media/media_45490 .html.

Voris, Van. *Carrie Chapman Catt: A Public Life*. New York: Feminist Press, 1987.

Walhout, Donald. "Recovering Our Predecessors: Julia Gulliver as Philosopher." *Hypatia* 16, no. 1 (Winter 2001): 72–90.

Walker, Margaret Urban. "Moral Epistemology." In *A Companion to Feminist Philosophy*, edited by Alison M. Jaggar and Iris Marion Young, 363–71. Oxford: Blackwell Publishers, 1998.

Webb, Beatrice. "A Fabian Visits Hull House." 1898. In *100 Years at Hull-House*, edited by Mary Lynn McCree Bryan and Allen F. Davis, 61–62. Bloomington: Indiana University Press, 1969.

Weeks, Kathi. *Constituting Feminist Subjects*. Ithaca, N.Y.: Cornell University Press, 1998.

Wells, Ida B. *Crusade for Justice: The Autobiography of Ida B. Wells*. Edited by Alfreda M. Duster. Chicago: University of Chicago Press, 1970.

West, Cornel. *The American Evasion of Philosophy: A Genealogy of Pragmatism*. Madison: University of Wisconsin Press, 1989.

———. *Race Matters*. New York: Vintage Books, 1993.

Willett, Cynthia. *The Soul of Justice*. Ithaca, N.Y.: Cornell University Press, 2001.

Winston, A. P. "The Significance of the Pullman Strike." *Journal of Political Economy* 9, no. 4 (September 1901): 540–61.

Young, Iris Marion. *Justice and the Politics of Difference*. Princeton, N.J.: Princeton University Press, 1990.

Zinn, Howard. *A People's History of the United States: 1492–Present*. San Francisco: Harper Perennial, 1995.

———. *The Twentieth Century: A People's History*. New York: Harper and Row, 1984.

———. *The Zinn Reader: Writings on Disobedience and Democracy*. New York: Seven Stories Press, 1997.

INDEX

Abbott, Edith, 26
Abbott, Grace, 26
Addams, Jane: biography of, 2–5; care ethics and, 58–61; cosmopolitanism and, 185–86; criticisms of, 119–21; democracy, her concept of, 39, 46–47, 54–56, 60–61, 76–84, 90–92, 96–97, 102–7, 117, 132, 137–39, 152–53, 161–63, 181; economic theories of, 127–48; educational theories of, emotions and, 62, 74; feminism of, 48–52; feminist pragmatism of, 69–70; feminist theorizing and, 58–66; historical influences on, 16–18; hope and, 183–85; inclusiveness, her theories of, 109–26; intellectual influences on, 18–31; lesbian ethics and, 61–67; pacifism of, 4, 89–108; philosopher designation of, 5–11; pragmatism of, 32–47; religion and, 166–80; women's issues and, 67–69. WORKS: *Democracy and Social Ethics*, 6–7, 18, 45–46, 50, 66, 72, 77–82, 97, 129, 139, 143–44, 147, 172; *The Long Road of Woman's Memory*, 56–57, 92; *A New Conscience and an Ancient Evil*, 10, 73, 82, 144–46, 156; *Newer Ideals of Peace*, 6, 76, 81, 83, 92, 97–98, 103; *Peace and Bread in Time of War*, 7, 92, 100, 106; *The Second Twenty Years at Hull-House*, 92, 157; *The Spirit of Youth and the City Streets*, 10, 36, 59, 72; *Twenty Years at Hull-House*, 19, 22, 38, 50, 62, 80, 92, 138, 157, 168–71, 189n1, 190n8
Addams, John, 11, 18–20, 169
Addams, Mary, 2

aesthetics, 21, 115
aldermen, 72–74, 137
American Civil Liberties Union, 4
American Federation of Labor, 26, 134
American philosophy. *See* pragmatism
American Railway Union, 134–35
ancient Greek philosophy, 30
Appiah, Kwame Anthony, 185
Applebee, Arthur N., 163
Armstrong, A. C., 105
Atwood, Charlotte, 101
Audoin-Rouzeau, Stéphane, 107
Augsburg, Anita, 63

Baier, Annette, 58
Balch, Emily Greene, 90, 92, 106
Barker-Benfield, G. J., 190n19
Barnett, Samuel, 23–25
Becker, Annette, 107
Bernstein, Richard, 40, 167
Blaisdell, Sarah, 169
Bok, Sissela, 101–2
Bowen, Louise de Koven, 140–41
Breckinridge, Sophonisba, 26
Brown, Victoria Bissell, 6, 19, 64, 150, 166, 170, 191n19, 205n4

capitalism, 50, 82, 128–39, 146–48, 160, 171
care ethics, 10, 58–61, 68, 70–71, 84–85, 115–19, 165, 195n43, 196n1, 197n46
Carey, Ida May, 62

Carlyle, Thomas, 20–23, 30, 97, 121, 170
Catt, Carrie Chapman, 52, 111
Charters, Jessie A., 189n13
Chicago Woman's Club, 112
Chicago World's Colombian Exhibition, 113
Children's Bureau, 26, 29
Civic Federation of Chicago, 134–35
Civil War, 2, 16, 18–19, 103, 118
Clapp, Elise Ripley, 42
Cleveland, Grover, 134
Code, Lorraine, 53–54, 58
Comte, August, 11, 30
cosmic patriotism, 103
cosmopolitanism, 4, 12, 54, 100, 118, 181, 185–86
Craig, John, 52
Cuomo, Chris, 108
Curti, Merle, 5, 9

Daly, Mary, 173
Danes, Gary, 165
Darwin, Charles, 2
Darwinism, social, 44
Davis, Allen F., 17, 27, 63, 146
Day, Dorothy, 183
Debs, Eugene, 50, 129, 133–35
Deegan, Mary Jo, 8–9, 38–39, 46–48, 50, 61, 122, 192n22, 200n11
Dell, Floyd, 194n2
devil baby, story of, 57–58, 65
Dewey, Jane, 37
Dewey, John, 6–8, 10–11, 15, 32–33, 35–43, 178, 183, 189n13, 190n26; on Addams, 7, 37–38; on education, 149, 151, 153, 158; on peace, 91, 100, 102–4
Diliberto, Gioia, 64
Dorcas Federal Labor Union, 131
Dreikurs, Sadie Garland, 29
DuBois, W. E. B., 109, 112, 117, 193n61, 200n11

ecology. See Oekology
education: Addams's theories of, 62, 74; Dewey on, 149, 151, 153, 158; at Hull House, 156–57; lateral progress and, 149, 159–61
Edwards, R. A. R., 171–72
Emanuel, Fannie Hagan, 17
emotion: action and, 76; emotivisim and, 74–75; knowledge and, 74–75, 145; patriotism and, 101–2; settlement work and, 60–62; sex drive and, 155; war and, 75, 92, 99
epistemology, 10–11, 21, 40, 48, 60, 120–21; disruptive knowledge and, 74–76; service learning and, 158, 164; social settlements and, 6, 24, 34–35, 60, 116, 141; standpoint theory and, 52–58, 94. See also sympathetic knowledge

essentialism, gender, 51, 95, 194n16
ethics. See care ethics; lesbian ethics; rights-based ethics

Faderman, Lillian, 61, 63–64
fallibility, 1, 39, 112–13, 121, 178
Farrell, John, 102
Feagin, Joe R., 193n61
feminism: cultural, 48, 50–51; liberal, 10, 49; pragmatist, 10, 42, 79–80, 179–80, 197n46; radical, 10, 49, 65
Fiorenza, Elisabeth Schussler, 173
Freire, Paulo, 181, 183–84
Froebel, Friedrich, 151–53
Frye, Marilyn, 51

gender essentialism, 51, 95, 194n16
Gilman, Charlotte Perkins, 7, 26, 111, 156, 167–68, 176–77, 194n1
Great Depression, 16, 128
Gulliver, Julia, 91–92

Hamilton, Alice, 26–27, 90, 92, 156
Harding, Sandra, 53–54
Harkavy, Ira, 158
Harkness, Georgia, 172
Hartsock, Nancy, 53
Haymarket Riot, 128
Hegel, G. W. F., 96
Hekman, Susan, 85
Heymann, Lida Gustava, 63
Hinton, Chase, 29
Hoagland, Sarah, 65
Holmes, Oliver Wendell, 190n26
Hooker, George, 27
hooks, bell, 183–84, 186
Hull House: adult education at, 157; aesthetics of, 115–16; children at, 28–30, 138–39, 151–54; civic church of, 170–75, 205n4; class struggles and, 128–29; description of, 3–4, 8, 17, 34, 45–46, 77, 150, 165; Dewey and, 37–38; diverse neighborhood of, 55–57, 78, 100, 110–13; feminist pragmatist utopia of, 175–82; funding of, 22, 133, 139–40; labor museum at, 159–61; labor organization and, 131, 134–35, 142; management of, 24; Mead and, 39; pacifism of, 61, 93; as philosophical center, 5, 10, 25; sex education at, 156; social housekeeping of, 94; social work and, 189n3; women of, 25–28, 51–52, 61–63, 66–67, 200n11
Hull-House Maps and Papers, 8, 110, 150
Hunton, Addie, 101

International Congress of Women, 90, 104–5

Jackson, Shannon, 28, 39, 116, 177
Jaggar, Alison, 53
James, William, 6–7, 9, 12, 33–36, 45, 97–100, 178, 180, 190n26
Jane Club, 142, 179
Joslin, Katherine, 98
Juvenile Court, 45, 59–60

Kant, Immanuel, 53, 104–7, 195n23, 199n62
Keller, Helen, 129
Kelley, Florence, 25, 27–29, 41, 50, 109, 131, 161, 191nn16, 46, 48
Kenney, Mary, 26–27, 50, 131
Kent, William, 139–40
Keyser, Mary, 143
King, McKenzie, 27
Knight, Louise W., 140, 200n10, 205n12
knowledge. *See* emotion: knowledge and; epistemology; sympathetic knowledge
Kropotkin, Peter, 50

Ladies Home Journal, 68–69
Lagemann, Ellen Condliffe, 150, 163
Lasch, Christopher, 38, 80, 91, 193n62
lateral progress: capitalism and, 129, 140, 147; care ethics and, 60, 77; Christianity and, 170; definition of, 11, 44; democracy and, 187; education and, 149, 159–61; fallibility and, 112–14; labor unions and, 132–33; patriotism and, 119; peace and, 90, 96, 105; racism and, 114, 123; radicalization of pragmatism and, 32, 43–47, 193n62; rights and, 82, 118; standpoint theory and, 56
Lathrop, Julia, 26–27, 30
Lears, T. J., 160–61
Leffers, M. Regina, 84–85
Lerner, Gerda, 7–8, 177
lesbian ethics, 61, 64–65, 195n56
Levine, Daniel, 97
Lincoln, Abraham, 16, 18, 44, 122, 174, 191n13
Linn, James Weber, 19, 63, 205n12
Lippmann, Walter, 146
Lissak, Rivka Shpak, 201n41
listening, value of, 23, 57–58, 137, 142, 193n61
Liu, Goodwin, 164
London, Jack, 129
Longo, Nicholas V., 164–65
Lorde, Audre, 155–56
loyalty, as supporting patriotism, 101–3
Lugones, Maria, 54–55
lynching, 110, 114, 122–24

Mahowald, Mary, 9, 15
Mann, Bonnie, 194n16
Martindale, Kathleen, 64–65

Marx, Karl, 9, 26–27, 79, 128–29, 140, 147–48
Mazzini, Joseph, 19–20
McDowell, Mary, 17
McKenna, Erin, 178–79
McKinley, Ada Sophia Dennison, 17
Mead, George Herbert, 8, 15, 38–39, 47, 51, 102, 104, 149, 152–53
Metaphysical Club, 10, 190n26
Mill, John Stuart, 53, 82
Mitchell, Lucy Sprague, 42
Moore, Earnest Carroll, 27
Moore, Michael, 96
More, Thomas, 175
Morgan, J. P., 128
Mosse, George L., 108
Muncy, Robyn, 18, 176

National Association for the Advancement of Colored People, 4, 111, 122
National Child Labor Committee, 139, 151
National Council of Colored Women, 112
Nelson, Julie, 147
Noddings, Nel, 17, 154, 165

Oekology, 113
Olasky, Marvin, 171–72

Parker, Wayland, 151–52
patriotism, 4, 49, 90, 101–3, 117–19
Peirce, Charles Sanders, 40, 183, 190n26
Penelope, Julia, 66
philosophy: American (*see* pragmatism); ancient Greek, 30
Plato Club, 37
play, in human development, 12, 38–39, 138, 149–55, 165
Playground Association of America, 151
playgrounds, 151
Pois, Anne Marie, 194n1
Polacheck, Hilda Satt, 155
Polikoff, Barbara Garland, 29
Pond, Allen B., 139–40
Powers, Johnny, 72
pragmatism, 6, 10–11, 77; criticisms of, 92; definition of, 1, 33, 36, 40; feminist, 10, 32, 42–43, 69–70, 79–80, 114, 179–80; prophetic, 40–41; radical, 32–47; religion and, 167; utopias and, 177–80, 190n15
Pratt, Scott, 38
progress, lateral. *See* lateral progress
Progressive Era, 1–2, 16, 158, 164, 170
Progressive Party, 4, 39, 68, 119–20, 190n2
prostitution, 73, 82–83, 142, 144–47, 183
provisioning, economics as, 147
Puckett, John L., 158

Pullman, George, 133–41, 202n40
Pullman strike, 12, 79, 132–38, 140–41,
  202nn21, 40

racism, 74, 111, 114, 120, 122–25
radical, definition of, 10–11, 43, 46–47, 49–50,
  148, 161, 193nn61, 62. *See also* feminism
Rankin, Jeanette, 93, 198n12
Reagan, Ronald, 127
Rice, Harriet, 111, 200n10
Richards, Ellen Swallow, 113
rights-based ethics, 46–47, 67, 72, 81–84,
  118–19, 161
robber barons, 44, 128, 133
Rockefeller, John D., 128–29
Rockford Seminary, 2, 20, 30, 62–63, 92, 149, 168
Romano, Carlin, 1, 5
Roosevelt, Theodore, 4, 120, 190n2
Rorty, Richard, 40, 180
Rose, Hilary, 53
Rosenberg, Rosalind, 66, 189n3
Ross, Dorothy, 30
Royce, Josiah, 32, 42, 84
Ruether, Rosemary Radford, 173
Ruskin, John, 20–22, 132

Saunders, Martha, 64
Sawaya, Frances, 30
Seigfried, Charlene Haddock, 2, 9, 33, 56, 78,
  116, 186; on Addams's influence on Dewey,
  38–39; on feminist pragmatism, 42–43, 179;
  on marginalization of women, 7, 47; on
  perplexity, 74
separatism, 51–52
settlements, social. *See under* epistemology
settlement work, and emotion, 60–62
Shaw, George Bernard, 98
Sill, Anna P., 169
Sinclair, Upton, 129
Sklar, Kathryn Kish, 24, 28, 64, 93, 171
Smith, Adam, 129
Smith, Dorothy, 53
Smith, Mary Rozet, 22, 140; relationship with
  Addams, 62–64, 66, 177
social Darwinism, 44
Spanish-American War, 92, 96
Spelman, Elizabeth, 54–55
Spender, Dale, 194n1
stakeholder theory, 201n14
standpoint theory, 52–58, 94
Stanton, Elizabeth Cady, 67, 166–68
Starr, Ellen Gates, 3, 5, 116, 143, 169–70; rela-
  tionship with Addams, 62–63, 66, 177
Stead, William T., 172
Stebner, Eleanor, 172, 176
Stevens, Alinza, 131

Stuhr, John, 177, 180, 190n15
Sullivan, Shannon, 12–21, 201n41
Swope, Gerard, 27
sympathetic knowledge, Addams's theory of,
  11–12, 15, 24, 65, 71–85; Carlyle and, 21; children and, 30; feminist theory and, 48; fiction
  and, 31; lateral progress and, 56; play and, 39;
  Ruskin and, 21

Taft, Jessie, 66
Taft, William Howard, 29–30
Talbert, Mary B., 101
Tarbell, Ida M., 3
Taylor, Graham, 171, 181
Terrell, Mary Church, 101, 112, 122–23, 200n11
Thirteenth Universal Peace Conference, 34, 98
Tolstoy, Leo, 22–23, 143, 175
Toynbee, Arnold, 20, 22–25
Toynbee Hall, 3, 24–25
transaction, social concept of, 36, 73, 93, 100,
  115–16, 131–32, 140–41, 149, 162, 164–65;
  Dewey on, 42; Sullivan on, 120–21

Universal Peace Conference, Thirteenth, 34, 98
University of Chicago, 8, 26, 37–39, 46, 157–59,
  189n13
utopian thinking, 26, 72, 172. *See also* Hull
  House

Vera, Hernán, 193n61
Vittum, Harriet, 17

Wald, Lillian, 17, 29
Walker, Margaret Urban, 75
Waring, Mary F., 101
Webb, Beatrice, 26–27
Weeks, Kathi, 55
Wells, H. G., 98, 129
Wells, Ida B., 112, 120–25
West, Cornel, 33, 40–41, 109, 125
Williams, Fannie Barrier, 17, 112
Wilson, Woodrow, 103
Women's Congress, 92
Women's International League for Peace and
  Freedom, 4, 104, 200n11
Women's Peace Party, 52, 106
women's suffrage, 47, 49, 67–69, 83, 120
World War I, 4, 17, 39, 47, 49, 61, 75, 91–93,
  103–8
Wright, Frances, 43

Yarros, Rachel, 26, 156
Young, Ella Flagg, 151–52, 158, 204n45
Young, Iris Marion, 185

Zinn, Howard, 187

MAURICE HAMINGTON is associate professor of women's studies and philosophy and director of the Institute for Women's Studies and Services at Metropolitan State College of Denver, where he teaches feminist philosophy and feminist theory. His interest in feminist philosophy and, in particular, feminist ethics led him to pursue Jane Addams's historically underappreciated work. In his view, Addams's social philosophy represents a critical and innovative approach to classic American pragmatism, especially with respect to race, class, and gender. Hamington's research has resulted in two dozen scholarly presentations and journal articles on Addams's philosophy. His previous books include *Socializing Care: Feminist Ethics and Public Issues* (Rowman and Littlefield, 2006), coedited with Dorothy C. Miller; *Embodied Care: Jane Addams, Maurice Merleau-Ponty, and Feminist Ethics* (University of Illinois Press, 2004); *Revealing Male Bodies* (Indiana University Press, 2002), coedited with Nancy Tuana et al.; and *Hail Mary? The Struggle for Ultimate Womanhood in Catholicism* (Routledge, 1995).

THE UNIVERSITY OF ILLINOIS PRESS
IS A FOUNDING MEMBER OF THE
ASSOCIATION OF AMERICAN UNIVERSITY PRESSES.

———————————————————————

COMPOSED IN 9.75/13.5 ICS SCALA
BY JIM PROEFROCK
AT THE UNIVERSITY OF ILLINOIS PRESS
MANUFACTURED BY THOMSON-SHORE, INC.

UNIVERSITY OF ILLINOIS PRESS
1325 SOUTH OAK STREET
CHAMPAIGN, IL 61820-6903
WWW.PRESS.UILLINOIS.EDU